REBUILDING EUROPE

The Postwar World
General Editors: A.J. Nicholls and Martin S. Alexander

As distance puts events into perspective, and as evidence accumulates, it begins to be possible to form an objective historical view of our recent past. *The Postwar World* is an ambitious new series providing a scholarly but readable account of the way our world has been shaped in the crowded years since the Second World War. Some volumes will deal with regions, or even single nations, others with important themes; all will be written by expert historians drawing on the latest scholarship as well as their own research and judgements. The series should be particularly welcome to students, but it is designed also for the general reader with an interest in contemporary history.

Rebuilding Europe
Western Europe, America and Postwar Reconstruction

David W. Ellwood

Longman
London and New York

Longman Group UK Limited
Longman House, Burnt Mill,
Harlow, Essex CM20 2JE, England
and Associated Companies throughout the world.

*Published in the United States of America
by Longman Publishing, New York*

First published 1992

ISBN 0582 02245 2 CSD
ISBN 0582 02244 4 PPR

British Library Cataloguing-in-Publication Data

A catalogue record for this book is
available from the British Library

Library of Congress Cataloging-in-Publication Data

Ellwood, David W.
    Rebuilding Europe: Western Europe, America, and postwar
reconstruction, 1945–1955 / D.W. Ellwood.
        p. cm.— (Postwar world)
    Includes bibliographical references (p.   ) and
index.
        ISBN 0–582–02245–2 (csd) – ISBN 0–582–02244–4 (ppr)
        1. Reconstruction (1939–1951) 2. Europe—Foreign relations—United States.
3. United States—Foreign relations—Europe.   4. Europe—Politics and
government—1945–5.   Europe—Economic conditions—1945– I. Title. II. Series.
    D825.E45 1992
    940.55—dc20   9147007
                                                                      CIP

Set 9b in 10/12 Baskerville
Produced by Longman Singapore Publishers (Pte) Ltd
Printed in Singapore

Contents

List of Tables

List of Abbreviations

CDL	Comité de Libération
CDU	Christian Democrat Union
CEEC	Committee on European Economic Cooperation
CGIL	Confederazion generale italiana del lavoro
CIA	Central Intelligence Agency
CRS	Compagnie républicaines de sécurité
ECA	European Cooperation Administration (Washington)
ECE	(UN) Economic Commission for Europe
ECSC	European Coal and Steel Community
EDC	European Defence Community
EEC	European Economic Community
EPU	European Payments Union
ERP	European Recovery Programme (= Marshall Plan)
FAO	Food and Agriculture Organization
IMF	International Monetary Fund
ITO	International Trade Organisation
MRP	Movement Républicain Populaire
NA	National Archives (Washington)
NATO	North Atlantic Treaty Organisation
NSC	National Security Council
OECD	Organisation for Economic Cooperation and Development
OEEC	Organisation for European Economic Cooperation
PCF	Partie comuniste français
PCI	Partito comunista italiano
RPF	Rassemblement du Peuple Français
RG	Record Group
UNRRA	United Nations Relief and Rehabilitation Administration
WEU	Western European Union

Editorial Foreword

The aim of this series is to describe and analyse the history of the World since 1945. History, like time, does not stand still. What seemed to many of us only recently to be 'current affairs', or the stuff of political speculation, has now become material for historians. The editors feel that it is time for a series of books which will offer the public judicious and scholarly, but at the same time readable, accounts of the way in which our present-day world was shaped by the years after the end of the Second World War. The period since 1945 has seen political events and socio-economic developments of enormous significance for the human race, as important as anything which happened before Hitler's death or the bombing of Hiroshima. Ideologies have waxed and waned, the industrialised economies have boomed and bust, empires have collapsed, new nations have emerged and sometimes themselves fallen into decline. While we can be thankful that no major armed conflict has occurred between the so-called superpowers, there have been many other wars, and terrorism has become an international plague. Although the position of ethnic minorities has dramatically improved in some countries, it has worsened in others. Nearly everywhere the status of women has become an issue which politicians have been unable to avoid. These are only some of the developments we hope will be illuminated by this series as it unfolds.

The books in the series will not follow any set pattern; they will vary in length according to the needs of the subject. Some will deal with regions, or even single nations, and others with themes. Not all of them will begin in 1945, and the terminal date may similarly vary; once again, the time-span chosen will be appropriate to the question under discussion. All the books, however, will be written by expert historians drawing on the latest fruits of scholarship, as well as their own expertise and judgement. The series should be particularly welcome to students, but it is designed also for the general reader with an interest in contemporary history. We hope that the books will stimulate scholarly discussion and encourage specialists to look beyond their own particular interests to engage in wider controversies. History, and particularly the history of the recent past, is neither 'bunk' nor an intellectual form of stamp-collecting, but an indispensable part of an educated person's approach to life. If it is not written by historians it will be written by others of a less discriminating and more polemical disposition. The editors are confident that this series will help to ensure the victory of the historical approach, with consequential benefits for its readers.

A.J. Nicholls
Martin S. Alexander

Acknowledgements

This work represents a development of interests which first emerged in the years when my attention was directed to the politics and economics of the Allied intervention in Italy from 1943 to 1945. At that time I was much struck by the contrast between the European and American approaches to postwar Italy and to postwar Europe in general. While the Europeans – and the British in particular – tended to make their calculations in terms of recent history, the Americans looked to the future, to a world remade according to designs which they were busy drawing up. The United Nations, the World Bank, the plans for global free trade all testified to their visionary energies. But one impulse in particular could be seen at work at every level, no matter how great or small the subject under discussion, and that was the urge to 'raise living standards everywhere'. Along with collective security and free trade, the desire to lead the rest of the world to the state of peace and prosperity generally thought to be enjoyed in America by the end of the Second World War must be seen as one of the great ambitions of Roosevelt and his men for the postwar world.

Tracing the fate of this drive by way of the Marshall Plan to the boom years of the late 1950s – when many saw full-scale Americanisation taking place in Western Europe – became a long-term research goal. The text which follows is the first product of this effort.

The work was greatly stimulated by the intense activity of research and debate which for almost a quarter of a century now historians have been dedicating to that first postwar decade. Everyone continues to assume that the key choices which made the Western world what it subsequently became for forty years were taken then, and the dramatic events unfolding in Eastern Europe while this text was being written have, if anything, heightened interest in the origins of Europe's postwar divide. But a wide variety of new approaches to the story has carried our understanding of the 1945–1955 era well away from the supreme preoccupation of the 1960s and early 1970s with the origins and impact of the Cold War. The arrival of economic historians in the field, especially 'historical political economists', has brought to the surface a whole new range of facts, considerations and analyses. These will take years to digest, and will continue to make their influence felt long after the end of the Cold War.

The British economic historian Alan Milward and the Harvard political historian and economist Charles Maier have been at the forefront of this new wave, and I should like to pay tribute here to their inspiration, which is often visible in the pages which follow. A Jean Monnet fellowship at the European University Institute in Florence enabled me to participate in Alan Milward's seminar in the academic year 1986–87, and I am pleased to take this occasion to thank the Institute for the award and Alan Milward in particular for his stimulation and example as scholar and teacher.

The work of writing the text began in St Antony's College, Oxford, in the autumn of 1989, and I am grateful to the college for the Senior Associate Membership which enabled me to do this, and to Sir William Deakin, the former Warden of St Antony's, for his support on that occasion. At St Antony's I was fortunate to find one of the General Editors of the series in which this book appears, Anthony Nicholls, whose encouragement and dedication throughout have been indispensable.

Florence and Bologna have been the crossroads for much good debate on the recent history of Europe over the years, and I have benefited greatly from the wider perspective which living in those cities and meeting their resident scholars and their visitors has brought. In Florence Professor Ennio di Nolfo and Antonio Varsori have offered many occasions of discussion, having themselves greatly contributed to the presentation and analysis of Italy's role in the postwar evolution of Western Europe. In Bologna friends and colleagues including Paolo D'Attorre, Vera Zamagni and Maurizio Vaudagna at the University of Bologna, together with Adrian Lyttelton, John Harper and Patrick MacCarthy at the Bologna Center of the Johns Hopkins University School of Advanced International Studies have shown their support and interest by reading the text or arguing over its themes. Their presence and sense of solidarity have been a constant sustenance.

A special word of thanks must be dedicated to the Library of the Johns Hopkins Bologna Center and its staff, Alfred di Martino (Director), Gail Martin and John Williams. The collection managed by them is ideal for the work necessary in preparing a text such as this one. Their dedication and willingness to help made it a pleasure to use their services.

The final recognition is due to my friends in London, Geoffrey Warner, formerly Professor of European History at the Open University, and Elizabeth Gill. Both read the text critically and thoroughly at decisive stages, and contributed greatly to ensuring that a valid product would eventually emerge. I alone of course answer to readers as to the final judgement on its validity.

David Ellwood
Bologna,
November 1991

The publishers would like to thank the following for permission to reproduce copyright material: The Macmillan Press Ltd, London, for tables 1 and 2 from *State, Economy and Society in Western Europe 1815–1975*, Peter Flora (1983); Cambridge University Press and WW Rostow for table 3 from *The Stages of Economic Growth* Second Edition, WW Rostow (1971); Greenwood Publishing Group, Inc., Westport, CT for table 4 from *The Marshall Plan Revisited. The European Recovery Program in Economic Perspective*, I Wexler (1983); University of California Press and Penguin Books Ltd for table 5 from *Prosperity and Upheaval: The World Economy, 1945-1980*, by Herman Van der Wee, translated by Robin Hogg and Max R Hall (Viking, 1986), copyright © Deutscher Taschenbuch Verlag GmbH & Co KG, 1983, 1984, English translation copyright © Robin Hogg and Max R Hall, 1986.

Even if the Soviet Union were a gentle and cooperative and even capitalistic member of our international society there would still be a tremendous and spontaneous pressure in the United States – economic pressure and social, moral and religious pressure – to use the overwhelming power and resources of this country to help men everywhere in the world satisfy basic social and economic needs.

Harlan Cleveland
European Cooperation Administration
July 1950

. . . policymakers [in Washington in 1949] assumed that Western Europe could not become self-supporting without first eliminating 'the stifling effects on the process of economic growth, on competition and on the spirit of enterprise' inherent in the 'tight compartmentalization' of national economies. Needed was one or more 'free trade areas' in which 'mass production for mass consumption and intensive internal competition can restore the dynamic of enterprise and economic growth.' The ultimate goal was a full-scale European union [in which] new 'supranational institutions' would manage the 'day-to-day co-ordination of national economic policies' . . . Envisioned here was a New Deal for Europe, a program, in other words, that would re-design Europe in the image of American neo-capitalism. The ECA urged the continental countries to commit themselves to this goal by early 1950.

Michael J Hogan
The Marshall Plan
Cambridge 1987

Elizabeth Gigou, France's Minister for European Affairs . . . rejects charges that France is moving inexorably towards a federalism that effaces national identities. 'No-one should imagine that Europe is going to be turned into the United States of America,' she says. 'We are not going to plough under the centuries-old traditions of Britain, France and other countries of the EC to transform them into Dakota and Kansas. We have never considered a construction of this kind.'

The Observer
8 December 1991

Introduction

With the end of the Cold War come new questions on the years after 1945, on the reconstruction and the division of the European world in that era. They concern not just the predictable issues: the redefinition of Germany, the rebuilding of France, the dilemmas of Britain. Today's questions go deeper. They invite comparisons with the first postwar era, trace the link between reconstruction and modernisation in each nation, highlight the distance between intentions and results. How could free market capitalism, discredited in Europe by two world wars and the upheavals of the 1930s, recover in the space of a decade to flourish as never before? How was it possible for the ruined nations of 1945 to carry through a revolution in production and consumption and at the same time keep up ever more costly defences in the Cold War? Was the division of the continent into two hostile blocs the price to pay for all this?

In reflecting on capitalism's crisis, many blamed exasperated nationalism. How then did new attitudes encouraging interdependence and cooperation contribute to the reconstruction? The prosperous part of Europe was more dependent than ever on the United States, so how did the comprehensive projection of American power influence the reorganisation and its outcome? Who contributed most, America or Europe, to the idea of the 'good life' which emerged in the Western European nations after the 'economic miracles' of the 1950s? And how did the good life then influence ideas on what 'Europe' itself now consisted of?

Not surprisingly a great deal of historical effort continues to be devoted to the very eventful years between 1945 and 1955. But as long as the experts have stuck to their specialities, the political and economic threads of the story have tended to remain separated. The aim of the present work is to propose a fresh synthesis of the main diplomatic, strategic and economic developments in the first ten years after the war, using the most significant of the new analyses available, as well as the most enduring among the older variety.

The perspective offered revolves round the arrival of the key modernising concept of 'growth' or rather 'growthmanship', as the Cambridge economic historian Michael Postan termed it in 1967:

> The most unprecedented phenomenon in post-war Europe was not so much the purely material record of her economy as the spirit which moved it. What was really remarkable ... was that economic growth was so powerfully propelled by public sentiments and policies .... In all European countries economic growth became a universal creed and a common expectation to which governments were expected to conform. To this extent economic growth was the product of economic growthmanship.

Henceforth societies defined progress less in political and more in economic terms; colonies and numbers of men under arms gave way to figures for gross national product as the highest expression of national prowess. Prosperity had always seemed liberal democracy's best response to its Fascist challengers; now, recast as 'growth', it set the terms for the competition with the Soviet system.

What the race cost the Soviets became clear after 1989 and is likely to be revealed in ever greater detail in the years to come. Now, as the inheritors of the Soviet empire's ruins rush to embrace the victorious creed, the political, social and economic limits of the growth vision impress themselves ever more heavily on the consciousness of the West. At the time of Europe's great postwar boom however, growth-manship promised to cancel out the memories of the continent's dreadful twentieth century civil war and even end the class war: the rising tide would lift all ships. 'How new will the better world be?' an American commentator asked in 1945. By 1955 everyone, affluent and excluded alike, had an answer.

CHAPTER ONE

The Lessons of Last Time

LOOKING THE DISASTER IN THE FACE

'If men will not learn until their lessons are written in blood, why, blood they must have, their own for preference', wrote Bernard Shaw in 1918 introducing *Heartbreak House*, his great play on the decadent Europe from which had sprung the Great War. In contrast to those who learned from the First World War simply how much better to prepare for a Second, there stood in Western Europe and America in 1945 a new class of politicians, high civil servants and experts determined not just that this time 'never again' would mean what it said, but that the survival of liberal civilisation itself demanded a positive, constructive response equal in scale to the disasters of the previous three decades.

'During the catastrophe, beneath the burden of defeat, a great change had occurred in men's minds. To many, the disaster of 1940 seemed like the failure of the ruling class and system in every realm':[1] General de Gaulle, the towering leader of the Free French, was only one of those, conservative and leftist alike, who understood the revolutionary character of the challenge and who feared a repeat of the Europe-wide chaos of 1918–26 should it not be met. A sense of shame and guilt pervaded those in Britain and America who had seen war coming as the outcome of the great depression of the 1930s, but had felt powerless to prevent it.[2]

But in the defeated and occupied countries nothing less than a top-to-bottom change of regime could be contemplated by the new men. 'The issue of progress versus reaction has characterised every example of genuine resistance in Europe', a *Manchester Guardian* writer proclaimed in August 1945; 'Europe is in a revolutionary mood, a mood that forces comparison with 1848. Nothing is finally decided, and loyalties remain open in a way they have not been for a hundred years.'[3]

The distinguished historian and *Times* editorialist E.H. Carr had declared as early as 1942: 'The most encouraging feature of the present situation is the prevalence, especially among the younger generation, of a deep-seated conviction that the world of the past decade has been a bad and mad world, and that almost everything in it needs to be uprooted and replanted.' The radical impulses of the First World War towards self-determination, international justice and 'a world made safe for democracy' – Woodrow Wilson's great call of 1917 – had produced the League of Nations. But, insisted Carr, these impulses and the League itself had been swamped within months by the craving of the traditional ruling classes in France, Britain and America for a return to the stability, security and prosperity presumed by all of them to have been the supreme characteristics of the world before 1914. Now, from the wreckage of this mentality and all the disasters it had produced, from the very successes of the warmongering, 'dissatisfied' powers of the post–1919 era, had come a new agenda: social equality, economic democracy, supranational cooperation, the politics of participation, planning and welfare at every level, within nations and beyond them.[4]

Wherever involvement in the Second World War required something like total mobilisation of a nation's people and resources, there was intense debate on the postwar world – the more complete the mobilisation, the wider this debate ranged, the more numerous those involved in it. In times such as these it was conceivable in America for a former Republican Presidential candidate, Wendell Willkie, to publish in 'One World' (1943) a grand international peace plan and to see it enjoy the most phenomenal sale of any book ever published in the United States.[5] In Britain the confrontation on the shape of the country after the war had started almost immediately upon its outbreak: 'The pros and cons of social change, the high hopes of some for a more just world, and the scepticism of others, were perpetual talking points', (writes the historian Paul Addison). 'The issues were debated in air-raid wardens' posts, in factory canteens, at mothers' meetings, on trains and buses when strangers fell into conversation.'[6]

In occupied Europe Resistance itself was inconceivable without designs which went far beyond the expulsion of the invader and the liquidation of his accomplices, towards conceptions of renewal which could inspire the appearance of new leaders and new social groups. Political exiles and those incarcerated in relatively tolerable conditions such as the St. Michielsgestel hostage camp in Holland or Mussolini's island prisons, carried on 'interminable discussions on politics and liberty', according to the pioneer federalist, Altiero Spinelli, who spent sixteen years in this situation. Governments in exile, such as the Belgian and the Dutch in London, spent their time partly in drawing up detailed plans for the work of renewal and reform to be started on their return home.

E.H. Carr identified the nature of the Europe-wide search for renewal as a revolt against 'the three predominant ideas of the nineteenth century: liberal democracy, national self-determination and *laissez-faire* economics', and he proceeded, in a book widely read not just in Britain but also in countries such as Holland and Denmark, to illustrate the nature of the crisis in each of these conceptions brought on by the rise of totalitarianism and the outbreak of a second world war only 20 years after the end of the first. Almost fifty years afterwards, it is easy to perceive the limits of this view, its inability to foresee the Cold War and the division of Europe, the impact of decolonisation, the role of America in Western Europe's future, or even the many continuities of institutions, ideas and methods from the discredited prewar era. But it did succeed in highlighting the supreme importance economic priorities would play in settling the fate of the other two areas of crisis. In spelling out these three key lessons written in blood, Carr provided a key to the plans being so intensely prepared in Europe and America for when the war was over.

RENEWING DEMOCRACY

The expectations of the liberators

By 1945 the question of political renovation had quite changed in complexion when compared to the assumptions reigning in the central years of the conflict. The reason why was explained by Stalin in a famous speech to a visiting delegation of Yugoslav Communists early in 1945: 'This war is not as in the past; whoever occupies a territory imposes on it his own social system. Everyone imposes his own system as far as his army has power to do so. It cannot be otherwise.'[7] So no longer were the Allies responible for simply 'liberating' the territories that fell to their military advance: liberation and occupation would henceforth not be so easily distinguishable.

Against Nazism and Fascism, the Allies guaranteed the right of every nation to choose democratically its own future. But by the end of the war it had become clear that the conceptions of democracy brought by the armies were reduced to two, and that liberated peoples would be obliged to adopt the version sponsored by the great power or powers to whom they owed their deliverance. In the West the classic formulations of parliamentary liberalism and popular sovereignty would clearly bring back a model, however deeply modified in its methods and aims, of traditional class collaboration, based on consensus and the rule of law. In the areas taken over by the Red Army democracy would be that embodied in the anti-Fascist forces who had led the fight against the enemy.

Earlier in the war, when principles had to be settled for the treatment of the first of the liberated territories, Italy, it had been possible for the Allied Foreign Ministers to agree at a special conference in Moscow in October, 1943 that the democratisation of government meant the elimination of Fascist institutions and the introduction of recognised anti-Fascist elements – generally gathered in broad-ranging 'committees of liberation' – into the political life of that country.

But by the time Churchill, Roosevelt and Stalin met in Yalta (February 1945), London and Washington had become convinced that the forces dominating anti-Fascist fronts everywhere were Communist parties loyal to Moscow, and that social revolution in the name of the working classes would be the consequence of their efforts at democratisation, inevitable where accompanied by the Red Army, imaginable even where the armies were Anglo-American. One result was the Declaration on Liberated Territories produced by the Yalta summit, a lame compromise formula which committed the Big Three powers to promote free elections throughout the nations they controlled as soon as possible.[8] Within a matter of weeks the Declaration was a dead letter, and the conference began to acquire the baleful reputation it has kept to this day. Among those who followed its proceedings, diplomats, journalists and anti-Fascist leaders who were not invited – such as General de Gaulle – there spread the conviction that a new division of Europe had begun.

Expectations on the ground

The forces of democratic renewal were everywhere surprised by this outcome to their struggles. From the majesty of de Gaulle's position at the head of the French Provisional Government to the outposts of the Greek mountains, a common illusion had taken root that freedom to choose what came next would – within national boundaries – be limitless. Had not the lavish propaganda of the fighting United Nations guaranteed self-determination and the right of each people to choose its own destiny at the war's end? But when the end finally arrived, it quickly became clear that democracy could only be renewed on the basis of certainty concerning the essential elements of civil life: *food, work, law, order*. Whoever could guarantee these possessed the keys to the future. But such was the chaos and disruption prevailing in most liberated territories that only the liberating armies and the victorious great powers who had sent them were in a position to provide these means to restart normal life. And their help, it soon emerged, would not be unconditional or automatic.

The plans prepared by the Resistance and its allies all reflected other priorities. In Italy, Germany and France a change of regime came at the head of the list. The collapse of democracy in these countries – Italian liberalism in 1922, the Weimar Republic in 1933, the Third Republic in France in 1940 – all ignominious and often violent events, demanded the invention of new systems of representation with much stronger bases of legitimacy. But how? What political *method* would build the new relationship between the state and civil society, between the institutions and the electorate?

The rebirth of politics

This was the question the reborn political parties of Continental Europe all hastened to answer. Although radically changed in appearance and tone, almost none of them were new: even a substantial part of their leaderships had survived in most cases. They proved to be a stronger force for continuity with the past than almost any other in the postwar years. On the question of democratic renewal the major blocs or areas presented their case as follows (moving from left to right across the political spectrum).

The Communist parties which existed in every European country stood for popular participation. The Italian party told its swelling ranks in July 1944:

> Only the participation of all the people in the insurrection will guarantee victory and it is this participation which is the essential prerequisite for the democratic renewal of the country. The reeducation of the Italian people, the radical elimination of Fascism and its economic roots, these will only be possible if all kinds of employees, not only workers, actively intervene in political life, in first person, as conscious creators of the new democracy. The first act of intervention of the Italian people in the forging of its destiny is the war of liberation.[9]

Officially such an approach excluded any action aimed at armed revolution, and events in Greece, where an insurrectionary movement led by two Communist parties began in December 1944, soon to be crushed by the British, only served to confirm this attitude in central committees elsewhere.

They saw their main task as carrying out the Moscow line of broad anti-Fascist cooperation, which they expected to continue well after the war. Monarchy was certainly to be replaced by republicanism, but only in due time, when legality had been guaranteed by local and parliamentary elections, and when each party had been able to establish securely its broader conception of participation, in the form of loyal trade unions, youth groups, women's organisations, partisans' circles, etc. In this way might be managed the difficult transition from élite underground group to legitimate mass party which they all now faced.

Unlike the Communists, reformist parties of the socialist or social democratic variety, such as the British Labour Party, the French Popular Front veterans or the Danish Social Democrats, could often count on a heritage of direct governmental experience. They took it for granted that renovated parliaments would provide the highway to influence and power. By bringing in youthful new elements from the Resistance, from the 'progressive' or 'productive' (as opposed to the 'reactionary' or 'parasitical') sections of the middle classes, and from their following in reconstructed trade unions, the socialists thought they would be able to develop local versions of the New Deal, or the British Beveridge Plan for social security, each of which had many admirers in their ranks.

In contrast to the period after the First World War, few activists from this area of the political spectrum now had any illusions about the 'transition to socialism'. Most of these had been abandoned in the 1930s, when the Depression had brought the realities of power much closer, as in the case of the followers of the French Socialist leader, Léon Blum, who had participated in the Popular Front, or the Dutch Social Democratic Party, which entered government in 1939. Talk persisted about the collective will and the socialisation of the means of production, but it remained vague and never entered into detail. References to modernisation, planning and the enlarged responsibilities of the state almost always concentrated on economic policy and had little to say about bureaucracy, the institutions, or the rights and obligations of citizens outside the economic sphere.

Socialists and social democrats knew they were against totalitarianism in all its manifestations, and against confessionally based political culture, whether Catholic or Protestant. In countries such as France,

Italy, Holland and Belgium, this 'lay' mission of the non-Communist Left provided it with a useful form of camouflage which would facilitate tactical moves leftwards or rightwards, but provided it with few constructive ideas for the longer term.

The parties which would later form the centre and right of the political spectrum were not to be outdone in this phase in their ardour for renewal, and can most easily be characterised by their position in relation to one of the great religious camps. Not surprisingly, the weight of past experience and now the war itself had led to a flowering of particular national groupings – 'actionists', radicals, liberals, unionists and others – as parliamentary democrats of all sorts tried to place as much distance as possible between themselves and the parties which had helped bring on national disasters, or had been hopelessly compromised in collaboration with the enemy. This common pattern of behaviour gave an illusion of unity, and effectively if temporarily concealed the issues which would soon divide the conservatives from each other.

The hardest job of distancing faced the new generation of Catholic leaders. Their Church had furnished Mussolini with his Concordat in 1929, had provided the Vichy regime with its most prestigious supporters in bishops' palaces throughout France, and by means of the strong national Catholic party, had thrown its weight behind the compromised Leopold III in Belgium. Yet no force proved more successful in establishing itself in West European politics at this time, providing a group of leaders – De Gasperi in Italy, Adenauer in West Germany, Bidault in France, van Zeeland in Belgium and others – whose legacy was to be of crucial significance.

Anxious to establish mass parties with the numbers and effectiveness of the Communists, the Christian Democrats in Italy, the MRP in France, the CDU in Germany and the Catholic Party in Belgium built on hitherto minority populist and liberal elements in the modern Catholic tradition. In this way they were able to arrive at syntheses of voluntarism and republicanism, liberal reformism and 'sense of the state' which would enable them to compete in all parts of the political spectrum. For them democracy was incomplete without the spiritual and intellectual development of the individual in a context of social *solidarity*. This meant in practice the construction of the Catholic version of the welfare state in an atmosphere of national reconciliation: between the Resistance and its enemies, between the state and the citizenry, between employers and workers, between city and country.

Protestants too could agree, as in Holland, a nation where nineteenth-century liberalism had long flourished, that 'opposite the free play of social forces and the unbridled pursuit of one's own egoistical interests, should be placed the public spirit'. In a country where the two major confessions had shared domination of parliament and the stagnant public life of the prewar years, it was possible to imagine the construction of a state system which took welfare responsibility from the old confessional parties and their support systems to distribute its benefits more equitably throughout the population.

Holland was notably a country where the future of the monarchy was not a significant issue, in contrast to the situation in Belgium, Italy and Greece. There crowned heads saw their positions fatally threatened. But Queen Wilhelmina was a fervent adherent of renewal, learning from exile experience in England how monarchy could serve to bridge the distance between rulers and masses, which she saw as traditionally far too great in her own realm.[10]

What the political parties unwittingly shared in their outlook on postwar European democracy was a belief that they themselves should be the supreme arbiters of its fate: they would interpret the popular will through channels such as parliaments, trade unions, voluntary associations, under arrangements which they would turn into law in new constitutions, designed by themselves. Maximalists who wished to continue the Committees of Liberation experience of the Resistance era were soon brushed aside. So too were reformists such as the Italian Action Party, perhaps the truest expression of the Resistance impulse to renewal, who sought a significant modernisation of the institutions of state (including local government), alongside the common objectives of welfare and economic advancement. General de Gaulle was alone in complaining of the 'passionate desire (of the French parties) to give themselves all the powers of the Republic in full and at the earliest opportunity, and their incapacity, which they revealed in advance, to wield them effectively'. 'Revolution by law!' was the cry of Bidault, leader of the Catholics; but what would lie behind it? Nothing more than tactical calculation and demagoguery?[11]

De Gaulle's challenge was no less appropriate as the reborn political parties faced up to the second great lesson of twentieth-century history.

AFTER NATIONALISM

The basic analysis

The revolt against nationalism and in favour of institutionalised international cooperation as one of the keys to peace was remarkably uniform across the political spectrum and between nations. The general assumption was not only that Nazi-Fascism had perverted nationalism beyond redemption, but that the ailing democracies of the 1930s had responded to the crisis by beggaring each other economically and politically, so hastening their collapse. The Versailles emphasis on self-determination and the rights of minorities was reviled as having produced nothing but 'Balkanisation' and international anarchy, and of course the settlement had totally ignored, had in fact aggravated, the economic dimensions of the problems supposedly being dealt with.

It was the breadth of this consensus, shared by many on both sides of the Atlantic, which impressed the pioneers of European integration with the rightness of their cause, and which has helped stimulate in recent years – as the European Economic Community has come to maturity – an outpouring of historical research on the origins and conditions of the integrationist 'movement'.

In reality, this impulse was directed at a quite distant future, and came far behind the strategic outcome of the war, national survival, the need for relief, the search for stability, the fate of empires, in the consideration of the reborn parties and their leaders. Dutch commentators note now that 'the resistance movement . . . was far too occupied with everyday worries and the Netherlands' future to dedicate themselves to the working out of concrete plans for European cooperation after the war. This took no priority.'[12] Still, the Dutch underground press, Catholic, Liberal and Socialist, agreed that the German invasion proved no nation could stand alone, and that thoroughgoing cooperation in Europe would be essential after the war. Suggestions were floated for a military alliance with Belgium, France and Britain as a basis for a customs and currency union, and there was a clear understanding that Britain would be the power overseeing the reorganisation of the Continent.

Postwar federalism and its impact

Governments-in-exile such as that of Belgium, containing three former prime ministers and such figures of future significance as Paul-Henri Spaak and Paul van Zeeland, were better placed than most to muse on the possibilities for Europe's postwar reorganisation. Able to count on an impressive study organisation, CEPAG (Commission Belge pour l'Etude des Problèmes d'Après-Guerre), the government witnessed a lively debate on the role of the United Nations, the possibilities of federalism, and the relationship of small nations to the emerging superpowers. Even if its impact on subsequent events was small, the

11

confrontation was a significant one in that, in microcosm, it anticipated many of the opposing positions which would emerge when the construction of the new order effectively began: between the universalists and the regionalists, between out-and-out federalists and those who saw cooperation as a means of reinforcing the nation-state internally, between those who put economic reorganisation in a European framework first and those who looked to defence and the Anglo-American connection: 'It was the sea that made possible the early and immortal flowering of our Flemish towns', wrote the Catholic ex-minister and Belgian delegate to the League of Nations, Frans Van Cauwelaert, in the *Washington Post* in May 1942; 'It is the sea that will once again condition the moral and material renaissance that we are expecting after the war. . . . Our international orientation should be maritime and not continental, Atlantic not European.'[13]

And it was from the Belgian political forces-in-waiting that the first concrete plan for integration came, the Benelux initiative of 1944, aimed at Holland and Luxemburg (but originally intended to include France also). Starting with the London Customs Convention of September 1944 it would evolve into a full-scale free-trade area by the end of 1949.

But for most of the anti-Fascist forces new schemes of supranational collaboration came under the heading 'spiritual reconstruction', and only took on real significance when confronted with the notion of 'collective security', coined in America in the era of the old League of Nations and soon to be recast in the concept of the United Nations Organisation. The declaration in favour of European federalism promulgated in May 1944 in Geneva by representatives of Resistance movements from Italy, France, Germany, Holland, Czechoslovakia, Yugoslavia, Poland, Norway and Denmark was impressive, even if it derived some of its urgency from the first perceptions of a Europe overshadowed by America and the Soviet Union. But it was completely ignored by the Allies, even by Winston Churchill in London, whose own enthusiasm for a large-scale European reorganisation was by this time well established.[14]

The impulse to overcome nationalism should not be underestimated. If it was Eurocentric, it did realise what all the years of subsequent history amply confirmed, that the use of force to settle disputes between them was henceforth inconceivable for European powers. The steps towards free trade in Europe which began in the early 1950s would not alone have acquired the political momentum necessary for their realisation without the feeling that they were steps to a higher ideal – the European Community.

Specifically, the formal recognition in a number of the new constitutions introduced after the war, that national sovereignty must be limited if the peace was to be secure, brought tangible proof that a historical lesson had indeed been learned. As D.W. Urwin points out, the preamble of the French Constitution of 1946 stated that 'on condition of reciprocity, France shall accept the limitations of sovereignty necessary to the organisation and defence of peace'. Likewise, Article II of the Italian Constitution of 1947 asserted that 'Italy consents, on condition of parity with other states, to limitations of sovereignty necessary to an order for assuring peace and justice among nations; it promotes and favours international organisation toward that end.' The West German Basic Law passed in 1949 was similarly endowed, while the new Danish model of 1953 anticipated the explicit delegation of powers from the national state to authorities charged at the international level with promoting rules of law and cooperation.

From all this to the signature of the Treaty of Rome in 1957 creating the European Economic Community and the European Atomic Energy Community, there lay a direct political and cultural lineage. Born under the auspices of France, Germany and Italy, among others, the new communities represented, as Urwin comments, 'the most advanced experiments of abrogation of national sovereignty' yet seen.[15]

THE REVOLT AGAINST LAISSEZ-FAIRE

What Versailles left out

It was no coincidence that those most ardently in favour of an integrated Europe should have seen economic results and economic structures as the supreme means to their goal. The total incapacity of the inter-war system to face up to its responsibilities in this area was the lesson most dramatically spelled out by the great collapse, only partially redeemed by the new systems of mobilisation for goods and people the war brought forward. Commenting on these issues and the new relationship he saw between self-determination and economic power, E.H. Carr pointed out that the nineteenth-century political rights accorded to minorities by the Versailles treaties did not extend to the right to work or 'the right not to starve'. A new compromise was needed 'between the claims of national independence and the imperative exigencies of economic interdependence'.[16]

None had been more eloquent on the failure of the earlier settlement to face up to the nature of economic exigencies than Keynes, whose famous tract of 1923, *The Economic Consequences of the Peace*, boomed out:

> To what a different future Europe might have looked forward if either Mr Lloyd George or Mr Wilson had apprehended that the most serious of the problems which claimed their attention were not political or territorial, but financial and economic, and that the perils of the future lay not in frontiers and in sovereignties, but in food, coal and transport. . . . The fundamental economic problem of a Europe starving and disintegrating before their eyes was the one question in which it was impossible to arouse the interest of the Four.[17]

The language and very meaning of political action was transformed in the Second World War as economic goals – full employment, stability, more production and consumption – rose to dominate the horizon of all those who now sought power and legitimacy. The change was rooted in what Carr called 'the socialisation of the nation', the process started by the entry of the masses into the political scene in the industrialised economies of the late nineteenth century. In addition the power of the state over the economy had been transformed by the two world wars. In the 1930s John Maynard Keynes had demonstrated in theory how the state could operate to smooth the ups and downs in the economic cycle; he was brought into the British Treasury in 1940 to show how the new war could be paid for and to point the way forward for the peace. His work was aided by the new techniques of macroeconomic measurement essential to bring planning to economic policy spelled out in Colin Clark's milestone volume of 1940, *The Conditions of Economic Progress*. Meanwhile in wartime Washington, Roosevelt's New Deal administrators had brought coordination and organisation to the American economy, stimulating the release of extraordinary productive powers.

All these examples, together with the practical intelligence gathered by a generation which had seen two world wars, finally gave the politicians the degree of control over real economic processes they needed to pledge the arrival of a new era.[18]

The economic challenge in Europe

Fear of failure also had much to do with the urgency of their claims. In occupied Europe the rise of Communist parties everywhere left no doubt that liberal capitalism itself was on trial. The collapse of the Greek economy in a welter of inflation and misery directly contributed to the insurrectionary outbreak right after liberation at the end of

1944. More than any other, this event convinced Allied observers that if similar conditions to those prevailing after the First World War were to reappear as the Second World War ended, they would bring a second wave of revolutionary outbreaks. With Churchill's 'hot rake of war' proceeding agonisingly up the peninsula, post-Fascist Italy would be next in line.

But in countries such as Yugoslavia and Greece, and even in Italy to some extent, the challenge was not relief or recovery in any contingent sense, but national unification, industrialisation, and development from levels long forgotten in most of northern Europe. In Yugoslavia average per capita income before the war had been no more than $70 per annum, and while industrialisation was clearly seen to be the essential national task, ethnic divisions and the usual vicious circles associated with low incomes, low savings and low investment guaranteed perpetual stagnation. It was growing economic dependence which had provided Germany's influence in the Balkans in the 1930s. As for the rise of the Left in the area, not only did it usually prove the only dynamic, nation-wide force capable of organising armed opposition to the invader, it also came equipped with something like an analysis of the causes and consequences of underdevelopment.[19]

Italy

The Italian case was more complex. In industrial terms the country had progressed during the Fascist era in the heavier sectors and in electrification. New industrial zones encouraging light industries and based on advanced technology had appeared. But the occupational structure was hardly more advanced when the war began than in 1922 when the Fascist regime had begun. Then some 55 per cent of the active population worked in agriculture; by the late 1930s the figure was just under 50 per cent, with the overwhelming majority of industries still concentrated in the triangle based on Genoa, Milan and Turin.[20] The economic gap between this area and the 'underdeveloped' South had worsened, and it was no coincidence that when the crisis of Fascism came in 1943, the northern working class expressed protest and discontent, first in a great strike wave during March 1943, then, after the armistice and the German invasion of September, in participation in the Resistance. The South meanwhile, though restless, remained passive and resigned to its fate.

The length and destructiveness of the liberation process had exacerbated this division, and brought home to Italian industrialists, politicians and Resistance leaders before anyone else in Europe how much their future would depend on outside help. Indeed so great was the sense of helplessness and dependence that no-one saw any sense in planning for reconstruction; competent experts were few and played little part in active anti-Fascism. The northern Resistance command in Milan organised its economic planning round the aims of dismantling the Fascist economic system, keeping production going, and reining in the revolutionary spirit of large parts of the working class.

But there was another factor at work in the wait-and-see attitude of the leading groups: a widespread backlash against Mussolini's incessant modernising rhetoric and the paraphernalia of state agencies, corporations and patronage systems which seemed its inevitable accompaniment. Though united on little else in economic policy, the conservative parties had no time for grand designs, assuming it would be possible to restore the situation in this area much as they imagined it to have been when 'interrupted' by Fascism.

The Communist Party was caught up in the same currents, ruling out nationalisation and planning in its economic statements and emphasising the need to control inflation and expand production. Structural reform would certainly be necessary, said the party, but to dismantle Fascist autarky and industrial monopolies. In this view the future was vague: Italy would be an industrial country rather than an agricultural one, but could be developed only in proportion to available capital and raw materials. This meant 'industries related to agriculture and food production, textiles, light and precision industries'. Even so investment from the outside would be essential: not from the USSR as the underground party in the north imagined during the struggle, but from the Anglo-American world, which the post-liberation Communist Party wooed with a special economic conference in English put on in Rome in December 1945.

FIAT also assumed that external aid – from America, not from anywhere else – would be essential. But in the vision of its all-powerful managing director of those years, Vittorio Valletta, this could only be effective if accompanied by a wide-ranging reform and modernisation effort promoted by the state. The true key to stability though was 'internationalisation', said Valletta, the establishment of a new and dynamic international division of labour, favoured by the gradual reduction of tariff barriers. Only in that way could living standards be raised everywhere.

But Valletta's voice was a lone one among industrialists at the time, and only with hindsight did the significance of the FIAT picture of Italy's future become clear. As the liberation took place the overwhelming demand coming from the Rome government and the Italian ruling classes was for the immediate provision of food and work, law and order for the masses of the cities and the North, 'because it is feared that if this does not happen', wrote the prime minister to the Allied command, 'there will be a most serious agitation'.[21]

France

General de Gaulle was equally disturbed by the conditions he found on return to his native Lille in September 1944: 'too many faces whose smiles effaced neither their pallor or their emaciation . . . '; without 'a profound social change' it seemed inevitable to him that 'the embittered and suffering mass of the workers would founder on disturbances which ran the risk of depriving France of what remained of her substance'.[22]

De Gaulle was no economist but in his first major speech in liberated Paris he provided, together with a list of immediate economic measures, a statement of the 'principles of recovery which it had been the aims of the resistance to realise'; they included attacks on vested interests, nationalisations to reduce the weight of private power, raising production, renewing the administration of the economy and resonant guarantees of 'work . . . security and dignity'.

But behind these unremarkable aims there lay a deep impulse towards another, supreme objective: that of national modernisation. Gaullists, socialists and reformists of all persuasions saw that stagnant, largely rural France had been overwhelmed by technology, industry and economic dynamism in 1940, not just by the diabolic fury of the Nazis. Modernisation meant bringing the nation to a par with the most advanced industrial economies, continuous renewal and restructuring, expansion and urbanisation. It meant new powers for the state, powers to organise and above all to plan.

The drive to economic modernisation was common in anti-fascist forces everywhere, but nowhere was it transformed into such specific plans as in the French Resistance. Around de Gaulle in London a commission of experts including technocrats of the future such as Hervé Alphand, Etienne Hirsch and Robert Marjolin, had been working as early as 1942 to produce a French response to the grand Atlantic Charter of the Anglo-Americans (of August 1941, described below). Influenced by the British wartime experience, the Beveridge plan and the writings of Keynes, the result was the Alphand report, a typical wartime compromise between socialists and liberals, embracing economic stabilisation and full employment, nationalisation and free

17

trade. It assumed there would be an economic planning ministry and a world economic organisation.

Attempts to blend a managerial vision with elements of socialism characterised several of the efforts of French underground study groups to plan for the reconstruction, and even the 'Report on Postwar Economic Policy' of a more conservative group of economists, produced in November 1943, took for granted that redistribution, *dirigisme* and planning would be the order of the day, since 'the operation of (economic) mechanisms is better known and public authorities possess the principal instruments for an interventionist policy'. In this vision, galvanised market mechanisms, investment, education and expansion were to be the keys to social policy, which would be progressive and clearly aim at full employment. As the historian Richard Kuisel points out, the significance of this document was that it represented the views of the liberal faction which would eventually dominate postwar policy in France.[23]

Expectations at the time were different. The National Resistance Council in France had published its own official 'action programme' in March 1944, calling for structural reform aiming at full employment, but as liberation approached de Gaulle appointed a new commission on postwar problems, headed by a socialist. Keynes's influence was clearly felt here also, not least through the commissaire for finance, Pierre Mendès-France (briefly prime minister between 1954 and 1955, but significant over a much longer period). In the Commission's report, 'Structural Economic Reforms' presented in July 1944, there were proposals for 'comprehensive planning and Keynesian counter-cyclical policies to sustain full employment and economic development', all coordinated by a powerful new economic ministry.

But it was not until the businessman and international civil servant Jean Monnet returned to France, after the war had ended, that the path to the future would open. He had spent the war years in Britain and America organising supplies, making friends and winning admiration for his particular combination of vision and practicality. With his experience of Anglo-American ideas and methods, Monnet would turn out to be the man to turn all the talk into policy and decisions.[24]

Belgium, Denmark

Who, if anyone, wished to fulfil this role in Belgium was uncertain. The CEPAG study groups looked to the creation of a regime of 'organised freedom' for their country, where expansion and flexible planning would combine to bring comprehensive social security and realise the right to work henceforth guaranteed by the Constitution. How they planned to impress these ideas on the political scene after the liberation remained to be seen. In Denmark too there was talk of full employment, social reforms and state regulation of the economy. When the most significant party on the Left, the Social Democrats, produced their programme 'The Future of Denmark' in 1945, very specific plans in these directions were spelled out, embracing as elsewhere economic democracy and industrialisation.[25]

In Europe, then, the people who expected to wield power after the war shared a common agenda: avoiding the mistakes of last time, planning, welfare, modernisation. But thinkers such as the great Scandinavian social democrat Gunnar Myrdal saw all these visions overshadowed by one supreme immediate consideration: what would America's role be in the postwar phase? A repeat of 1919, when the great hopes for world reorganisation and peace aroused by Woodrow Wilson had been betrayed by Congress, with its refusal to allow America to join the League of Nations? Unaware of the lessons Americans too were learning from their recent history, the conviction spread among European reformists that when the war ended a massive transition crisis would start in the United States and then engulf Europe. Meanwhile conservatives such as Churchill were thinking in geostrategic terms: who if not the Americans would buttress the crippled nations of the West against the advancing Russians? Yet here was Roosevelt at Yalta insisting that his forces would leave the Old World for home as soon as possible after the fighting was done.

The nearer the war's end came, the more Europeans looked expectantly to the United States: for food and money obviously, but for more: for inspiration and action. America however had different priorities – its own – and of these very few Europeans knew anything, beyond the slogans of the propaganda machines.

BUILDING THE AMERICAN CENTURY

First principles

'What we must win now, during the war, are the principles ... ', declared Roosevelt's old Republican rival, Wendell Willkie early in 1943. In the Four Freedoms, 'Mr Roosevelt again states the same major purposes in America's participation in this war – a second crusade to establish American ideals', added another of Roosevelt's former opponents, ex-president Herbert Hoover, recalling in true bipartisan spirit Woodrow Wilson's efforts in the First World War.[26]

The Four Freedoms were America's most successful contribution to the ideological battle of the Second World War. They were announced in Roosevelt's Annual Message to Congress of January 1941:

> The first is freedom of speech and expression everywhere in the world.
> The second is freedom of every person to worship God in his own way – everywhere in the world.
> The third is freedom from want – which, translated into world terms, means economic understandings which will secure to every nation a healthy peacetime life for its inhabitants – everywhere in the world.
> The fourth is freedom from fear – which, translated into world terms, means a world-wide reduction of armaments to such a point and in such a thorough fashion that no nation will be in a position to commit an act of physical aggression against any neighbour – anywhere in the world.[27]

There was much more than rhetoric in this vision of the human future. The Lend-Lease concept providing aid to Britain without a full-scale American war commitment, had just been invented, and by March 1941 had passed into law. It was based on the idea that Britain and eventually all the other allies would not buy outright the arms and materials they needed for the war, but would 'lease' them from the US government, paying for them or returning them at the end of the war. If this was the theory of Lend-Lease, its operation proved highly technical. But in the 'Master Agreement', on which all the relationships were modelled, the Washington administration took pains to ensure that in return for this help its practical long-term concerns were recognised. They were included in Article VII of the accord and spelled out priorities which were above all economic: 'the expansion . . . of production, employment and the exchange and consumption of all peoples . . . the elimination of all forms of discriminatory treatment in international commerce . . . the reduction of tariffs and other trade barriers'.[28]

In August of the same year came the Atlantic Charter, a joint pronunciation of ideological principle by Roosevelt and Churchill which echoed with calls for the respect of sovereign rights, of freedom of trade, of international peace and security. Again economic objectives were made especially prominent. The fifth principle expressed the urge of both governments 'to bring about the fullest collaboration between all nations in the economic field with the object of securing, for all, improved labor standards, economic advancement and social security'.[29]

The supremacy of economics

Like Wilson, Roosevelt was convinced of the universal significance of the American historical experience. 'The essential validity of the American Bill of Rights was accepted everywhere at least in principle', he is reported to have said on one occasion. But the Americans of the Roosevelt and Truman administrations were convinced that in the experience of the New Deal they had specific confirmation of the determining role of economic ingredients in any strategy of social and political stabilisation. As Roosevelt told Stalin at Yalta:

> ... in his [Roosevelt's] opinion any leader of a people must take care of their primary needs. He said he remembered when he first became President the United States was close to revolution because the people lacked food, clothing and shelter, but he had said, 'If you elect me President I will give you these things', and since then there was very little problem in regard to social disorder in the United States.[30]

By the summer of 1944 State Department planners had developed a comprehensive prognosis for the past, present and future situation of liberated countries in Europe. At its heart it stated that: 'American policy is based on the premise that the economic well-being of a country is a primary factor in its internal stability and its peaceful relations with other states.' For this reason Washington looked forward in the case of a country like Italy to: 'An economic reconstruction designed to create an expanding economy which will offer the Italian people genuine opportunities for their economic betterment.'[31]

The American executive itself was more attentive to the possibilities of expansion than to the needs of stability. The Hot Springs Agriculture Conference of March 1943, promoted by Roosevelt to 'do something about world agriculture', dealt with food not in terms of relief but in terms of trade. Likewise the epochal Bretton Woods conference of July 1944 set out to reform the world's financial system and succeeded in making plans for the International Bank for Reconstruction and Development and the International Monetary Fund. But here too non-American negotiators such as Keynes were struck by the assumption that good times were just around the corner; that a new American-run economic system of free trade and constantly expanding incomes would soon come into being. The venerable Secretary of State, Cordell Hull, explained the reasoning in a famous passage in his memoirs:

> To me, unhampered trade dovetailed with peace; high tariffs, trade barriers, and unfair economic competition with war. Though realizing that many other factors were involved, I reasoned that if we could get a freer flow of trade – freer in the sense of fewer discriminations and obstructions – so that

one country would not be deadly jealous of another and the living standards of all countries might rise, thereby eliminating the economic dissatisfaction that breeds war, we might have a reasonable chance for lasting peace.[32]

Planning for world reconstruction

In Hull's State Department and at the Council on Foreign Relations research centre in New York committees were at work throughout the war developing this line of analysis, which can be traced consistently from the middle of the 1930's to the postwar period in the Department's public statements. It built on the thought of men like 'the great elucidator' Walter Lippmann, the authoritative commentator whose 1934 essay, 'The Method of Freedom' was among the most widely read discussions of the impact of mass democracy on popular economic demands. Lippmann insisted that 'the modern state cannot endure unless it insures to its people their standard of life' and he contrasted the narrowness of national politics with the cosmopolitan trends in economic life.[33] Inside the Administration Vice President Wallace had by 1942 established himself as the spokesman for 'a messianic liberalism of abundance', writes the American historian Charles Maier. Wallace saw the war as 'an act of millenial liberation that would usher in "the century of the common man".'[34]

Roosevelt and his men believed that the way to do this was to project abroad the American experience in general and the New Deal model in particular. Even before America's entry into the war, discussions in the State Department in 1941 were looking to goals which were economic and social as well as political, 'a common effort on the part of all to improve living conditions and to attain democratic participation'. This meant the Far East and Europe, said the planners, in order to realise the major objectives of American foreign policy: 'world stability and economic advancement'.[35] Among the favourite Administration models was the Tennessee Valley Authority, the great New Deal system of dams, hydroelectric plants and irrigation projects which had transformed the prospects of a once-backward rural region. Former Under-Secretary of State Sumner Welles pinpointed the Danube and the Balkans as the most suitable terrain in Europe for a similar scheme. In October 1944 he wrote:

The poverty of the masses underlies every problem of the Balkan peoples. Only through a higher standard of living can they develop the social foundation upon which to construct stable national governments. . . . The potentialities inherent in some vast power project which might be established in the Danube valley are almost unlimited. The electrical power derived from such an installation, cutting across all the national lines of

Eastern Europe, could within twenty years create an entirely new industrial civilisation in the area.[36]

Schemes such as this one were typical of the work being done in the network of State Department committees planning the postwar world and how America would build it. Outside the Department they could count on the collaboration of eminent congressmen, journalists specialising in international affairs, businessmen and academic experts, as well as the research resources of the Council on Foreign Relations in New York.

So the plans which emerged were the product of an entire political culture, generally internationalist but not necessarily New Dealer, convinced of the rightness of Roosevelt's vision of collective security but anxious to know how to put it into practice, determined to make sure that America's public and her allies understood the dominant role the United States would naturally play in the postwar world. Although generically aware of the rise of the Left, the evolving political and economic situation in the European countries was largely beyond the ken of this élite. Rarely was any thought ever given by these people, sophisticated and worldly as they were, to the possibility that the liberated nations of Europe might have evolved their own ideas on what should happen to them when the war was over.

The one exception to this rule was European integration. Churchill's visit of May 1943 introduced official Washington to the prime minister's views on a regional Council, even a kind of 'United States of Europe'.[37] This was practically the only time during the war that the American planners reacted to a proposal from outside. The Council on Foreign Relations decided however that gains from a loose regional organisation in Europe were 'likely to be of far more modest dimensions than their advocates appear to realise'. Yet the economic prospects were taken seriously: removing internal barriers to trade and forming a larger market, said a State Department economist, 'would lead to a higher degree of regional specialisation and hence to a higher level of real income in Europe, from which American trade with Europe would be likely to benefit'. At the same time opinions were expressed to the effect that America's attitude would necessarily depend on this union's external commercial policy: it might turn out to be very damaging to US interests. For this reason, and on the basis of worries that any regional arrangement would detract from the world security organisation – the United Nations – 'extreme reserve' was chosen as the official US posture on moves towards European unity.[38]

Of course it had always been understood that free trade meant closer economic collaboration, and that sovereignty as traditionally understood was a 'fetishism' or 'curse' standing in the way of this process. As far back as 1942 the Council on Foreign Relations had asked how the Big Three could pool their sovereignty and how the 'popular association of sovereignty with national freedom and independence [could] be effectively broken'. At this stage the economic objectives were still being defined as 'economic security' and 'social welfare', including full employment, on an international scale, and the means proposed were almost exclusively functional and institutional. This was the road which led to the Bretton Woods conference of July 1944 which founded the World Bank and the International Monetary Fund. They were 'a high-water mark in human attempts to order the world economically', in the words of a leading player in the postwar order they created.[39]

But in their 'Progress Report on Postwar Programs' of September 1944, the State Department experts specialising in economic and social policy were even more ambitious. They spelled out their view of US objectives in the world as:

(1) An expansion of economic activity.
(2) The maintenance of high and stable levels of employment.
(3) Rising standards of living.[40]

Specific policy approaches to realise these objectives in fields ranging from commodity policy to cartels, from reconstruction finance to reparations, were detailed in separate plans.

Other experts were conjuring up the vision of the 'chain reaction' that might be set off by huge, planned capital inputs into countries such as Greece. Roosevelt was searching for a country which could be transformed by American capital and methods from virgin desert into a fully developed modern state. The country he was inclined to choose for the experiment was Iran. The planners in the State Department were now ready to propose 'a thoroughgoing reorientation of its economic and social life' for France, a revolution in its values which would 'place less emphasis on security and more emphasis on risk and enterprise', with the state providing 'direction, coherence and encouragement' in a 'general scheme of industrial and agricultural development'. By this time, however – December 1944 – reality on the ground was beginning to catch up with the visionaries in Washington.[41]

COMMITMENTS TO THE FUTURE

The so-called 'revolution of rising expectations', normally associated with the booming Europe of the 1950s, took place in reality during the

Second World War. 'The demand for prosperity has spread and deepened', noted E.H. Carr, who insisted that it could only be met if the logic of economic interdependence was recognised politically. The US was obviously the country where this recognition process was furthest advanced, but remoteness from the chaos of Europe meant that no practical plans existed at the end of the war to bring it to bear on reality. America had defined her peace aims even before joining the war, in the Four Freedoms Speech, the Lend-Lease Master Agreement and the Atlantic Charter. In these the language was all about collective security for the world, free trade among nations, and greater prosperity for individuals (even the Four Freedoms declaration was prefaced by the assertion that among the basic democratic expectations was 'the enjoyment of the fruits of scientific progress in a wider and constantly rising standard of living').

In Europe in contrast the key priorities revolved round drawing up new social contracts. Under these dispensations full employment would be guaranteed, welfare for all assured and industrial relations orchestrated. By implication the role of the state would expand enormously and when reconstruction of industry and trade began, it would take place in a recognisable framework of modernisation: 'profit was to be ruled out as the prime goal of economic activity', said Belgian observers. In Britain, reports Paul Addison,

> Social security for all, family allowances, major reform in education, a National Health Service, Keynesian budgetary technique, full employment policies, town and country planning, closer relations between the state and industry – all these had been set on foot by the spring of 1943. . . . All three parties went to the polls in 1945 committed to principles of social and economic reconstruction which their leaders had endorsed as members of the Coalition.[42]

If there was one moment when the highest aspirations of the Europeans and the Americans came together it was in the design and launching of the United Nations Charter. In the grand structure where Roosevelt's hopes now resided, a key article (no. 55) explained the economic and social aims of the new world government:

> With a view to the creation of conditions of stability and well-being which are necessary for peaceful and friendly relations among nations based on respect for the principle of equal rights and self-determination of peoples, the United Nations shall promote:
> (a) higher standards of living, full employment, and conditions of economic and social progress and development.

Within months of its launching at San Francisco in June, 1945 the United Nations and its charter were practically forgotten. The conditions existing in Europe at war's end had little or nothing to do with the dreams of the utopians in Washington and elsewhere. Yet the lessons read in America and Europe in the bloodshed of the Second World War were destined, this time round, not to be forgotten.

NOTES

1. General de Gaulle *War Memoirs. Salvation 1944–1946* 1960 p 96
2. Mortimer E *Roosevelt's Children. Tomorrow's World Leaders and Their World* 1987 Ch 1
3. *Manchester Guardian* 2 Aug 1945
4. Carr EH *Conditions of Peace* 1942 p xxi
5. Divine RA *Second Chance. The Triumph of Internationalism in America During World War II* New York 1967 pp 104–5
6. Addison P *Now the War is Over* 1987 p 1
7. Cited in Djilas M *Conversations with Stalin* 1963 p 90
8. Foreign Relations of the United States (henceforth FRUS) *The Conferences at Malta and Yalta. 1945* Washington DC 1955 pp 972–3
9. Ellwood DW *Italy 1943–1945* Leicester 1985 p 159
10. Paragraph based on Blom JCH and ten Have W Making the New Netherlands: Ideas about renewal in Dutch politics and society during the Second World War. In Smith ML and Stirk PMR (eds) *Making the New Europe. European Unity and the Second World War* 1990 Ch 7
11. De Gaulle op cit pp 103–4
12. Blom and ten Have, op cit p 12
13. Emerson B 'Belgian Political Parties and European Integration 1940–1944'. Paper presented at the conference, 'European Unity in Context' Hull 1988; Henau BP Shaping a new Belgium: the CEPAG – the Belgian Commission for the Study of Postwar Problems (1941–44). In Smith and Stirk op cit Ch 8
14. Lipgens W *A History of European Integration* vol 1 1945–47 Oxford 1982 pp 53–8
15. Urwin DW *Western Europe since 1945* 3rd edn 1981 pp 24–5
16. Carr op cit pp 57–8
17. Keynes *The Economic Consequences of the Peace* 1919 p 134, 211, cit Carr 57
18. Carr EH *Nationalism and After* 1945 pp 20–21; Arndt HW *The Rise and Fall of Economic Growth* Melbourne 1978 Ch 3
19. Tomasevich J *The Chetniks, War and Revolution in Yugoslavia, 1941–1945* Stanford 1975 pp 12–19, 84; for the condition of Greece at the end of the war, Nachmani A Civil War and Foreign Intervention in Greece 1946–49. In *Journal of Contemporary History* Oct 1990
20. Zamagni V *Dalla periferia al centro. La seconda rinascita economica dell'Italia 1861–1981* Bologna 1990 p 343, 368
21. Ellwood *Allied Occupation Policy in Italy 1943–46* PhD thesis Reading

University 1977 Pt III, Conclusions; (summary in *Italy 1943* op cit Pt III)

22. De Gaulle op cit p 23
23. Kuisel R *Capitalism and the State in Modern France* Cambridge 1981 p 169
24. Ibid pp 178–9. The French debate on postwar society is the only one to have attracted a comprehensive new study: Shennan A *Rethinking France: Plans for Renewal 1940–1946* Oxford 1989
25. Henau op cit; Sorensen V *Social Democratic Government in Denmark Under the Marshall Plan, 1947–1950* PhD thesis European University Institute 1987 Ch 1
26. *Prefaces to Peace. A Symposium* NY 1943 pp 121, 292 (this volume, also a bestseller, contains the full text of Willkie's book, together with essays by Hoover, Wallace and Sumner Welles)
27. *The Public Papers and Addresses of Franklin D. Roosevelt. 1940 Volume* NY 1941 p 672
28. Council on Foreign Relations *The Problem of Lend-Lease: Its Nature, Implications and Settlement* NY April 1944
29. Atlantic Charter reproduced in *Documents on American Foreign Relations 1941–42*, World Peace Foundation Boston 1942 (henceforth DAFR) p 11
30. FRUS 1945 *The Conferences at Malta and Yalta* p 923
31. State Dept document n. CAC–248, 'The Treatment of Italy' 31 Aug 1944, in National Archives (NA) Record Group (RG) 59 Records of Harley A. Notter ('Notter File')
32. Roosevelt and Hull cited in Gaddis J L *The United States and the Origins of the Cold War 1941–1947* NY 1972 p 11, 19
33. Lippmann W *The Method of Freedom* NY 1934 pp 12–14, 36
34. Maier CS The Politics of Productivity: Foundations of American International Economic Policy after World War II. In Katzenstein PJ (ed) *Between Power and Plenty. Foreign Economic Policies of Advanced Industrial States* Madison, Wisconsin 1978 p 28
35. Précis of the Discussion of the General Advisory Committee on the Future Cultural Relations Program 18 Sept 1941 in NA RG 59 'Notter File'
36. Welles S *The Time for Decision* NY 1944 pp 152–3
37. See Woodward Sir L *British Foreign Policy in the Second World War* 1962 p 446
38. Council on Foreign Relations: Studies of American Interests in the War and the Peace, Memorandum of Discussion, Political Group, P-B71, 'European Regionalism and Postwar World Organization', 27 Sept 1943; Committee on European Regional Organisation, Mins of Meeting of 15 Oct 1943 n NA RG 59 'Notter File'
39. Council on Foreign Relations doc P-B48 'National Sovereignty and the International Tasks of the Postwar World' 31 Aug 1942 by Walter R Sharp,(a comprehensive paper anticipating many themes and objectives of postwar American foreign economic policy); on Bretton Woods, Roll Sir E *The World After Keynes. An Examination of the Economic Order* 1968 Ch 8 (cit at p 91)
40. 'Progress Report on Postwar Programs' 1 Sept 1944 in NA RG 59 'Notter File'; a substantial selection of this material is available in

Notter HA *Postwar Foreign Policy Preparation 1939–1945* Washington DC Dept of State 1949

41. Greek case cited by Reitzel W *The Mediterranean: Its Role in America's Foreign Policy* NY 1948 p 145; Roosevelt quoted by Secretary of State Stettinius in Stettinius ER *Roosevelt and the Russians. The Yalta Conference* NY 1949 p 180; French case discussed in State Dept, Committee on Territorial Problems, doc T-556, 'The Future Industrial Development of France: Problems and Prospects' 12 Dec 1944 in NA RG 59 'Notter File'

42. Henau op cit p 1; Addison P *The Road to 1945* 1975 p 14

CHAPTER TWO
The Realities of Survival 1945–47

THE COLLAPSE OF EUROPE?

In the middle of March 1945 the British deputy prime minister, Clement Attlee, returned from a tour of liberated Europe. The message he brought back was not comforting. The *Economist* noted how 'gradually realisation is spreading that the plight of Europe is grave beyond words, and that a new attitude to its problems is absolutely necessary'. In the same days the shrewd American journalist Anne O'Hare McCormick wrote in the *New York Times*:

> The human problem the war will leave behind it has not yet been imagined, much less faced by anybody. There has never been such destruction, such disintegration of the structure of life. . . . The liberated cannot be fed or put on the way of recovery. The sharp increase in the death rate and tuberculosis rate in France during the first winter of liberation . . . is typical. In Italy the relief sent from the United States, though considerable, is only a drop in an ocean of need. In Belgium the situation is politically critical; in Holland it is worse.[1]

American writers and commentators often supplied the most telling surveys of the life of the peoples of liberated Europe in the months after the end of the war. They were freer to travel than most and so made more effective comparisons; also they had a much clearer conception of 'Europe', of what the societies and cultures of the 'Old World' shared, than their national counterparts in England or France.

In a country such as Italy, where they had followed the armies much more closely then any other journalists, they had long predicted what was likely to happen when hostilities finally ended. There the length and destructiveness of the war, barely alleviated by a hapless Anglo-American military government regime, brought economic breakdown and widespread near-starvation in the wake of liberation. The Communist Party counted over two million members by the end of 1945 and it was automatically assumed in the British and American camps that this was a direct outcome of the general misery. Some on the spot saw further. Anne McCormick had written in September 1944 that no political or territorial settlement, no security organization meant anything while people were starving:

> ... the danger in Italy – and this goes for all the poor, broken nations of the Continent, is not that it will go Communist ... [instead] it cannot be too strongly stressed – and the left parties here are keenly aware of it – that the prospect is not a violent but clearly directed shift from one system to another; it is an uncontrolled breakdown of the whole social structure.'[2]

In one of the first surveys offered after hostilities ended, Raymond Daniell of the *New York Times Magazine* dwelt on the moral problems left by the era of ceaseless mass destruction and totalitarian propaganda: the ruthlessness everywhere of the struggle for survival, the self-pity of those Germans who still believed in Hitler's 'defensive' war, the vindictiveness on display in countries like France where settling scores with 'collaborators' seemed far more important than seeking out those responsible for the collapse of 1940, the impulse in Resistance fighters to take the law into their own hands and turn to guns whenever their word was challenged. While black markets flourished on all sides, whingeing and resentment was already appearing against the needs of the rescuing armies: 'it will be a hungry and embittered Europe, with a people frustrated and cynical, that emerges from this war', said Daniell.[3]

By mid-summer it was clear that no effective plans existed to cope with the scale of the drama. It was easy to point out the essential need for 'a large measure of social reform and at the same time a rapid restoration of economic life', but concretely this meant tackling on a broad European, even trans-Atlantic, scale questions such as coal supplies. The problem was rarely mentioned in public, 'but it is coal that keeps statesmen awake at nights', another American commentator wrote in July; they feared what the US Supply Secretary Ickes called 'the race between coal and anarchy'.[4]

In Germany the coal crisis set off a spiral of disorder. It was due in part to the lack of pit-props. 'But the foresters refused to work in the rain because they lacked clothes or shoes, which in turn were in short supply in part because of low coal supplies to consumer-goods industries.' If all the coal promised to Italy arrived, it would meet one quarter of industry's needs, the *New York Times* revealed in a Europe-wide survey carried out in September. Meanwhile, of the 70,000 tons of building materials requested by Greece from UNRRA only half had arrived because of the shipping shortage. 'Economically, central Europe is in a state of suspended animation', wrote John MacCormac from Vienna in September. So far as industry in the region was concerned, 60–70 per cent had been carried off by the Russians, with the result that the most basic necessities were lacking, even nails to hold down coffin lids. With the winter approaching no household coal at all was available for a city which normally consumed 850,000 tons.[5]

For clothing the Viennese would have to depend on what could be converted from rags. All the clothes shops were said to be closed in Oslo, while Holland and Greece were also reported to be totally without clothing supplies. In the French clothing industry no more than 'one new suit yearly for every eight Frenchmen' was produced, though for $400 one could be had on the black market. Even in Britain, where clothing on the wartime 'utility' pattern was available by rationing, the king was moved to complain of the situation: 'I said (to the prime minister) we must all have new clothes and my family are down to the lowest ebb.'[6]

At the end of 1945 one of America's most senior commentators, C.L. Sulzberger described the twenty million 'desperate and homeless people . . . milling east and west, north and south, across the Continent'. Officially known as 'displaced persons', this immense army of refugees was made up of 'Germans pouring westwards into the devastated Reich from Slavdom, Poles and Czechs moving hard upon their heels into the devastated towns . . . Hungarians trudging into the Pannonian plain'. Throughout Europe, said Sulzberger, 'the freedom for which so many nations fought is far from evident', while in the east in particular conditions were similar to those which had prevailed after the First World War: 'Dictatorship succeeds dictatorship.'[7]

The future had never looked further away: ambitious reform schemes would have to be set aside, rising living standards and European unification now seemed dreams far over the horizon. Instead national survival and stability imposed themselves as the immediate priorities: reliable supplies of basic food, work for the masses, functioning law and order. 'By stability is meant not prosperity but freedom from want and freedom from unemployment', said the Executive Commissioner of the Allied military government in charge of Italy in May 1945. And everywhere, said the US Press, 'all are asking "what will America's policy be?"'[8]

THE NECESSITIES OF LIFE

Food and Politics

Contrary to the impression often given by commentators and historians who lived through the period, Communism and Communists were not the supreme preoccupation of the populations of Western Europe in the years after the war. A January 1946 opinion poll in France revealed that 49 per cent of those interviewed gave the satisfaction of basic needs as their principal concern, compared with 26 per cent who cited health and 15 per cent money. J.P. Rioux reports that these proportions would remain unchanged until as late as 1949, generating a 'durable and legitimate obsession with food supplies' and provoking political repercussions in all directions.[9]

In September 1945 the official ration in France stood as follows:

Fats	1 lb per month
Meat	8 oz per week
Sugar	1 lb per month
Cheese	5 oz per month
Wine	1 qt pr week
Potatoes	4 lbs per month
Ersatz coffee	4 oz per week
Milk	children only
Coal	100 lbs for entire winter
Fresh vegetables	unlimited[10]

As elsewhere, rationing, imports, prices, distribution and quality were all assumed to be direct government responsibilities, and as in other occupied countries, it was taken for granted that the end of German depredations would unlock plentiful supplies for domestic consumption. Instead 'deep social conflict' over food was soon evident in the French provinces as black markets flourished and restaurants prospered. Meanwhile the mass of the population faced a reality which was 'often quite desperately bleak'. CDLs (Comités de Libération), Patriotic Militia, the CGT trade union and the Communist Party itself all mobilised, producing in the course of 1945 witch-hunts for profiteers, strike waves, looted bakeries, the storming of *préfectures* and the ritual burning of ration cards in mass protests.[11]

Looking at Greece, Yugoslavia, Romania, Hungary, Austria and Italy, Allied Force Headquarters in Italy produced in June 1945 an unusually thoughtful analysis of the consequences of food shortages in liberated areas, an analysis which would reappear in economic surveys of postwar Europe all the way down to the Marshall Plan. This concentrated on the breakdown in economic relations between town and country as a cause of social unrest, noting that most of these countries were largely agricultural in nature while possessing significant numbers of industrial workers who depended on the surplus from the country for essentials, together with a margin of cheap imports. The workers in return supplied the country with basic manufactured products, from shoes to textiles and tools. With the disruption of production and trade brought by the war, money had lost almost all its purchasing power, the town-country exchange had broken down and the black market flourished. The reaction of the starving workers was to press for ever more aggressive action from their representatives, who were of course Communists and socialists.[12]

Everywhere there was resentment against the obvious gains made by the peasants and farmers from the war. A British observer reporting on northern Europe from late 1944 to the end of 1945 spoke of

> the unveiled hostility of the townsman everywhere from Normandy to the Rhine, who accuses the peasant of being the only war-profiteer. . . . In Flanders in the autumn of 1944 it was the farmers' wives and daughters who dressed in the height of fashion, not the ladies of the towns. In short, any peasant who failed to clear his mortgages on land and property during 1940–45 was an exception.

By this analysis only when overseas food and products arrived again would the old balance of supply and demand be restored, and social harmony reappear.[13]

But this was a relaxed view of a situation which was deteriorating towards catastrophe by the end of 1945. Even in relatively intact Denmark – where rationing was imposed to create a food surplus for others – there was worse dislocation than during the war, since the Germans had paid high prices for bacon and butter, and had kept up a fairly effective flow of coal supplies, on which Danish industry was totally dependent. Now the breakdown of Germany, the diminished import capacity of the British and the world shortage of shipping exposed the country to severe difficulties.[14] Everywhere people discovered the physical meaning of economic interdependence and the incapacity of the structures dreamed up in wartime to deal with those conditions which were foreseen, let alone those which developed in Germany all the way to 1948–49, far beyond the limits of imagination until then.

The aid challenge

The Economic and Social Council of the United Nations was told that in Europe in the summer of 1946:

> ... 100 million people were being fed at a level of 1,500 calories or less – the level at which health suffers severely and working capacity is quickly reduced or destroyed. Another 40 million were living at the little less dangerous level of between 1,500 and 2,000 calories. These people were also desperately short of housing, domestic equipment, tools, clothes and footwear.[15]

The Hot Springs Agriculture Conference of May 1943, which set up the UN Food and Agriculture Organisation (FAO) had warned that food shortages on a world scale were already appearing and that the transition from war to peace would be difficult. But the FAO was aimed at the grand Rooseveltian objective of 'freedom from want everywhere in the world' – in a context of harmonious liberalisation. So a separate organisation was needed to cope with the inevitable but hopefully brief transition period. Hence the birth of UNRRA – the United Nations Relief and Rehabilitation Administration, created in November 1943 to organise essential supplies and services in liberated areas in the time between the end of hostilities and the restoration of effective local control.

UNRRA was a remarkable achievement, 'tantamount to a declaration of the moral solidarity of the whole human race', proclaimed the great British historian Arnold Toynbee. Financed to the extent of 75 per cent by the United States, it made a decisive relief contribution in much of Central and Eastern Europe, as well as in Yugoslavia, Greece and (in 1946) in Italy. But UNRRA did not involve Western Europe – nominally self-supporting – and did not command the resources or supplies even to meet its own minimum targets. Above all it had no control (except through its massive displaced persons operation) over relief in Germany, heart of the great European food crisis of 1946–48.[16]

In June 1946 a commentator in London wrote:

> ... it was as late as December 1945 before it was generally recognised that a food crisis actually existed and the spring of 1946 before much was done about it, although UNRRA had been pointing out the prospects months earlier. . . . The 1945 output of bread grains in Continental Europe was little more than half the prewar average, and for bread consumption to be maintained at former levels imports would have had to be some 32 million tons as against 3.7 million annually. Many adverse factors contributed to this: an overall shortage of fertilisers following on low output and exhaustive farming during the war years; war damage and curtailment of sowing caused by military operations, minefields and fortifications; lack of equip-

ment, requisitioning of livestock, mass population shifts, insufficient labour, hasty land reform, and, finally, unfavourable weather. . . . The food problems of Germany reflect all the above factors with particular intensity.[17]

The division of Germany according to the wartime interallied agreements had partitioned the country into tightly insulated zones and had handed over to Poland and Russia areas containing a quarter of the country's food potential. From them, from the Russian zone and from much of the rest of Central Europe, came successive waves of refugees which meant that by October 1946 the western zones were filled with a destitute population more than four million above that of the same area in 1937. The result was inevitable: rations down to 1,014 calories in the British zone by the end of February 1946, to 1,180 calories in the American zone by the end of May, to 910 calories in the French zone. Less than 900 calories were said to be available in Vienna in May, with supplies even at that level about to end.[18]

The Dutch, Belgian and Danish economies, all dependent structurally on the prosperity of Germany, felt the weight of its collapse immediately. Meanwhile the British were forced in the course of June 1946 to bring in unprecedented levels of rationing at home, in part to free supplies for their zone in Germany. But they were also obliged to divert wheat to India, where exceptional and catastrophic droughts – which swept Africa and Asia from Morocco to Australia in the latter months of 1945 – transformed the European crisis into a worldwide drama and put pressure on the producers beyond anything yet seen.

In America, however, source of over half the world's wheat exports, there appeared to be little sense of crisis. As an expert in London observed: 'it is a peculiar commentary on world organization that, in what is perhaps the greatest food crisis of all time, over twice as much wheat as before the war is still being fed to animals'.[19] Getting wheat off the farms and into ships meant restoring price, production and distribution controls which the government in Washington was most reluctant to do at a time when revulsion was mounting on all sides against the war experience and all its commitments. In the course of 1946 the effort was made, step by step, and relief programmes were improvised to prevent the worst happening. But no one was satisfied with the results, and everywhere pressure arose for a different kind of American approach, a new politics which would link all the economic factors together in a system of practical transatlantic cooperation to replace the failed or yet-to-be-realised utopias of wartime.

Instead, under American pressure, UNRRA was wound up at the end of 1946. The *Economist* believed that by this time Washington saw UNRRA as too generous to governments in the Russian zone and an obstacle on the road to world free trade. In this way was undone 'one of the only successful essays in international cooperation achieved so far'.[20]

WORK AND WANT

When Ernest Bevin, the great trade unionist and Minister of Labour, went to Portsmouth to see the men of the 50th Division off for the invasion of France in June 1944 (reports Paul Addison), he was asked 'Ernie, when we have done this job for you, are we going back on the dole?'

> Hindsight supplies the answer [Addison goes on].They would not have to return to the dole. A new deal for the working classes was already in the making, and not for the working classes alone. The hopes of soldiers and civilians for a better life, and the plans of social reformers for an all-embracing Welfare State, were converging. In the general election of July 1945 they met, and the Labour Party was returned to power in a sweeping victory.[21]

This victory was greeted by the Left everywhere as proof that history was on their side. In northern Italy there were huge demonstrations to celebrate it: in Turin alone 40,000 marched. The Socialist party paper *Avanti!* commented:

> These were not the tough, menacing processions of strikers defending their right to live. There was something new . . . there was the serenity and joy of knowing that England's workers, triumphant in their conquest of government, will not want to deny the right to work and to democracy of any nation.[22]

Conditions in industry

The British running Allied military government in northern Italy were not amused. They had been relieved to discover that only 10–15 per cent of industrial capacity had been destroyed. But in the short term there was inflation – up to 3,000 per cent with respect to 1939 – mass unemployment, forecast at 1.5 million by sources in Milan, and severe shortages of food, coal and raw materials. Strikes accompanied by demonstrations and factory occupations were an everyday occurrence, inevitably raising the spectre of Communist orders and organisation. In the case of FIAT itself, 'the direction of the concern has been almost entirely Communist-inspired' said a military intelligence report in

36

July. But an American civilian analysis looked beyond the gates of FIAT, and referring to demonstrations involving up to 70,000 people, expressed the conviction that: 'they are not being instigated by the radical parties but they are rather spontaneous outbursts on the part of the working masses against their enforced idleness and against conditions in general'.[23]

Damage to factories alone was not the key factor in determining the fate of an industrial economy after the liberation. In the French case, writes Rioux, the greatest threat to recovery came from the breakdown of the transport system – 4,000 kms of railway, five-sixths of the locomotives, three-quarters of the goods wagons had been destroyed – and the shortage of coal, France being the world's largest importer. The French Finance Minister told an American expert shortly after VE (Victory in Europe) day that in his country it was coal that represented the key to the entire economy and hence to stability.[24]

Everyone desperately needed coal, the expert told a New York audience in November 1945, and since the two major prewar suppliers, Britain and Germany, could no longer produce anything for export, almost no one – except the United States – was in a position to supply it. The list was endless: 'France needs coal, Luxemburg needs coal, Belgium needs coal, the Netherlands . . . Denmark . . . Norway . . . Italy . . . Finland . . . Czechoslovakia . . . Greece . . . the Neutrals.' Even Russia, the Iberian peninsula and North Africa had to be included to complete the picture, which was of course dominated by the German situation. There it was certain that supplies would not reach the minimum level needed to prevent 'disease and unrest'. Clearly:

> . . . unless coal is made available to France, and to other European nations, talk of free trade, the value of the franc or other currencies, the Four Freedoms, etc., is only academic. The French national income is several billion dollars below that necessary to maintain a stable government.[25]

At a time when increased production in all sectors was desperately needed, 'an exhausted and demoralised workforce' was expected to bear the brunt of food, coal, gas and electricity shortages and a tripling in the cost of living compared to 1938, as inflation proceeded to 'put down deep roots in the French economy'.[26]

The most devastated country, however, was Holland. Here too the greatest damage was to the transport sector, with over 60 per cent of its value being destroyed. Industrial output was less than 25 per cent of its prewar level, and 219,000 hectares of land had been deliberately flooded by the Germans, including over 77,000 under salt water. But

37

in spite of a baby-boom and a housing situation reported as 'even worse than that [of Britain]', the Dutch were seen by contemporary commentators as a law-abiding people who cooperated well with their government, and so were likely to be the first to complete their reconstruction. In this view their future seemed assured, if their colonial relationships could be restabilised, international financial support assured and, above all, if Germany could be rebuilt quickly.[27]

Responses from below

Workers and trade unionists in Denmark and Belgium, countries whose strategic situation was not dissimilar to that of the Dutch, did not wait for these conditions to materialise. The Danish Communist Party received 12.5 per cent of the vote in the October 1945 elections, forcing the long-ruling Social Democrats into opposition. The stage was thus set for a lengthy season of industrial strikes over inflation and wage restraint, since it was the Liberal–Conservative bloc which had the largest vote and now took power, having campaigned on the slogan of 'away with restrictions' and ostentatiously renouncing anything like a long-term economic strategy.[28]

Belgium's economy had emerged among the least ruined at the end of the war, with little destruction to manufacturing industry and the key port of Antwerp almost intact. But her dependence on Germany and the loss of skilled workers during the war – 40,000 German prisoners of war were employed in the mines till October 1947 – soon brought dislocation and inflationary pressures. Food, fuel, transport shortages and financial measures to restrain inflation caused government crises from the liberation onwards, and only when a Communist leader was made Minister for Food and the coal situation eased, did the focus of political discontent shift elsewhere.

In this sort of context, democratising the factories was never as important to the forces of the Left as restarting production and defending employment: the 'troisième bataille de France' as it was called in Paris, by authorities, parties and unions alike. Rioux writes:

> The Communist Party threw its weight totally and continuously behind the efforts which were to lay the foundations for the 'renaissance nationale'. . . . Speaking in the mining regions of the Nord on 21 July 1945, Thorez defined production as the highest class duty of the French worker and identified increased output as the weapon with which to defeat the forces of reaction.[29]

In Italy the message was accompanied by appeals for wage and price controls, but found an enthusiastic response among those in work, a positive reaction against the stagnation and alienation prevalent under Fascism and the Germans.[30] The ability to stimulate work and output thus appeared as one of the key currencies of their legitimacy everywhere left-wing parties aspired to government. Conversely the ability to restrict it was soon confirmed as their key currency of power.

British workers initially slackened off after working fifty-six hours a week for six years in typical factories, but the manufacturing economy was swamped with demand from the Empire and from areas of the world formerly served by Germany, Japan and the other war-damaged producers, as well as by the desperate need to earn dollars. The result was the Labour government's spring 1946 production campaign across the whole of industry to convince all sides of what was at stake in the economic situation: 'Fill the ships and we will fill the shops', promised the official slogan.[31] The Labour government was fortunate: the unions and the governing party in Britain made up one vast area of organised consensus for a Cabinet determined above all to continue the well-established wartime programme of social reform. Days lost through strike action in the first five years after the war were one-twentieth of what they had been in the corresponding period after the First World War; unemployment vanished. The British had recovered their prewar level of income and output by 1946 and increased it a further 8 per cent by the end of the following year.

But in much of Western and Southern Europe, by way of contrast, decisive battles on 'who governs?' which had begun even before liberation, were still being fought in 1946, and often they were being fought on the streets and in the factories.

THE RETURN TO LEGALITY

The Resistance and the Communist question

In January 1945 the future prime minister, Harold Macmillan, was busy as the British political adviser to the Supreme Allied Commander in the Mediterranean. He was preoccupied in particular with the likely behaviour of the northern Resistance in Italy, dominated by the Comunist Party, during the final phases of the war. 'The lesson of Greece', he told his diary, 'is that nothing matters except "disarmament". The political questions are the excuse for retaining armed power.'[32] Churchill of course was more eloquent: 'Democracy is no harlot to be picked up in the street by a man with a tommy gun', he told the Commons in December 1944, in a debate on his government's decision to face down the Communist insurrection in Athens with force.

In both Greece and Italy the Allies deployed an extraordinary range of military, political and psychological techniques to guarantee the continuity of constitutional government and the machinery of state – no matter how compromised – until elections could be held. When Belgium was liberated the section of the Resistance movement dominated by the Communists could count on some 10,000 men and women, while the Belgian police contained no more than 8,000 unarmed gendarmes. Again the threat of Allied intervention was thought necessary to secure the neutralisation of the armed potential of the Resistance, opening a long period of political turmoil in which the disarmament process itself was a key issue.[33] In France de Gaulle had tackled the problem unaided, incorporating well-established Resistance units into the armed forces (as was done to a certain degree in Italy, Belgium and Holland), and dissolving the Communist-dominated Patriotic Militia by decree.

The Communist rank-and-file in most countries were astonished by this outcome to their struggles, discovering only at this hour the new realities of national sovereignty the war had brought. A Milanese militant complained of '[the] moral liquidation of everything that was best, historically new in the Resistance and the insurrection, namely a clandestine government which made laws and created respect for them'.[34] Communist Party leaders were participating in coalition governments in France, Italy, Belgium and Denmark by the war's end. Everywhere they made strenuous efforts to ensure that the men from the mountains and the Maquis understood that if all went according to plan, their days of armed struggle against the invader would be a source of pride, but not a prelude to revolution. 'The task of the [CDLs]', said the Secretary General of the French Communist Party, Maurice Thorez, 'is not to substitute themselves for the administration, but to help those who are administering.'[35]

Referring to the euphoric liberation moment a Communist member of the FIAT labour-management committee recalled: 'One thing was clear: out with the bosses, power and leadership to the workers.' But it was the the Communist Party and the all-party trade union, the CGIL, dominated by the Left, which did most to restrain the insurrectionary impulse in the factories and demobilise the political organs of the Resistance. The official explanation was the need to avoid Allied military government intervention, but the pattern was identical in France where military government did not exist.

In both France and Italy the Communist Parties put their recognition as legitimate mass parties at the head of priorities. To this end they presented themselves as 'the essential anchor of social stability', suggests the labour historian Walter Kendall:

> Only by means of their aid did the established order accomplish the difficult transition to a new normality and re-establish the old organs of state power, military and judiciary, substantially unchanged from an earlier age. This was not a development which anyone could have prophesied in advance.[36]

Doubtless true in part, this view nevertheless exaggerates the effective political power of the Communist Party leadership. Participation in government did not give the Communists the ability to penetrate the state, nor were their allies on the Left, the socialist parties, likely to concede any more political space to them than was strictly necessary.[37]

Left parties and trade unions of all kinds gained strength in numbers in these years, just as they had done during and after the First World War, and independently of political context or national situation. The French Communist-affiliated CGT went from two million members in 1939 to almost 5.6 million in 1946; the Belgian Confederation of Christian Unions passed from 305,000 in 1937 to 402,00 in 1946, the British TUC from just under 4.5 million to just over 7.5 million in the same period.[38] The French Socialist Party which emerged from the war was over 20 per cent larger in members than it had been at the end of the 1930s and added another 20,000 members between 1945 and 1946. But the PCF far outstripped it, passing from 545,000 members in June 1945 to 809,000 in January 1947. In Italy the Communist Party had grown by the end of 1946 to be two-and-a-half times as large as its socialist rival, which peaked in that year at 860,000. Yet in electoral terms the socialists were ahead of the Communist parties everywhere in Europe except France in 1946, and all of them had to reckon with the immediate mass strength of the reborn Christian Democrat parties.[39]

Hence the socialist-communist power potential was put to various uses according to time and place, and throughout the Left gaps soon appeared between rhetoric and realisation, between the leadership and the mass base. At stake were basic definitions of power and legitimacy in the new era. Communist parties across Western Europe faced up to the need to construct a following in electoral as well as in militant terms, thence to the discovery that the socialist parties were indispensable but were not easy or predictable allies. Public administrations, armed services and police forces were impervious to outsiders, especially Communists (indeed, said the *Economist,* in these circles had taken refuge the majority of 'ex-Nazis, ex-Fascists, ex-Vichyites and ex-collaborators of all sorts').[40] The links with Moscow were a factor which started to turn against the Communist parties when Russian policy in Eastern Europe, in their zone in Germany and over Trieste became public knowledge. A background of constantly mounting suspicion was thereby added to the diffidence their ruthlessness and conspiratorial ways had always provoked.

In reality there were many on both sides of the barrier separating Communists from non-Communists who were convinced that the insistence on legality was nothing more than a tactical smokescreen, and that at an eventual X Hour – when the Allied armies left, after a wave of mass strikes perhaps – the magic password for the insurrectionary break-out would be given. While unstable provisional governments began the difficult task of purging and reforming their police forces, arms caches were hidden away in remote parts of France and Italy or actually deployed in countries such as Greece or cities such as Trieste.

In the lugubrious pre-civil war atmosphere which characterised much of Southern Europe and France until well after 1948, it was inevitable that banditry and the black market should flourish and the far Right make a surprisingly quick recovery. A 'Rightist' terror quickly replaced the former 'Leftist' terror in many parts of Greece after the Resistance army was officially disbanded.[41] Italian neo-Fascists were active with propaganda as early as May 1945, and a powerful clandestine association built up by industrialists to fight Communism with force was detected by Allied Intelligence in June. From 'the usual coalition of frightened and compromised people . . . [as exists] in any liberated country' (said the *Economist*), there sprang the reactionary, corrupt, entirely cynical Uomo Qualunque (Average Man) movement which spread rapidly in 1946, and which would have its French parallel in campaigns against '*Résistentialisme*' and the anti-state agitations of the early 1950s.

The new parties in practice

The system of parties which had emerged from the war was the target of much of this resentment, accused of legitimising Communists and usurping moral as well as political authority by way of new constitutional settlements. The most clamorous protest was that of de Gaulle, who resigned in January 1946 in a climactic gesture of contempt at the sacrifice of national interests as he perceived them – the specific object of contention was the size of the army – to the manoeuvrings of the parties.

It was in part to appease the anti-party forces that purge processes in France and Italy were quickly abandoned or turned into amnesties: the spiral of recrimination purge trials set in motion threatened to delegitimise what little authority the new coalition governments possessed. In the same compromising spirit, prominent symbols of the Italian Resistance, such as the Milan underground leader, Parri, who had become prime minister in June 1945, were soon set aside. By November he was thought to be altogether too representative of the 'wind from the north' and was obliged to make way for the Christian Democrat De Gasperi, whose distinguishing 'sense of the state' would usher in a one-party hegemony unique in postwar European politics.[42]

The major surprise facing the Left in all its forms was the strength – quite unforeseen until the Resistance experience – of the new Christian Democrat parties of the centre.[43] By the middle of 1946 Catholics had emerged as the strongest party in Belgium, Holland, Luxemburg, Southern Germany, Italy, France, Austria and Hungary. In most of these countries they came from an identifiable if not strong political tradition, usually agrarian in its roots. Only the German CDU/CSU parties and the French MRP were substantially new.

All managed to combine conservatism based on traditional views of the authority of the state with the new impulse to social reform. This they did by entrusting government responsibilities to the party leaderships, while organising their popular base in affiliated trade unions and other voluntary associations. Their links with the Church were complex, and depended much on national traditions. But this was a time when the Vatican's authority was hard put to recover its prewar standing and seemed to have little response to the changes brought by the war other than to warn of the dangers of Communism. Anxious to establish their popularity on as wide a basis as possible, this was just one of the reasons why the renewed Catholic parties chose to create their political identities in the language of perceived national rather than confessional priorities.

The short-term results could be seen in the urge to renew the authority of the state and to promote national reconciliation in the name of reconstruction. Any impulse to settle the scores left by the war in purge processes or war crimes trials would be played down. Thus in France there was no question of applying the standards of 'indignitié nationale' invented for certain categories of collaborators to the institutions of the Republic. Instead, writes J.P. Rioux, the leading historian of the France of these years:

43

Conciliation and indulgence would contribute to the creation of unity and greatness. The State was the source of all legitimate authority and it repudiated disorder ... the *épuration* had to be curbed in the interests of returning to order and overcoming the material problems; the restoration of the State had priority in the struggle to survive and to stand up to the Allies.[44]

NOTES

1. *Economist* 17 March 1945, *New York Times* 14 March 1945
2. *New York Times* 11 Sept 1944
3. *New York Times Magazine* 13 May 1945
4. *New York Times* 8, 21 July 1945
5. Carlin W Economic Reconstruction in Western Germany, 1945–55: The Displacement of 'Vegetative Control'. In Turner ID (ed) *Reconstruction in Post-war Germany. British Occupation Policy and the Western Zones. 1945–1955* Oxford 1989 Chs 2, 3, 4; *New York Times* 16, 30 Sept, 13 Dec 1945
6. Ibid 30 Sept 1945; cit in Robertson AJ *The Bleak Midwinter 1947* Manchester 1986 p 5
7. *New York Times* 13 Dec 1945
8. *New York Times* 23 Sept 1944
9. Rioux JP *The Fourth Republic, 1944–1958* Cambridge 1987 pp 23–8
10. *New York Times* 30 Sept 1945
11. Rioux op cit
12. Ellwood *Italy 1943* op cit p 229
13. War Damage in Western Europe *The World Today* April 1946 p 147
14. Survey of International Affairs 1939–1946 *The Realignment of Europe* ed by Arnold Toynbee and Veronica M. Toynbee 1955 (henceforth 'Survey') p 570
15. Cit in ibid pp 38–9
16. Ibid Part I
17. The World Food Crisis *The World Today* June 1946 pp 246, 249
18. Ibid p 247
19. Ibid p 252
20. *Economist* 24 Aug 1946. (The Paris Peace Conference took place from the 27th July to the 15th October 1946.)
21. Addison *Now the War is Over* op cit pp 1–2
22. *Avanti!* Turin 28 July 1945
23. Ellwood *Italy 1943* op cit pp 227–9
24. Mayne R *Postwar. The Dawn of Today's Europe* 1983 p 25; Potter CJ Europe's Coal Problem. In *European Recovery* Proceedings of the Academy of Political Science Columbia University NY Jan 1946
25. Potter op cit
26. Rioux op cit pp 19–21
27. Griffiths RT *Economic Reconstruction Policy in the Netherlands and its International Consequences, May 1945–March 1951* European University Insti-

tute Working Paper n 76 Florence 1984; Recovery in the Liberated Countries of Western Europe *The World Today*, Feb 1947 p 93

28. Sorensen op cit pp 33–8
29. Rioux op cit p 63 and Ch 5 in general
30. Foa V La ricostruzione capitalistica nel Secondo dopoguerra. *Rivista di Storia Contemporanea* n 4 1973. Foa is a veteran left trade union leader and intellectual.
31. Crofts SW The Attlee Government's Economic Information Propaganda. *Journal of Contemporary History*, vol 21 1986 p 453–6. (This shows that the campaign was a failure, half the population at the end of it not even understanding 'the basic message that the country needed exports to pay for imports'.)
32. Macmillan H *The Blast of War* 1967 pp 677–8
33. Warner G *The Belgian Crisis of November, 1944: A Case Study in the Politics of Liberation* unpublished paper
34. Ellwood *Italy 1943* op cit p 190
35. Cf Warner G Belgium, France and Italy 1944–1950. *History Today* Sept 1983 p 12
36. Kendall W *The Labour Movement in Europe* 1975 pp 317–18
37. Eg Warner Belgium, France and Italy op cit
38. Kendall op cit pp 336–9
39. Ibid pp 380–7
40. *Economist* 1 Dec 1945
41. 'Survey' cit p 46, 399–400
42. Ellwood *Italy 1943* op cit p 218
43. Maier CS The Two Postwar Eras and the Conditions for Stability in Twentieth-Century Western Europe *American Historical Review* April 1981 p 332
44. Rioux op cit p 36, 40

CHAPTER THREE

Managing the Shift to Peace

RECONVERSION AND THE USES OF ADVERSITY

Across Europe, the British authorities were undoubtedly those in greatest control of their national economic and social situation. In the first instance this meant they knew with greater precision just how precariously their financial and supply circumstances stood. Hence the Cabinet's decision in August 1945 – when the end of Lend-Lease aid from America was suddenly announced, right after the Japanese surrender – to maintain a vast range of production, distribution and consumption controls inherited from the war for a further five-year transition period.

'Almost all the European countries tried to plan their adjustment through a system of controls', recalled an American commentator in the early 1950s. Few of them were new: 'The war had left a heritage of currency controls, rationing controls, export–import controls. The earlier depression years had provided a tradition of tariff controls, quota controls, allocation controls.'[1] How many of them were necessary or useful was impossible to say. Wherever the state had broken down they were unenforceable. In the early years of emergency, rationing systems for food, raw materials and money were essential. But as political energies returned they were criticised for producing bureaucracy and demoralisation, stagnation and illegality.

Apart from the United States, only in Britain had there been systematic thought during the war about planning relief and reconstruction on an international scale. Such reflections as the 1942 Fabian conference in Oxford had correctly identified the key problems, their likely dimensions and the desirable principles of collective action for tackling them. Action which integrated the work of the suppliers and set in motion a continuous process of relief, reconstruction and modernisation, on a world scale, was the goal of such visions, which found their concrete expression in part in the United Nations Charter, UNRRA, FAO, UNICEF and the related agencies.[2]

The experts and visionaries behind these developments had always taken care to insist they were not simply idealists, and had learnt the lessons of the failed pacifist internationalism of the 1920s. But even they could never begin to glimpse the distance between their well-written, technically convincing blueprints – which foresaw Britain 'taking the lead' in Europe – and the dislocated horrors which emerged on the ground after 1945. There impulses to survival and revival usually took on the most spontaneous localistic or nationalistic forms.

Italian textile manufacturers restarted production by black-market bartering of finished product against raw material and coal supplies. The 'rates of exchange' tended more and more in their favour as the general clothing shortage was aggravated by floods of refugees and home-coming soldiers. UNRRA later declared that not one kilo of the early imports of textiles remained in the country; all was re-exported clandestinely by profiteers.[3]

In France it was 'popular demand' which forced the government to concede an immediate, large wage rise in September 1944 to make up for the years of Vichy or German austerity, and likewise nationalisation of the mines was pressed forward by spontaneous strikes in the coal regions in protest against collaborationist coal owners and conditions in general.[4]

Planning and its limits

But the French authorities were the first in Continental Europe to see how the opportunity for radical change hidden in the confusion all around might be realised. The new men with experience of the wartime New Deal and British welfare planning now appeared on the national scene. Their economic culture and ability to mobilise facts were deployed to convince politicians, industrialists, workers, public opinion and 'the world' (i.e. the United States) that their comprehensive vision of reconstruction and modernisation offered the only way forward, deserving all-out support. The most famous of them was Jean Monnet, the founding father of French economic planning and among the patron saints of European integration. Amidst the doom and gloom, he was able to sense that 'France had in fact become a new country, full of fresh energies which lacked only a setting to work in, a method of action, and objectives on which to converge'.[5] These of course he set out to provide, armed with a faithful band of experts, a distinctive command of the true facts of the situation and his own techniques for managing the relationship between economics and politics in a world of rising expectations.[6]

Monnet's team gathered the scarce data available, developed a series of targets for production and imports and appointed 'Modernization Commissions' to construct programmes for the six industries identified as crucial: coalmines and electricity, steel and building materials, transport and farm machinery. Against a background of deepening political chaos and worsening inflation, Monnet succeeded between 1945 and spring 1947 – with the decisive support of de Gaulle as well as the Left parties and unions – in making sure 'the Plan' was 'firmly rooted in the customs of the country'.[7]

The first official Dutch estimates for recovery appeared in July 1945. They assumed that national income would not rise in the short term above 80 per cent of the 1938 level and that consumption would be held to a 'basic minimum'. Even so, and taking an optimistic view of the possibilities of controlling the rampant inflation potential, at least five years and more probably 'a longer period' would be required to complete recovery. In fact later plans were more precisely pessimistic, the Central Economic Plan for 1947 (published in March 1946) putting the date for the end of reconstruction back to 1952, and the end of physical rebuilding to 1960. Full employment was openly mentioned as a key objective in this view, but if it did arrive as planned, in 1952, this would be at the cost of per capita consumption, likely to be still 6 per cent below the 1938 level. In the meantime the government managed to replace the currency and reduce significantly the amount of money in circulation, thus avoiding the explosive inflationary consequences of too much liquidity chasing too few goods.[8]

This circumstance, which 'was to bedevil the recovery programmes of so many European countries', overwhelmed the conscious efforts of governments to avoid the mistakes which had led to the monetary chaos of the years after 1918.[9] As in the similar but unsuccessful action in France, (where the national debt had multiplied four times and the money supply by five between 1938 and 1945), the model for the Dutch plan had been Belgium.

The Belgian government tackled the money situation first, within weeks of the liberation. The currency was replaced and extremely tight monetary controls fastened on to the economy by means of restricting the release of the new variety, the first 60 per cent of it being held back as an obligatory loan to the state and the rest put into circulation as activity picked up. A series of other deflationary and stabilising measures in the course of 1945 put the country in the strongest financial position in Europe by the end of that year, with inflation falling and strikes scarce. The Belgian economy was the first to witness the abandonment of wartime controls and the return of something like abundance. But of the elaborate wartime plans for nationalisation and planned reconstruction there was little trace by the end of 1946. The Socialists did not pretend to have any definite economic programme (besides a social insurance package 'surpassing the Beveridge plan'), while the Communist Party – still sticking to the basic internationalist line of cooperation at all costs – now found itself the junior partner in a coalition dominated by conservative industrialists.[10]

In the case of the Italian economy the key problem left by Fascism and the war was, as Vera Zamagni has written, 'not *reconstructing* but *projecting a new future* on the basis of a new development strategy to be substituted for the nationalistic, autarkic, war-oriented strategy that had been followed up to then and had miserably failed.'[11] This challenge set off a vast debate on the presumed alternatives which came to a climax in the Constituent Assembly, elected in June 1946 to draw up the new, post-Fascist Constitution. The Left supplied a range of theoretical analyses, notable for ignoring the evolving international context. The fragile government coalition meanwhile confined its activity to a limited range of public works, to removing obstacles to exports and to ever more desperate pleas for immediate relief aid from the United States. Long-term decisions were inevitably put off in a situation where the government lacked the authority to carry through monetary reform even though inflation raged, and was unable to prevent unemployment rising to 2.5 million by the end of 1946. Officially firms were prevented from laying off the extra numbers they had taken on in the war years.

Gradually it became clear that the vast public sector built up by Fascism would be kept on and developed, and that exporting and reorientating the economy to foreign markets would be crucial. At the same time it was obvious that the country would not, in the foreseeable future, dispose of anything like the elementary resources to maintain the whole population: 'in 1946 per capita private consumption was 90 per cent of the *1913* level', says Zamagni. Yet very soon observers were beginning to marvel at the speed and vitality of the physical reconstruction in Italy. In this way, a gap destined to be permanent emerged between the almost inexplicable workings of the real economy on the one hand, and on the other the pronouncements of policy-makers and their critics in the endless debate on what might be a politically, morally or conceptually desirable strategy of development.[12]

OCCUPYING GERMANY

The destruction

But in Italy, as elsewhere, reality began to impinge from the moment when import programmes had to be redrawn in the new situation created by Germany's collapse and what came after it. Whatever their plans or intentions, in practice the Allies too had often fought the war as though there would be no tomorrow; for the Nazis of course there was none, hence the furious destructiveness of their last stand:

> Samson pulled down the pillars of the Temple on the Philistines, [wrote an eloquent British witness], but the German Army, moved by Fate, pulled down the bridges on the bleeding body of Germany, at once the most senseless and suicidal act of the war, and possibly the greatest economic disaster experienced in Europe in modern times.[13]

The allusion referred to the total destruction of the inland waterway network linking northern France, the Low Countries and western Germany, mainstay of the area's exchange system and indispensable parallel to the no less wrecked road and rail networks. In Germany the elemental relief moment was far longer and harder than expected, the preplanned steps to reconstruction immediately lost sight of, and the armies overwhelmed with tasks they were not prepared for or interested in. The Allies had decided in the course of the war that the large-scale destruction of residential areas by a thousand or more aircraft at a time was the most effective way to hit significant targets and undermine the German ability to resist. The result was that more than 50 per cent of housing in the major cities – up to 80 per cent in some – lay in rubble. The central administration in Berlin had meanwhile collapsed, leaving only the armies and the remnants of local government to face the appalling conditions. But as a former Pentagon official confirmed in 1987, the 'whole project' of the military was to re-establish local civilian government and get out as rapidly as possible.[14]

But this was only one of the contradictions which transformed Germany and its occupation by the erstwhile Allies into the central problem of European reconstruction in the years after the war.

The allied approaches

Five key aspects of Germany's fate had dominated discussion among the Big Three in their wartime conclaves, but on only one was there any kind of accord by the time Nazism collapsed. The five were: unconditional surrender, dismemberment, frontiers (specifically the Polish–German border), the destruction of Germany's capacity to make war, and reparations. Only on unconditional surrender was there an uneasy agreement by the time of Yalta, and even then the Allies refused to specify its precise meaning. On all the others there had been intense but fitful confrontation, and no agreed plans had emerged.

A common criterion in the Anglo-American camp inevitably was to avoid the errors made during the period after the First World War, and it was on this basis that the United States and the UK had opposed the repeated Russian insistence on reparations, before eventually giving way at Yalta. Yet the American economic plan revolved round versions of the scheme drawn up by the Treasury Secretary Morgenthau, which envisaged the handing over of large parts of Germany's territory to her neighbours, forced labour by German prisoners of war as reparations, and the general transformation of the nation to a subsistence agricultural basis by the total dismantling of heavy industry and mining. As Alfred Grosser, the leading French historian of postwar Germany, pointed out in 1955, the 'Morgenthau Plan' was never official Anglo-American policy in Germany, and was repudiated by Truman just before the Potsdam conference. Yet,

> . . . a great part of its content is embodied in two essential documents, the Potsdam agreements and J.C.S.1067 of the American Chiefs of Staff Committee which were the text-book of American policy in Germany up to July 1947. As no complete agreement was ever reached in Washington . . . there was a long period when the American government had no coherent German policy.[15]

At the Potsdam conference in July 1945 the Allies appeared to agree on a unified system of political and economic control; on denazification, 're-education' and political reconstruction; on Poland's frontiers; on the destruction of war-potential and reparations. They set aside dismemberment plans, but insisted on their positions in zones preassigned separately, by nationality (including, on British insistence, one for the French).

But the last conference of the wartime allies was the scene of acrimonious discussion on every issue set before it, of the solidification of deep mutual suspicion and hostility between Americans and Russians, with the British convinced that they would have to face up to the Soviets in the key area – Germany. Almost nothing was concluded definitively, ambiguity abounded. The British negotiator Lord Franks cited the case of economic relations:

[The accord] ... talked about Germany as a unity, administrative and economic ... But it also made arrangements about reparations which presupposed a divided Germany. ... The Russians wanted their form of economic unity, we wanted our form of economic unity. Therefore what prevailed was the division.[16]

Likewise the French – who had not been invited to Potsdam but who had veto power in the Control Commission set up to enforce the Potsdam accords – made clear that they believed in dismemberment, including the assignment of the Saar mines to their sovereignty and the Rhine–Ruhr area to permanent international military supervision. 'This meant', Grosser wrote, 'opposing all measures of a centralising tendency and especially the creation of political parties for the whole of Germany and the setting up of centralised German administrations.'[17]

In practice, says the German scholar Kurt Düwell, 'each of the four Allied powers chose its own way of carrying out [the] general objectives'. This was to some extent the result of different war experiences, but was a product too, especially in the French and Russian cases, of unreflecting attitudes to German history and the rise of Nazism. In their urge for revenge and compensation both powers set out to strip their zones of every industrial plant they could lay their hands on.

The French and Russian zones were more evidently agricultural and though not self-sufficient – especially with the grain-producing Eastern provinces occupied by the Poles – the armies encamped in them sought to live off the country. The British and Americans in contrast, soon found themselves spending 700 million dollars a year between them to import food for the industrial and urban areas in their charge. As to denazification and democratisation, again there could be no consensus:

The English, for example, [in Grosser's view], acted on the assumption that nazism was an unfortunate accident, a sort of horrible mask which had been forced upon Germany's features; once the mask was torn off, a democratic Germany would be revealed. For the French, every German had been a potential nazi even before the appearance of Hitler, and indeed from the moment that Germany became a unified nation. She must therefore become a federation again before she could be cured.[18]

The Americans were vague on the nature of Nazism but clung to the Rooseveltian view (which Churchill shared) that militaristic and authoritarian 'Prussianism' was the evil disease to be extirpated, and that there was no separation to be made between the people and the regime. The Soviets turned against this attitude in Stalin's victory message, but reserved to themselves methods to get rid of the economic and social structures which in their view had produced Nazism.

The experience of occupation

A flood of memoirs, diaries, histories, films and novels makes German – especially West German – experience by far the best-documented of all in postwar Europe. In a hundred different ways, these voices all bear witness to the appalling effects of Potsdam and the ensuing occupation upon everyone involved, including of course the German population. The Americans fretted over the paradox of 'forcing people to be free', and faced the fact that none of their prepared plans for the postwar world had any practical relevance in the German catastrophe. The ironic gap 'beween ambition and realisation' dominated the efforts in the US zone to manage and transform nearly every aspect of German life, reports a recent American study. In March 1946 the German-born State Department consultant Hans Speir wrote from Bad Homburg:

> It is difficult to maintain that we are working toward the 'reeducation' of the Germans – whatever that may mean – or are making progress in a definite direction. In the Western zones, the food problem almost seems to be growing worse by the day; the Germans do not know what our policy is regarding the Ruhr, or what policy we pursue on the issue of a central government ... the Germans learn what is going on from the Swiss broadcasting station Beromünster, the Swiss *Weltwoche* and from *Stars and Stripes*, published for the US occupation forces. In view of all this, the futility and naïveté of our efforts toward 'reeducation' are apparent.[19]

The British were seriously worried that the frustrations of the Americans would lead them to pull out of Germany and out of Europe, just when the Russians were becoming more and more intractable. The British had insisted on taking the zone which was the largest in population, the most industrialised and the most destroyed. There British military government improvised, without policy directives from London, unable to conceive an overall plan of economic action, and undecided between direct and indirect control of the ever-swelling mass of natives and refugees. The result, said the *Economist*, was that policy was entirely negative in character, lacking in defined political purpose, 'its underlying conception (being) that there is democracy hidden somewhere below the surface in Germany which can be called into being by a majority vote in politics and by *laisser faire* in economics'. For political strategy it substituted efficiency, but, 'efficiency depends in the very first place on food, and the food is not there.'

Constrained to barter for food shipments from the Russian zone as American supplies faltered, the British had arrived at 'a complete industrial impasse' by the end of 1946, according to another expert witness of the time. They were described as unable to restart large-scale coal-mining and undecided as to which was more important: rehabilitation to save the British taxpayer expense or economic disarmament to avoid the errors made after the First World War.[20]

With the benefit of hindsight the British record does not appear so negative. They were the first to understand the Russian danger, and to predict the division of the country. Partly for this reason they were in advance of the French and the Americans in betting on the revival of the German peacetime economy, and they saw the necessity to plan for this strategy. But the shortage of leadership and above all the desperate shortage of physical resources – of cash, food and raw materials – brought their position to crisis point by the spring of 1946.[21]

The American turn-around

It was the Americans who broke the British deadlock. As all efforts to go beyond the Potsdam system and aim at a comprehensive settlement for Germany failed amid ever more bitter recriminations at the international level, the key American officials in Germany decided to make a unilateral effort to bridge the widening gap between America's stake in the country and her declared objectives there. Using the Communist danger as its principal argument, the military government led by the distinctive figure of General Lucius Clay set out on a 'pragmatic stabilisation policy' which aimed to prime the German economy with local means and resources, supported where necessary by relief supplies. Clay argued in March 1946 that the inhabitants of the western zones were constrained to live off 1,000 calories a day, while even in the Russian zone 1,500 calories were supplied. The consequences looked obvious:

> We have insisted on democratic process in the US zone and have maintained a strict neutrality between political parties. As a result the Communist Party has made little inroad. However, there is no choice between becoming a communist on 1,500 calories and a believer in democracy on 1,000 calories. It is my sincere belief that our proposed ration allowance in Germany will not only defeat our objectives in middle Europe but will pave the way to a Communist Europe.[22]

On this premise, the Americans began from early in 1946 to reorganise their priorities and actions in the country, proposing as a test of Russian intentions a twenty-five-year four-power treaty to keep Germany disarmed and, separately, a full-scale merger of the British and American zones. Both proposals the British accepted, though the second one only reluctantly. Bevin saw clearly its likely antagonistic effects on the Russians, while welcoming its signs of further American commitment to Europe, and its solution to the economic problem. The Americans, of course, would be expected to provide the greater part of the capital investment to make the 'Bi-zone' functional and self-sufficient, London suggesting a ratio of 4:1, as in UNRRA.[23]

In spring 1946 the British Foreign Secretary had been convinced that the Americans were 'not ready' to increase their responsibilities in Germany and face up to the logic of the divisions clearly emerging. But in September the American Secretary of State, James Byrnes, made a speech the historical significance of which was clear to all concerned. He told an audience in Stuttgart: 'We are not withdrawing. We are staying here. As long as there is an occupation army in Germany, the American armed forces will be part of it.' The American response was finally emerging now – in Western Germany – to what Winston Churchill in June had called 'the ceaseless degeneration at the heart of Europe'.[24]

THE SEARCH FOR STABILITY

Only with the benefit of hindsight does it become clear that the months between the end of the war and the emergence of a new kind of American presence in Europe represent an integral part of the development process which eventually produced the mixed economy and the welfare state. At the time they seemed to be a downward spiral in chaos and misery whose outcome could only be catastrophic. It is the generation which went through this experience which attaches so much psychological importance to the chain of American interventions leading from the relief programmes, through Brynes's Stuttgart speech, to the Marshall Plan. Norbert Gansel, a Social Democrat member of the German Parliament recalled in 1987:

> ... now as a politician I consider myself very lucky to have these experiences. In my generation ... those like me who were born in 1940 are the last to remember what hunger really meant and how it feels, how it looks when the last slice of bread is shared amongst five members of the

family and you have no butter . . . to put on it and it's put in the hot pan to give it some colour – well, it's a good thing to be able to remember that.[25]

Politics became economics in a very literal sense in those times and few among the ruling groups which emerged from the war were in a position to do more than react to local circumstances as best they could, while directing their daily prayers and exhortations westwards, across the Atlantic.

In this sense if a Catholic conservative like Adenauer continued to declare his faith in 'socialisation', or the governments of countries such as France and Britain carried out programmes of nationalisation an important tactical purpose was served. By so doing the new generation of politicians continued to recognise that among the physical hardships of the moment, radical collective aims – the pursuit of full employment and 'social justice' – remained the goals of reconstruction.[26]

But the ways of thinking and the rancours of wartime weighed heavily, long after the fighting had ceased, and clearly determined much of what happened in this phase. They explain in part why in most countries 'stability' was as far away at the end of it as at the beginning: France had three referenda and three general elections in just over a year as the Fourth Republic was born (October 1946). Italy passed from monarchy to republic in the June 1946 referendum by a margin which clearly divided the traditionalist south from the more reform-minded north. Belgian politics was deeply split over the fate of the monarchy. Greece was on the brink of civil war. And everywhere Communist parties loyal – if each in its own way – to an ever more truculent and alien Soviet Union appeared ready to inherit the fall-out of cynicism and bitterness. 'It is the fatal, unforgiveable error of conquerors to ordain the destinies of men and nations according to wartime views and circumstances', said the dissident, disillusioned Yugoslav communist Milovan Djilas reflecting forty years later on the meaning of victory for Stalin and Tito and their followers.[27]

In reality Communists foresaw the arrival of the East–West split no better than anyone else, and soon found themselves in an authentic division of loyalties which caused all but the most fanatical of their militants intense confusion. The case of the Italian party's situation with respect to the Trieste issue is but one of many which might be cited. Loyalty to Stalin meant supporting the Yugoslav demands on the city; loyalty to the government of which they were part meant opposing Tito. No matter how moderate or accommodating their stand on any number of daily domestic questions, this division of allegiance inevitably kept them beyond the pale of respectability in the eyes of 'the world'. Hence the task of striking the balance between national and international politics in the new era of inter-dependence was translated into an ever-lengthening series of questions on *security*.

But all the witnesses insist that the situation was still fluid up until the spring of 1947. 'Germany as *the* enemy still loomed over international relations for a while, then, after 1946, the Soviet Union slowly began to fill this role', says a German historian.[28] The atomic bomb arrived just as the wartime alliance was breaking down and the horrors of Germany were being discovered. The fear which spread in 1945–46 as Europeans saw the Continent dividing before them into two hostile blocs was a source of deep existential anxiety at every social level. Churchill commanded the words to express it. He told a Zurich audience in September 1946 how

> . . . over wide areas a vast quivering mass of tormented, hungry, careworn and bewildered human beings gaze on the ruin of their cities and scan the dark horizon for the approach of some new peril, tyranny or terror. . . . Among the victors is a babel of voices, among the vanquished a sullen silence of despair.[29]

Churchill's response was a grandiloquent call for European unity, based on 'something that will astonish you': a renewed Franco-German partnership.

Exceptionally the former prime minister did not mention the role America might play in such a scheme. That was spelled out instead by a Republican international lawyer with increasing experience of post-war negotiations, the future Secretary of State, John Foster Dulles. In a speech in New York in January 1947 Dulles presented a complete elaboration of the European future: political resistance to Soviet expansionism, federation on the American model, economic unification with a redeveloped Germany included as a whole (to create a market 'big enough to justify modern methods of cheap production for mass consumption'), leadership and assistance from America.[30] Ill-fitted for the Europe of 1945–46, the great wartime dreams were being rejigged. American power would soon be felt in new ways in the Old World.

NOTES

1. White TH *Fire in the Ashes. Europe in Mid-Century* NY 1953 p 55
2. *When Hostilities Cease. Papers on Relief and Reconstruction Prepared for the Fabian Society* 1943
3. Ellwood Classe operaia e occupazione alleata in Piemonte, 1945–46 *Rivista di storia contemporanea* n 3 1974
4. Kuisel op cit p 190
5. Monnet *Memoirs* NY 1978 p 231
6. Kuisel op cit Ch 8
7. Monnet op cit Ch 10 p 257
8. Griffiths op cit pp 4–5,7–10
9. Ibid; 'Survey' p 48
10. Papers on The Socialist Party, Economic Problems of Liberated Belgium and Financial Reconstruction of Belgium, in *Belgium in Transition* vol 247 of the Annals of the American Academy of Political and Social Science Sept 1946; 'Survey' pp 543–9
11. Zamagni V Betting on the Future. The Reconstruction of Italian Industry, 1946–1952 In Becker J and Knipping F (eds) *Power in Europe? Great Britain, France, Italy and Germany in a Postwar World, 1945–1950* Berlin/New York 1986 p 284, (henceforth *Power in Europe*)
12. Ibid pp 283–6, cit at p 285 n 8 (emphasis added); cf Italia 1945–50. Ricostruire, ma come? *giovane critica* n 34/35/36 primavera 1973
13. War Damage in Western Europe cit pp 156–7
14. Ernest Gross cit in Mortimer op cit pp 29–30
15. Grosser A *The Colossus Again. Western Germany from Defeat to Rearmament* NY 1955 p 19
16. Cit in Mortimer op cit pp 51–2; cf Alec Cairncross *The Price of War. British Policy on German Reparations 1941-1949* Oxford 1986 pp 86–99
17. Grosser op cit pp 34–5
18. Düwell K Germany 1945–1950 Problems of the 'Economic Miracle'. *History Today* Sept 1983; Grosser op cit pp 34–5
19. Montgomery JD *Forced to be Free: the Artificial Revolution in Germany and Japan* Chicago 1957; Ninkovich FA *Germany and the United States. The Transformation of the German Question Since 1945* NY 1988 p 46; cit from Hans Speir *From the Ashes of Disgrace. A Journal from Germany 1945–1955* Amherst 1981 p 63
20. The *Economist* 6 April 1946; The British Zone in Germany. *The World Today* Dec 1946; Cairncross *The Price of War.* op cit Ch 6, 7 (especially pp 156–8), pp 229–33; Turner ID op cit Chs 2, 3, 4
21. Cf contributions by Turner, Deighton and Carlin in Turner op cit
22. Schröder HJ The Economic Reconstruction of West Germany in the Context of International Relations 1945–1949. In *Power in Europe.* op cit; Clay cit p 305; cf Turner op cit pp 81–2
23. Bullock A *Ernest Bevin. Foreign Secretary 1945–1951* Oxford 1985 pp 267–71, 309–10, 320; Cairncross *The Price of War.* op cit pp 160–2
24. Bullock op cit pp 268, 276, 309
25. Cit in Mortimer op cit p 17

26. Cf Van Der Wee H *Prosperity and Upheaval. The World Economy 1945–1980* Harmondsworth 1987 pp 34, 290–313
27. Djilas M *Wartime* NY 1976 p 424
28. Overesch M Senior West German Politicians and their Perception of the German Situation in Europe 1945–1949. In *Power in Europe* op cit pp 118–19
29. Complete text in Rostow WW *The Division of Europe after World War II* Aldershot 1982 Appendix F
30. Complete text in ibid Appendix G

CHAPTER FOUR

The Reinvention of American Power

HOW THE AMERICAN VIEW EVOLVED

American observers in Europe had complained widely at the end of the war that a gulf was evident by that time 'between visible American power and the purposes for which it was being used'.[1] When liberation came, Henry Stimson, the veteran American Secretary of War, suggested that the way to bridge this gap was simple: put two million tons of wheat per month into Western Europe throughout the summer. 'This would be good psychology', urged Stimson; 'We could turn the tide of Communism in all those countries. Hoover stamped out Communism in this way in Central Europe [after the First World War].'[2] The United States did of course provide relief supplies on a large if chaotic scale after the liberation as well as during it. But there was no question of tackling the threatened breakdown of countries such as Italy, France or Greece in a similar fashion. A holding operation was all that could be tried, while local politicians tried to assert some sort of control over the situation until new constitutions had emerged and the peace treaties were signed.

So it was again left to the American press to point to the next step forward for America in the old world. In an article which appeared in the *New York Herald Tribune* at the beginning of July 1945, the feature writer John Chabot Smith began with the Italian case. He declared: 'Everyone said win the war first. Now no one knows what to do.' Smith's article was one of many signalling the start of an important shift in American thinking on economic problems in liberated Europe. As the scale of need began to appear in its true dimensions, planners and policy-makers faced the task of transforming the abstract designs of wartime into credible proposals to deal with it.

According to Smith, the objective circumstances were clear to all concerned: there was a general consensus that everything in Italy depended on US aid in economic and military terms. But the army had big plans to demobilise and/or send large contingents of its forces to the Pacific theatre. Those who had originally pressed for maintaining a strong US presence in Italy had been conservatives fearing mob rule and civil war; but now many high-level Americans were coming round to the same opinion. They were concerned, said Smith, that the forces of the Left sought totalitarian rule and might well provoke civil war to get it. As for the democrats who in the beginning had asked for nothing more than Allied charity, they were now more concerned with those conditions of poverty and civil war which fed Leftism: 'there is a growing disposition among some Italian and American officials to look deeper into the problems of economic reconstruction', Smith reported, 'and into the possibilities of developing a permanently higher standard of living in Italy'.

In Smith's opinion, instead of merely asking for large public loans, Italy might have done better to interest US businessmen in providing technical know-how and money, the essential resources necessary 'for rebuilding and developing Italy on a profit-making basis'. The essential political premises of course were stability and public order, so that the days of a 'hands-off' attitude on America's part were probably numbered. Many Italians and Americans, Smith concluded, 'would like to see the United States take a more direct hand in Italian politics'.[3]

Looking deeper into the economics of reconstruction then, meant connecting up the long-standing plans for expansion everywhere with responses to the now generally recognised challenge of Leftism in Europe, and to the circumstances thought to be at the root of it. Conceptually the shift was almost effortless, even too much so since the original distinctions made intuitively between stability, (= food, work, law and order), development (= industrialisation), and expansion (i.e. raising living standards everywhere) disappeared as the Cold War set in, not to been seen again until the late-1950s.[4] But politically and practically at least a year and a half passed by before the United States was willing or able to take 'a more direct hand' in European politics, months of drama and confusion as America paid the price for Roosevelt's old tactic of 'putting off politics' till the end of the war.

The inventions of the Truman Doctrine in March 1947 and the Marshall Plan in June of that year demonstrated that the United States had by this time decided unequivocally to project its power abroad, and had conceived a whole variety of means to do so, with short-term and long-term applicability. The objectives? Not simply to stop Communism, but to put forward a positive vision based on America's own experience: 'A higher standard of living for the entire nation; maximum employment for workers and farmers; greater production', as a Marshall Plan propaganda booklet would tell Italians in 1949.

AID PLANS, LOANS AND THE COLD WAR

British suggestions

Whatever influence the British possessed in Washington at the end of the war, it was they who had done the most detailed thinking on the economic logic of the new circumstances. An anonymous British official used the influential platform of the quarterly *Foreign Affairs* in July 1945, to ask: 'Do we want the "more abundant life" of an "expanding economy?" Do we want "full employment?" Do we seek peace and wish to pursue it?' If these phrases were be more than the 'catchpenny slogans' of journalists and economists, then the bare facts had first to be faced, said the author, specifically that:

> ... 180,000,000 people living in twilight, on an insufficient diet, largely without coal, without adequate means of communication, and under-employed are neither good customers nor good neighbours and cannot be either good customers or good neighbours unless they are helped to become so.[5]

A conception of the help needed going far beyond the kind of relief and credits approach familiar from the first postwar era had already been spelled out by the *Economist*. Up until the end of the latest war it had been clear simply that the United States would be called upon by all to supply large quantities of relief aid and also – except in certain special cases such as Sweden, Switzerland and Belgium – the means to pay for it. Very few reflected on what basis the United States would carry out this function for the major West European nations, whose needs went far beyond the scope or mandate of UNRRA. The *Economist* had noted at the beginning of 1945 how difficult it was to persuade anyone to think beyond the end of the war, and envisage the continuity of useful arrangements such as Lend-Lease and its two-way Anglo-American elaboration, 'Mutual Aid':

> Shall we have to go through the whole tortuous process again, starting with "cash and carry", advancing to "Lend-Lease" in the form of *ad hoc* credit

arrangements, and finally after costly and heart-breaking delays, arriving at new methods which incorporate at least something of the spirit of Mutual Aid?

Short-sightedness looked like bringing back old-fashioned charity, which meant, said the magazine, either grants of basic necessities or long-term loans which would probably never be repaid. Instead, there should be 'cooperation': 'a much more potent and lasting form of assistance: mutual aid by reciprocal endeavours to expand mutually advantageous trade'. The challenge to the economic arm of the new United Nations Organisation was clear: 'An international economic body without a policy for international expansion, would be as dangerous an anachronism as a national government without a policy for full employment.'[6]

The journal's fears were of course realized, and only after costly and heart-breaking delays of all sorts was the new conception brought to fruition in the Marshall Plan, which did not start in tangible, practical terms until more than three years after the end of the war. The reasons why are well-known: the break-down of the anti-Hitler alliance made the United Nations almost unworkable. Then again America proved not to have a plan to test the visions of wartime against reality, much less any means to turn them into effective action on the ground. And American politics – for reasons of its own – discouraged any large-scale thinking in such directions.

Hence applicants for aid were advised at first to put their own houses in order, to look to private investment, and to address special claims to the still-to-be-founded World Bank. Above all they were expected to demonstrate what they were willing to do to cooperate with America's great plans for universal trade liberalisation.[7]

But it was the Europeans, with the British in the lead, who eventually forced American thinking in new, more realistic directions, by the scale and urgency of their demands on Washington in the months between the spring of 1945 and the spring of 1947.

Loans and strings

Everyone wanted loans, and by mid-1947 most countries had received them. Between July 1945 and June 1947 the British received $4.4 billion, France $1.9 billion, Italy $330 million and the Benelux countries $430 million. Eastern Europe as a whole however received 'only' $546 million. The East Europeans had hoped for much more, but soon came up against Washington's unwillingness to assist nations falling ever more deeply under Russian control.[8]

The Soviet Union itself had been persuaded that support for institutions such as the International Monetary Fund and the World Bank would be rewarded with reconstruction aid. In January 1945 Moscow had proposed $6 billion as an appropriate sum. But while a figure of $1 billion did seem plausible for a time, by the end of the year, after bitter struggles over such issues as Russian insistence on German reparations, it had become clear that nothing less than the end of Stalin's regime and Russian influence in eastern Europe would be regarded by Congress as acceptable preconditions for its award.[9]

French tactics had been in many ways the most successful. The most famous of France's former prime ministers, the Socialist Léon Blum, together with Jean Monnet, led the French delegation which travelled to Washington in spring 1946. They had taken care to tell the State Department precisely what it wanted to hear. The American Embassy in Paris reported:

> French adoption of American commercial policy is contingent on large scale US credits. (France will modernise production in the absence of such credits, but more slowly and necessarily within the framework of a closed economy.)
>
> Lump sum credit should be granted at one time to cover modernisation period of 3 years. Piecemeal credits would handicap planning procedures and would prevent proper synchronization of France's modernisation program with production trends in the US ... Western Europe is also important and credit decision *vis à vis* France will be of key importance in determining commercial policy trends in this area.[10]

As became the norm in most West European countries in these years, the local case was taken up with fervour by the American Ambassador on the spot, who rapidly became a national figure of prominence. From Paris Ambassador Caffery sent a message in February 1946 whose refrain was by now familiar to the State Department, but which they would be destined to hear repeated from many parts of the globe for decades to come:

> At this time ... I desire to emphasize my belief that it is in our national interest to grant France a substantial dollar credit even though to a banker's eye France might not be considered an A–1 risk.
>
> There is little doubt that the political situation in recent weeks has seriously deteriorated. The average man is still cold, hungry, unable to buy what he needs and frustrated by the feeling that not enough progress has been made.
>
> Extremists today are not in control. It is in our interest that public discouragement should not reach the point where extremists appear to offer the only chance of improvement in leadership and in material things.
>
> Today France looks primarily to us for help. If coal is not forthcoming from the Ruhr the US is the only country that can squeeze out an export

surplus. When the French wheat crop fails, it is to the US she turns. Also important, it is only from the US that the industrial machinery and equipment necessary to modernise her plants can be secured.

With import requirements far beyond available gold and dollar reserves and export earnings marginal, the financial pressures were evident. But in his conclusion Caffery emphasised the political import-ance of a decisive gesture of support: 'To refuse it or (reduce) it . . . will pull out one of the last props of substance and of hope from those in France who want to see France remain an independent and democratic country'.[11]

The wide-ranging accord which resulted – just in time for crucial national elections – brought the French government $650 million (only months after obtaining $550 million from the Export–Import Bank), and reconverted the national war-debt into a low-interest loan to be employed in reconstruction. Beyond assurances on the future of nationalisation and free access for American products on French markets, the team 'refused to assume any precise obligations'.[12]

The loan the British obtained in July 1946 was far more controver-sial. Its scale – £1.5 billion was originally talked of, as a grant – and its implications forced a major political crisis in Washington and set in motion the first general rethink on aid to Europe. An American official economist sympathetic to the British case recalled how the force of the British request struck an American public unprepared for such demands and unaware of what the war had cost the British, 'nor at the time did the President and the Secretary of State possess the vision, the economic insight, and the determination needed to win over Congress'.[13]

Within days of the ending of Lend-Lease in August 1945 Britain found itself in a major sterling crisis, with Attlee in parliament talking of a deficit of £1,200 million, and Keynes of 'a financial Dunkirk'. The *Economist* calculated that $2 billion would be needed just to face the coming two years, while the sum required to restore long-term solvency was likely to be no less than $6 billion. Meanwhile, said the magazine, it looked as though the United States was thrusting the country back on its own last-ditch resources while at the same time constantly talking of non-discrimination and expansion.[14]

The ensuing Anglo-American loan negotiations have been widely debated, usually in terms of their sealing the fate of the British Empire as an independent economic entity and guaranteeing Britain's subor-dinate relationship to Washington.[15] The British government and the negotiators, famously led by Keynes, were surprised by the diffidence which greeted them and the extent of the efforts needed to explain to

American opinion just how and why their country was so desperate. A Gallup poll found 60 per cent of those interviewed opposed to any loan to Britain, and only 27 per cent in favour.[16]

Meanwhile, as the discussions dragged on in the closing months of 1945, the Truman administration published its latest 'Proposals for Expansion of World Trade and Employment'. This effort had very little to do with what was going on at that moment in Britain or anywhere else. It was rather the next stage in realising the great designs for world economic reform announced in Article VII of Lend-Lease, the Atlantic Charter, the Bretton Woods accords and Article 55 of the UN Charter. With the FAO, the World Bank and the International Monetary Fund in the process of being created, the American government now put forward a full-scale suggestion for an International Trade Organisation of the United Nations. Its members, said the State Department, would dedicate themselves to the realisation and subsequent regulation of free trade on a world scale, 'in order to make possible an effective expansion of world production, employment, exchange, and consumption'.[17]

As one of the many conditions for making a large loan to them, the British had little choice but to join the scheme, in whose name they were obliged, over the strenuous objections of the whole negotiating team and the London government, to declare sterling fully convertible into dollars (for non-residents) within fifteen months. In the Commons Churchill called this clause 'a proposition so dubious and perilous that the best hope is that in practice it will defeat itself, and that it is in fact too bad to be true'. The Opposition abstained, but all felt the humiliation as the terms were agreed. In this way British support for the ITO became a fundamental part of the enormous effort needed by Truman and his men to persuade Congress to authorise the loan. The process involved over six months of exhaustive debate and caused intense resentment in the UK: 'in the country there is a feeling that as victors we are being asked to pay reparations', said the *Sunday Times*.[18]

Aid in the perspective of the Cold War

The lesson of the British affair was clear to American economists working on the ground. As W.W. Rostow, then a medium-level State Department economist, later the doyen of American economic historians, recalled:

> . . . it was palpable that a vastly larger flow of American aid to Europe would be required and for a much longer period than anyone had yet envisaged if Europe was, in fact, fully to recover. If this were to happen,

The Reinvention of American Power

however, a new basis for US congressional support would be required. . . .
The appeal in terms of British requirements and its wartime service to the
Allied cause in standing alone from 1939 to 1941 only barely succeeded. It
was clear that, if additional US aid to Europe was going to be organized, it
would have to be in terms of a large enterprise that looked forward rather
than backward.[19]

In fact by the time the British loan reached its final vote in Congress
in mid-1946 a 'new basis' for supporting such moves in Congress had
already been found: anti-Communism. 'The period of late February
and early March 1946, marked a decisive turning point in American
policy toward the Soviet Union', writes one of the leading American
historians of the Cold War, John Lewis Gaddis. Up to this time, says
Gaddis, attitudes to the Soviet Union had developed on an *ad hoc* basis,
with little consistency besides the assumption of shared basic interests
in peace and stability. But by March 1946 criticism within the United
States of this stance was forcing a change. Soviet behaviour gave less
and less room for hope: when it was analysed by George Kennan, the
Soviet expert in the American Embassy in Moscow in a famous
telegram to Washington of February, the view began to spread among
all concerned on the American side 'that Stalin and his associates were
ideological zealots who viewed conflict with the West as necessary to
attain their objectives'.[20]

The impact of Churchill's 'Iron Curtain' speech in March was
correspondingly enormous. Against a background of ever more bitter
confrontation lasting most of the spring at the Council of Foreign
Ministers' meetings in Paris, leaders in both Houses of Congress now
expressed the basic issue of the British loan in terms of fundamental
political choice. The Speaker of the House of Representatives, Ray-
burn, descended from his lofty position to give a short speech on the
floor of the chamber:

> I do not want Western Europe, England, and all the rest pushed further into
> and toward an ideology that I despise. I fear if we do not cooperate with this
> great natural ally of ours, that is what will happen. If we are not allied with
> the great British democracy, I fear somebody will be and God pity us when
> we have no ally across the Atlantic Ocean, and God pity them too.[21]

TO THE 'TRUMAN DOCTRINE'

The British crisis in Greece and Turkey

Within months the Americans were again being asked to 'pull British
chestnuts out of the fire', as suspicious congressmen put it. In fact

67

Bevin had long hesitated before asking the Americans to take more responsibility anywhere in the world. 'It was essential to give them time, be patient and not try to force the pace', writes Bevin's biographer, Alan Bullock. In the Foreign Secretary's view, the political risks were too great, 'the American Government's new-found sense of purpose too brittle, American opinion too unsettled for Britain to surrender her own independence of action into American hands'.

But by February 1947 the Attlee government could postpone no longer: Washington was officially informed that as a result of its ever more serious financial difficulties, Britain would no longer be able to continue economic and military aid to Greece and Turkey, and would cut its support to their governments within weeks. History reveals the irony of this announcement: this was the very time when the Labour government was taking the portentous decision to develop its own atomic bomb, in order – among other things – to guarantee Britain's long-term status as a Great Power and avoid dependence on the unpredictable Americans. Yet here were Attlee and Bevin, obliged to admit that the country's immediate financial position was so grave that they were forced to abandon an area which British governments had always insisted was vital to national security.[22]

The Americans had been aware for some time of Britain's inability to face up to the challenges countries such as Greece and Turkey presented. When insurrection broke out in Athens at the end of 1944, the perceptive American Ambassador on the spot, MacVeagh, blamed the British, pronouncing the British Empire and its ways to be 'anachronistic, perfect for the 18th century, impossible for the 20th'. In his experience 'every day brings its evidence of weakness and dispersion, of consequent opportunism and dependence on America's nucleated strength'. The Ambassador spoke of 'the new growth of class-consciousness and proletarianism' and claimed that his Russian counterpart had told him the Soviet Union had no need to carry on subversive activities in such countries as Greece, since conditions in them would do all that was necessary. 'Eventually [concluded Mac-Veagh] what goes on in the Balkans and the Near East generally will have to be recognised as of prime importance to us.'[23]

By the spring of 1947 the United States had been providing aid on a modest scale to Greece for some time but had temporised when the Greek government requested a large-scale reconstruction loan in the autumn of 1946. In contrast, by a show of battleships, Washington had faced down the Soviet Union over Moscow's attempts to reform in its own favour Turkey's geostrategic position on the Black Sea Straits. The Americans had signalled a stepping up of their long-term presence by establishing a new naval command in the Mediterranean in October 1946 and beginning military planning talks with the British.[24]

But the latest Greek–Turkish challenge was different, since it came at a time when a new Congress had just been seated in which budget-cutting Republicans held sway. The Americans noted too that it arrived when the government in London was announcing imminent withdrawals from India, Burma and Palestine as well as from Greece and Turkey. Consequently a massive mobilisation of public opinion at home was ordered up in Washington. A senior member of the State Department's Office of Public Affairs wrote:

> I think we must admit the conclusion that Congress and the people of this country are not sufficiently aware of the character and dimensions of the crisis that impends, and of the measures that must be taken in terms of relief, loans, gifts, constructive development programs and liberal trade policies – all of these on a scale hitherto unimagined – if disaster is to be avoided. . . . The State Department knows. Congress and the people do not know.[25]

The doctrine announced

The outcome was the deliberate transformation of the moment into a national emergency, climaxed by Truman's famous speech to a joint session of Congress on 12 March 1947. This was the occasion when America announced its determination henceforth 'to help free peoples to maintain their free institutions and their national integrity against aggressive movements that seek to impose upon them totalitarian regimes'. The president went on: 'This is no more than a frank recognition that totalitarian regimes imposed on free peoples, by direct or indirect aggression, undermine the foundations of international peace and hence the security of the United States.' Then came the standard analysis, economic in nature, of the causes of totalitarianism: 'The seeds of totalitarian regimes are nurtured by misery and want. They spread and grow in the evil soil of poverty and strife. They reach their full growth when the hope of a people for a better life has died. We must keep that hope alive.'[26]

The so-called 'Truman Doctrine' represented 'the opening gun in a campaign to bring people up to [the] realisation that the war isn't over by any means', said the president's Special Adviser Clark Clifford. It was 'a form of shock therapy' (writes the historian Gaddis): 'a last-ditch effort by the Administration to prod Congress and the American people into accepting the responsibilities of the world leadership which

69

one year earlier, largely in response to public opinion, Washington officials had assumed by deciding to "get toung with Russia" '.[27]

While claiming that the message of the Truman Doctrine would be read with hope 'throughout the vast area from the Dardanelles to the China Sea', not to mention in Western Europe, the US Administration was at pains to point out that the Greek–Turkish proposal was in practical terms an emergency measure valid only in those two countries. Their long-term reconstruction needs, it was emphasised, would be handled by the FAO, the World Bank and other agencies of the United Nations.

Underneath, as the Americans well knew, the fundamental questions persisted: not the intentions of armed bands or the fate of fragile government coalitions but industrialisation and economic progress. Although it would soon emerge that the entire $100 million for Turkey was destined for its armed forces, Truman told Congress that the country needed American support, 'for the purpose of effecting that modernisation necessary for the maintenance of its national integrity'. The American international historian W.H. McNeill, an observer of Greece's evolution from wartime to the present day, explained the link between economic and political modernisation in the following terms in 1947:

> If economic conditions could be so improved that every Greek was able to live as well as he had been brought up to expect, it seems probable that the excessive concern and fanaticism which the people now manifest for political parties and programs would diminish. Circumstances might then become propitious for the gradual emergence of a community of ideas that would embrace almost the whole population, and permit genuine democratic government to be established. Economic prosperity could not guarantee stable and popular government, but it would certainly make its achievement more probable.

The Americans were destined to learn the hard way that this could only be a long-term hope. In the short term, as Attlee noted with disgust, the Truman Doctrine meant appearing to support 'vested interests and reaction against reform and revolution in the interests of the poor'.[28]

The immediate impact of the Truman Doctrine

The resounding call to ideological crusade which accompanied the mix of support proposed for Greece and Turkey would give the new American position historical notoriety. The statement's 'shock-therapy' effects on the American public were ambiguous. Authoritative commentators in Washington such as George Kennan in the State

Department and Walter Lippmann in the *Herald Tribune* foresaw certain of the dangers, while the *San Francisco Chronicle* was said to be typical of much cautious approval when it asked: 'where all this gets us. Are we to shoulder the mantle of 19th century British imperialism? . . . Are we to set up a 1947 model WPA (Work Progress Administration) on the world scale? And, finally, are we asking for a third world war?'[29] After two months of intense debate in Congress, there remained, according to observers at the Council on Foreign Relations: 'resentment over the way in which the Administration has handled the matter, regret that it seemed necessary to act unilaterally instead of through the United Nations, and skepticism toward claims that the program would bring stability and security to Greece and Turkey'.[30]

In Europe the most conservative wings of opinion were delighted. The Vatican, by now a well-established bastion of anti-Communism, published a cautious statement denouncing war, but in private there was exultation and congratulations for the president's personal representative to the Holy See, Myron Taylor.[31] In general, however, there was seen to be 'no . . . universal note of welcome'. The authorities in Britain were of course deeply gratified by this outcome to their long toils to get the Americans well embedded in Europe, but public opinion was said to be shocked by the blaring trumpets. The *Daily Herald*, official organ of the governing Labour Party, rejected the crusading vision and with it the idea that conflict with Russia was inevitable. Together with much liberal comment, the *Herald* insisted that by whatever means available, particularly the United Nations, every effort should continue to be made to reach a settlement with the Soviet Union.[32] In Eastern Europe, according to press surveys, commentators feared the Soviets would now see good reason to tighten their grip on the area, in ways which America would not be able to contest.[33]

But in countries such as Italy and France, where Communist parties continued to participate in government, the effects were deeply disturbing. 'In Italy the Truman speech blew apart the uneasy truce between De Gasperi and the Left', writes James Miller. This truce had held as long as De Gasperi's supporters were unsure of America's interest in their country, so that the Communist and Socialist parties had to be handled with caution: their help in the search for stability might still be needed. In fact the Italian prime minister had been in Washington in search of financial support at the beginning of January, but at that time had received little beyond gestures and publicity.[34]

Now both sides realised that a crisis was at hand. In government and in the machinery set up to produce a new Italian constitution the Communists continued to cooperate with the conservative parties. But violent clashes in the country towns and industrial cities threatened the government's authority daily. As the Left was seen to threaten force to gain its objectives, the police apparatus, the northern industrialists and the non-Communist Left began to organise an armed counter-revolutionary force. The logic of the situation was civil war.

The Italian Ambassador to the United States, recalled to Rome, told the prime minister that 'the Communists had to go if De Gasperi wished Washington's unconditional support'. Within weeks, after febrile consultations with Washington and in the midst of endless political and social convulsions, a new government was formed without the Communist Party. It received instant support from the State Department, just in time for the Secretary of State's epochal speech launching the Marshall Plan.[35]

In France, the moderates were reported to feel that the Doctrine 'heralded elimination of the middle ground both in French politics and on the international scene', with nations henceforth obliged to choose between dependence on Washington or on Moscow.[36] Far more significantly, de Gaulle chose this moment to launch his own political movement, the RPF, (Rassemblement du Peuple Français), born on 14 April 1947: 'Fear was rising all over Western Europe, and the Truman speech had galvanized the anti-Communist mood in the democracies [writes one of de Gaulle's biographers]. De Gaulle now proceeded to play on fear and anti-Communism to maximum political advantage.'[37] Within months the RPF had become a mass movement, with its own paramilitary potential, clearly ready to take on the Communist Party frontally. For its part the PCF, in spite of emerging from national elections in November 1946 as the largest party, had also been defeated in its effort to present itself as both a party of government and of mass struggle. In April it had been obliged to choose between the workers of the newly nationalised Renault company, on strike for higher pay, and the government's wage freeze. Having chosen the workers, and been dismissed from the government, the party at once shifted the emphasis of its mass action to the factories and the streets. The notoriety of the formidable French riot police, the CRS, dates from this era.

VIEWS OF EUROPE IN SPRING 1947

Economists dealing in large-scale trends and numbers had little interest in any of this. Their view of the West European situation in early 1947 was optimistic, as it is on occasion to this day. A British survey of February attested to the 'remarkably quick' pace of progress evident on a number of levels by that time. The raw materials shortage – apart from coal – had been overcome; the food situation was 'much improved'; the transport systems had been put back together. Industrial production was on average 80 per cent of the 1938 level, except in Holland (60 per cent) and Germany. Everywhere of course serious retarding factors persisted. In Belgium there remained labour shortages, political instability and historical dependence on Germany; in Holland, dependence on Germany – 48 per cent of the country's prewar invisible income had come from Germany's use of Dutch inland shipping and harbours – loss of trade with the Dutch Empire and the disastrous housing situation. In the case of Denmark a huge and growing foreign exchange debt hung over prospects; France was plagued by coal shortages, labour shortages and inflation. But the most fundamental problem of all was as serious as ever and was very clear: 'the dependence of recovery in Western Europe on the state of German industry. Until the future of Germany is settled, the other countries are unable to make satisfactory plans.' In the meantime, in the face of all the wartime talk on European integration, it was evident that 'national plans and policies had been made largely without reference to one another'.[38]

For the left-wing parties on the ground political life was never experienced in such detached and clinical terms. The greatest pressure on them, particularly on the Communists, all came from below. In Belgium, it was said, 'given the present delicate and uncertain character of the economic situation, everything depends on the attitudes of the workers, and it is not the parties in the [Catholic-Socialist] Government who control them'.[39] The Belgian Communists also made their exit from government at this time, and the issue they chose to make a stand on – coal subsidies – led observers to believe that they were afraid of losing their mass following as long as they stayed in administrations which proved incapable of carrying out structural reforms.[40] Orders from Stalin do not appear to have played a part; when the international propaganda organisation known as the Cominform was founded by the Kremlin in September 1947 there was bitter Soviet criticism of the political compromises made by the Western Communist parties for their place in postwar governments. In this way the Kremlin added to the humiliation of their expulsion, insisting that they had been incapable of improving either the political or the economic conditions of their members in Belgium, Italy and France.

Instead of improving, economic realities in France had in fact grown steadily worse. Instead of being used for reconstruction, American credits were forced to pay for day-to-day essentials. As J.P. Rioux describes the situation: 'the winter was hard, the population hungry and impatient; there were bottlenecks in raw materials, energy and labour; the commercial balance deteriorated and the currency reserves dwindled'. Along with falling output – 10 per cent in the spring – came a cut in the bread ration to 250 grammes (down to 200 grammes in September), and, inevitably, bread riots: 'Between January and July the money supply rose by 40 per cent and wages by 47 per cent; over the same period wholesale prices increased by 91 per cent and retail prices by 93 per cent.' After the Renault workforce, the gas, electricity and railway workers threatened or carried out strike action.[41]

Although the rail and road networks were largely repaired in Italy by 1947 and output was rising, particularly in exports, it remained still well below the 1938 levels. Meanwhile unemployment still stood around one million in the industrial sector alone, and was the immediate cause of most mass demonstrations and violence. Unable to impose rationing, the government faced the end of UNRRA's efforts with ever-more desperate appeals to friends in America, such as the one De Gasperi made to the mayor of New York in November, pleading for 50,000 tons of wheat to be sent immediately to stave off famine and tumult. With inflation persisting at an average of 50 per cent, the lower-middle and white-collar classes were particularly hard-hit and provided fertile terrain for neo-Rightist groups of various sorts; from just such a context had sprung Fascism itself, of course. Further humiliated by the surprisingly punitive peace treaty which was finally announced in February, the Christian Democrats leading the government coalition saw their support dwindle dramatically in regional elections in April.

But any rejoicing the Left may have felt was soon destroyed by the Portella di Ginestra massacre of the 1st of May. The bandit Salvatore Giuliano and his gang, acting on behalf of local Mafia bosses, opened fire on a May Day celebration in a Sicilian valley, killing eleven and wounding sixty-five of those present. In an overall comment, the American Ambassador in Rome wrote:

> Population generally and particularly more responsible banking and industrial leaders have lost confidence entirely in the Govt and are afraid to venture upon new or expanded enterprises. A flight from the Lira is beginning; rise in spiral inflation is unchecked. . . . There is such a real need of food in the country that responsible men are extremely concerned

over the possibilities of a starvation situation arising some time during the next six months.

As far as Ambassador Dunn was concerned, however, 'there could easily be a general confidence in the future if it were not for the political agitation of the Communists'.[42]

Even without a Communist Party to worry about, Britain was faced with the depths of the most difficult economic crisis any government had endured for many years. Winter conditions were the worst ever recorded, bringing a desperate coal shortage, power cuts, and the temporary reappearance of mass unemployment. The newly national-ised coal mines were not able to respond to the challenge and there was evidence that the government had been too complacent in the preceding months. Draconian wartime-style controls on every form of energy consumption were promulgated – from sport to advertising, from industry to hairdressing – but even so the railways were forced to commandeer household coal in transit for their own use and cancel 3,500 trains. As *The Times* commented in mid-February:

> The state of emergency through which we are now passing brings back memories of wartime. The darkness of the streets and roads; the austerity in domestic lighting . . . the feeling of being cut off from our friends and the desire to stay safe indoors; the tendency . . . towards avoiding unnecessary travel – all these things have a suggestion of bad times past.

In reality, with mass unemployment, soaring theft and the catastrophic effects on agriculture, things were considerably worse than wartime (though still not as bad as in most of Europe, as the government knew). The unplanted wheat was equal to one month's bread ration; steel production fell to the lowest levels of the 1930s depression and overall, two months of production for export were lost. With 42 per cent of its imports originating in the United States, $1.1 billion of the American loan had been used up by April 1947. Protagonists and observers agree that the Labour government's self-confidence never fully recovered, and that the illusions of great power status now began to be shed. The leading CBS reporter in Europe commented shortly afterwards:

> At the time, Britain was maintaining a great power's armed force of 1,250,000 troops and spending three billion dollars a year fulfilling her world-wide commitments – over four times more than richer, prewar Britain paid for her armed forces.
> The winter crisis made the impossibility of all this manifest.[43]

Inevitably a grim picture was that painted by the distinguished editor of *Foreign Affairs*, Hamilton Fish Armstrong, who reported on a new visit to Europe in the July 1947 edition of his magazine:

The 1947 visitor finds Europe abstracted and preoccupied . . . (transfixed) by one state which is universal – complete absorption in the problem of how to live. Every minute is dedicated to scrounging enough food, clothing and fuel to carry through the next 24 hours. Little energy is left for noticing what foreign nations think and say or for complicated reasoning and farsighted planning to please them and suit their requirements, even if they are benefactors and masters of the atom.

Production might have increased since the end of the war, but it was only a fraction of what people had been used to before it:

There is too little of almost everything – too few trains, trams, buses and automobiles to transport people to work on time, let alone to take them on holidays; too little flour to make bread without adulterants, and even so not enough bread to provide energies for hard labour; too little paper for newspapers to report more than a fraction of the world's news; too little seed for planting and too little fertilizer to nourish it; too few houses to live in, and not enough glass to supply them with window panes; too little leather for shoes, wool for sweaters, gas for cooking, cotton for diapers, sugar for jam, fats for frying, milk for babies, soap for washing.

Old Europe's political passions had gone: now a vote could be captured by a bucket of coal, an ounce of bread, a packet of cigarettes. The American–Soviet split meant nothing in such circumstances: 'the present currency for winning esteem is mainly material [so that] the advantage lies with us if we choose to exercise it . . . we can use our calories and our machines to reveal the weakness of the Communist apparatus of production and distribution'. Statesmanship was at a discount, as politicians struggled, each in his own myopic way, to fill the 'empty national bread-basket . . . empty national coalbin . . . empty national treasury'.

In this context the Truman Doctrine, while gladdening the hearts of America's friends, had worrying aspects, especially the casting aside of the United Nations and 'the intimation that everyone must now choose sides in an ideological battle'. In reality America's task was to move on from relief to reconstruction, Armstrong insisted: 'first we must give; then we must invest; whenever possible we must buy; and eventually we may hope to begin getting our money back'. What was needed was a plan, drawn up cooperatively by the Europeans, but with the best American brains involved 'to give it reality'. Capital goods and raw material imports, mutual aid principles, currency stabilisation measures would all be treated in the plan, which perhaps could be supervised by the new UN Economic Commission for Europe. Above all America would like to demonstrate her 'native confidence' in what she stood for: not just a political and economic system which had produced 'the highest standard of living the world has ever known', but one 'capable of extension and improvement to meet modern needs and desires', capable of projecting its example in the knowledge that, in contrast with the Soviets, 'Europe wants what we can give'.[44]

Even as Armstrong prepared his article, just such a plan was brought forth by the United States government.

NOTES

1. *New York Times* 26 Nov 1944; cf. Ellwood *Italy 1943* op cit p 119
2. Cit in Kolko G *The Politics of War. The World and United States Foreign Policy 1943–1945* NY 1968 p 498
3. *New York Herald Tribune* 8 July 1945
4. Cf. Rostow WW *The Stages of Economic Growth, A Non-Communist Manifesto* Cambridge 1960 Ch 9
5. 'A British Official' (sic) Liberated Europe: The Economic Inexorables. *Foreign Affairs* July 1945 pp 543–55
6. *Economist* 13 Jan 1945
7. FRUS 1946 vol V Washington DC 1969 pp 409–11
8. Lundestad G Empire by Invitation? The United States and Western Europe, 1945–1952. *Journal of Peace Research* n 3 1986 p 269
9. Gaddis op cit p 23, 190, 222–3, 259–61
10. FRUS 1946 vol V pp 399–400
11. Ibid p 413
12. Frank R The French Dilemma: Modernization with Dependence or Independence and Decline. In *Power in Europe?* op cit p 274; cf Rioux op cit p 84
13. Penrose EF *Economic Planning for the Peace* Princeton 1953 p 215
14. *Economist* 1 Sept 1945
15. Cf Gardner RN Sterling–Dollar Diplomacy in Current Perspective. In Louis WR and Bull H (eds) *The 'Special Relationship'. Anglo-American Relations Since 1945* Oxford 1986, and Kolko J and G *The Limits of Power. The World and United States Foreign Policy, 1945–1954* NY 1972 pp 65–9
16. Bullock op cit pp 121–5 (Gallup poll cit at p 122)
17. Excerpt from text of proposals in DAFR Vol VIII 1945–46 pp 625–7 (cit at p 627)
18. Ibid p 624, 627–8, 643–56; cf Penrose op cit pp 310–17; Bullock op cit pp 201–5 (*Sunday Times* 16 Dec 1945 cit at p 202)
19. Rostow *The Division of Europe* op cit p 56
20. Gaddis op cit pp 312–13. Kennan's analysis was contained in an 8,000 word telegram sent from the Moscow Embassy in February 1946 whose impact had been enormous; discussed in Gaddis op cit pp 302–4, reproduced in FRUS 1946 pp 696–709.
21. Cit in *The United States in World Affairs 1945–1947* Council on Foreign Relations NY 1947 (henceforth USWA) pp 368–9

22. Bullock op cit pp 348–54; cit at p 339
23. Cit in Iatrides JO *Revolt in Athens. The Greek Communist 'Second Round', 1944–45* Princeton 1972 pp 124–5
24. Gaddis op cit pp 336–7; Bullock op cit pp 315–16
25. Joseph M. Jones cit in Gaddis op cit p 346
26. Text in DAFR vol IX 1947 pp 646–50
27. Gaddis op cit p 351
28. Administration remarks in Statement by Acting Secretary of State Dean Acheson to Senate Foreign Relations Committee, 24 March 1947, in DAFR Vol IX 1947 pp 650–8; Attlee comment cit in Bullock op cit p 349; McNeill analysis in *The Greek Dilemma* 1947 pp 223–4
29. USWA 1947–48 pp 34–7 (cit at p 35)
30. Ibid p 48
31. Cf di Nolfo E (ed) *Vaticano e Stati Uniti 1939–52. Dalle carte di Myron C. Taylor* Milan 1978 p 518
32. USWA 1947–48 pp 40–1
33. Ibid p 38
34. Miller JE *The United States and Italy, 1940–1950* Chapel Hill 1986 pp 215–19
35. Ibid pp 226–30
36. USWA op cit pp 39–40
37. Cook D *Charles de Gaulle. A Biography* 1984 p 306
38. Economic Recovery in the Liberated Countries of Western Europe. In *The World Today* Feb 1947 pp 90–101
39. Ibid p 225
40. Belgium Changes Her Government. In *The World Today*, May 1947 p 223
41. Rioux op cit pp 122–3
42. Ginsborg P *A History of Contemporary Italy. Society and Politics 1943–1988* 1990 pp 145–8; De Cecco M Economic Policy in the Reconstruction Period, 1945–51. In Woolf SJ (ed.) *The Rebirth of Italy 1943–50* 1972 pp 165–6; Miller op cit pp 205–10 214–15; Dunn comment in letter to State Department, 3 May 1947, in FRUS 1947 vol III p 890
43. Eatwell R *The 1945–1951 Labour Governments* 1979 pp 80–2; Robertson op cit (*Times* cit at p 120); Smith HK *The State of Europe* NY 1949 p 28
44. Fish Armstrong H Europe Revisited. In *Foreign Affairs* July 1947 pp 537–49

CHAPTER FIVE

The Road to the Marshall Plan

THE IMMEDIATE BACKGROUND

Everyone, it turned out, had a plan. The Twentieth Century Fund had a plan, Republican Presidential aspirant Harold Stassen had a plan, former President Hoover had one, as did the leading Republican Senator Arthur H. Vandenberg, and a prominent Democrat, Senator Pepper. In April and May Walter Lippman in the *Washington Post* demanded abandonment of the piecemeal aid policies of the past in favour of 'a comprehensive recovery plan agreed to by the Europeans themselves and used to support the "unification of Europe".'[1]

The State Department hinted it had done some planning in a speech by the Under Secretary of State, Acheson, in Mississippi in early May. This listed the grim developments in the world since the war and suggested that existing aid programmes would cover only half the gap between America's imports from abroad and her exports to the rest of the world in the coming years. United States exports had quadrupled since 1939, said Acheson, and needed to be much higher if the means could be found to pay for them in the countries of Europe and Asia most threatened by disaster. In these areas of the globe 'emergency assistance' was required urgently, needed in building stability, promoting freedom and democracy, 'fostering liberal trading policies, and . . . strengthening the authority of the United Nations'. In his concluding remarks, Acheson, one of the key 'wise men' of Washington's foreign policy élite in these years, re-emphasised the fundamental American faith in the economic bases of freedom and democracy:

> Not only do human beings and nations exist in narrow economic margins, but also human dignity, human freedom, and democratic institutions.

It is one of the principal aims of our foreign policy today to use our economic and financial resources to widen these margins.[2]

By the spring of 1947 there was tumultuous debate in the foreign policy establishment about how to 'reconstruct a working world economy', 'stabilise democratic nations' and fight the 'Communist and Socialist propaganda threatening the American way of life', as various newspaper headlines cried. But the public opinion battle was only beginning: after the Truman Doctrine speech, enthusiasm for the administration's crusades seemed to wane. The State Department had been forced to promise its friends in Congress it would return with no more aid requests, large or small; proposals for post-UNRRA relief to a number of countries were almost reduced to $200m. before being grudgingly accepted at $350 million, while the Voice of America, the official US broadcasting system abroad, had seen its funds substantially cut. As Richard Freeland has written, 'the Administration had exhausted its ability to mobilise domestic support for foreign aid'.[3]

The end of the wartime visions

What then of the World Bank and the International Monetary Fund, the Export–Import Bank and the dream of the International Trade Organisation, all of which had promised to contribute to a liberalising, expansionary reconstruction of the world economy which would surely include Europe? What of the great dream of the United Nations itself, whose authority Under-Secretary Acheson had claimed he was anxious to reinforce as recently as May, and whose new Economic Commission for Europe was just beginning its work?

In reality very few of the hopes attached to these new institutions by their supporters in America and elsewhere had been fulfilled by mid-1947. At the close of the previous year the Export–Import Bank had announced that it was ending its emergency reconstruction credits in order to focus on trade and development financing on the basis of limited, bilateral relationships. The World Bank had been locked in structural and staff difficulties since its conception, and only appointed an authoritative president in February 1947. When it eventually began operations, the Bank too would 'carry out a more limited program of "safer" loans than had been originally expected', in the words of contemporary observers. The IMF also saw its remit reduced in scope by Washington in 1946–47, with the effect that it 'would limit itself to supplying foreign exchange to member countries with temporary deficits in their balances of payments'. It made its first advances, to France and the Netherlands, only at the end of May 1947.[4]

As for the United Nations, it had become apparent that while it could do much useful work, none of the great powers was interested in entrusting any truly significant element of its security to the majority vote in a world body. Instead the Council of Foreign Ministers was the forum where the key power struggles were taking place. The State–War–Navy Coordinating Committee in Washington pointed to major world problems to be settled outside the UN, 'such as peace treaties with Germany and Japan', and threats to US security which came from 'subversive and "boring from within" tactics in friendly countries'. Political instability which stemmed from economic weakness likewise fell 'outside the purview of the UN': this of course was the very basis on which foreign aid programmes were being determined by America.[5]

As the Canadian representative had told the UN General Assembly at its session in December 1946 it was evident already 'that we, the members of the Assembly, believe that the Security Council has yet to demonstrate that it is capable of doing the job the United Nations has a right to expect of it, and which is expected of it by the peoples of the world.'[6] However the highest authorities of the United States, led by the president but animated by the powerful Under-Secretary of State for Economic Affairs, William Clayton, still continued their drive to build the UN International Trade Organisation – 'the element in the postwar structure dearest to the American heart', in the words of the British banker and economist Eric Roll.

By early 1947 seventeen nations, including Britain and France, had declared support for this scheme and a new large-scale conference got under way in Geneva in April. Rules seemed to have emerged on eliminating commercial discrimination and on limiting the use of direct trade controls. But the next steps would pledge all involved to begin the work of tariff reductions, and at that point domestic opposition had begun to stiffen in America: 'it emerged that a policy which, without cutting tariffs, favored the ITO, would have strong popular support', said official observers. This total contradiction soon brought American public action to a complete halt. While the Geneva conference is noted as having established the still-surviving GATT (General Agreement on Tariffs and Trade) tradition, the ITO was doomed to extinction. During the heated confrontation in Congress on the Marshall Plan, the State Department found it necessary to 'suppress the entire issue of commercial and import policy . . . and to place the burden of its advocacy of that program on an anti-communist appeal', writes Richard Freeland.[7]

So of the great wartime reform edifice in all its articulations little of lasting significance had been put in place by the middle of 1947. From Bretton Woods the most enduring legacy would be the IMF with its limited mechanisms to help stabilise exchange rates. As for free trade, according to American commentators, it had turned out to be 'not the link which actually brought together postwar America and Europe. On the contrary, it was the issue that divided them'. New Deal universalism was obliged to shrink to a new, more finite regional perspective on the world. Harold Van Buren Cleveland, an economist who worked on the original formulations of the Marshall Plan, recalled in 1987: 'In retrospect it seems clear that the universalist approach to European recovery was abstract and unrealistic, considering the sorry state of most European countries' budgets.' The conditions of liberalisation attached to the British loan were soon to bring disaster: in Eric Roll's view, 'the loan agreement itself, though an absolutely indispensable part of the postwar structure, virtually proved that the new multilateral agreements and institutions were incapable, by themselves, of setting the world on the right economic road'. The British abandoned sterling convertibility after weeks in August 1947 as dollars poured out of the country. Yet the crisis 'served Europe well', says Cleveland, 'because it undermined the credibility of the American universalists' program, opening the way for a quite different approach.'[8]

THE BIRTH OF THE PLAN

The finest hour of the State Department

Historians and former protagonists alike are generally agreed by now on the major steps which brought the new approach to birth. Between the Truman Doctrine and the Marshall Plan substantial rethinking took place on how to project America's power into the European situation in new ways, ways intended to bring radical short- and long-term changes in economic structures and political prospects.[9]

The economist W.W. Rostow recalls three contingent developments of key importance. The first was the physical condition of the Continent after the setbacks caused by the extremely severe winter of 1946–47. Second was the failure of the Truman Doctrine to indicate a constructive way forward for all: as one of Rostow's colleagues in the State Department noted at the time: 'We have a great deal to gain by convincing the world that we have something positive and attractive to offer, and not just anti-Communism.' Thirdly was the gruelling experience of Secretary of State George Marshall in the Moscow Conference of Foreign Ministers in March and April, dedicated to Germany.

Marshall had been recalled to government by Truman at the beginning of 1947 after retiring from the Pentagon at the end of the war as Army Chief of Staff. His success in that job – Churchill had called him 'the organiser of victory' – and his personal qualities of incisiveness, integrity and self-abnegation made him the most authoritative public figure of the era. His patience and sense of duty were tested to the full in the six weeks of fruitless wrangling in Moscow. In Rostow's account:

> He concluded – as had many others over the previous year and a half – that Stalin did not intend to move toward a unified democratic Germany, but he did not stop there. Unlike [his predecessor] Byrnes he also concluded that the economic, social and political disarray of Western Europe, with all the opportunities it appeared to open for Soviet penetration, was a major reason for Stalin's complacency in the face of delay over the German problem . . . . George Kennan paraphrases Marshall's pithy view as of April 29, 1947: 'Europe was in a mess. Something would have to be done. If he [Marshall] did not take the initiative, others would.'[10]

Kennan and his new State Department 'Policy Planning Staff' – set up on Marshall's initiative – produced one of the master documents for the new approach. Another was provided by Under-Secretary William Clayton, whose sojourn in Europe in the spring, based at the Geneva ITO talks, and contacts with many of Europe's leaders, had convinced him too that the Continent was on the brink of 'economic, social and political disintegration'. Like the others he was certain that America must now provide relief goods on a massive, planned scale, but his rationale was slightly different from that of his colleagues: 'in order to save Europe from starvation and chaos (*not* from the Russians)'.

Kennan's paper, based on detailed long-range thinking among the State Department economists and in the State–War–Navy Co-ordinating Committee, looked to parallel, integrated programmes developed simultaneously in the United States and Western Europe. These would be constructed so as to bring self-sufficiency to America's partners in four or five years. There would be a special plan for Britain and safeguards against 'Communist sabotage or misuse'. The scheme assumed the Europeans would work on the basis of 'intramural economic collaboration', and that 'some form of regional political association of Western European states' would be a desirable outcome.

Although there was talk of clearing the proposal through the UN Economic Commission for Europe, Kennan insisted that the initiative must come from the European governments themselves, based on agreement between them. In any case the American zones of Austria and Germany would also be required to 'make the maximum contribution to economic restoration in Western Europe in general'.

It was Clayton who most openly recognised that 'we grossly underestimated the destruction to the European economy by the war', and who insisted on the structural difficulties, in particular the breakdown of the town–country relationship: 'More consumer's goods and restored confidence in the local currency are absolutely essential if the peasant is again to supply food in normal quantities to the cities.' Clayton too was the one who most clearly spelled out widely diffused fears of the impact of a European breakdown on the American domestic economy: 'markets for our surplus production gone, unemployment, depression, a heavily unbalanced budget on the background of a mountainous war debt'.[11]

When the leading State Department figures gathered to formulate the synthesis of the Kennan and Clayton approaches which would go into the announcement of the new initiative, they assumed that the UN Commission for Europe – where the Soviets participated as full members – would soon be dropped. But they explicitly left open the hope that Eastern European nations would participate, provided they 'would abandon [the] near-exclusive Soviet orientation of their economies'. The experts all agreed that institutionalised economic cooperation among the Europeans, 'perhaps an economic federation to be worked out over three or four years', was the only 'politically feasible basis' on which the United States could operate. Yet they insisted they were fully aware of the dangers of forcing 'the American way' on others.[12]

The new suggestion

But this was just one of the tensions the leading figures of the State Department had to take account of when turning to the tactics of how the new scheme would be launched. Marshall and his staff had to combine their intense sense of urgency with the need to avoid creating any more panic at home and abroad. They had to convince Congress that a qualitatively new kind of American initiative was demanded – only months after doing likewise with the Truman Doctrine – without provoking accusations of failure and a massive isolationist reaction. They were also obliged to foresee the likely political reactions in

Europe, giving the Soviets as little space as possible for objection while convincing the West Europeans that a decisive gesture to them was now on offer.

For all these reasons, Marshall, Acheson, Clayton and Kennan chose to launch their programme for European recovery in a single, low-key speech by the Secretary at a private gathering. Once this line had been decided the first suitably dignified occasion was seized on. It turned out to be the graduation ceremony on 5 June at Harvard University, where Marshall had just postponed an invitation to receive an honorary degree.

Hence when the famous plan named for George Marshall was born it took the form not of a specific programme or scheme but of 'a few remarks', expressed somewhat enigmatically in the course of an academic ceremonial, an unpredictable setting for an important diplomatic initiative. Only certain of the British had been warned − cryptically − that something important was about to happen, and even they made no special effort to take notice on the day.

In Marshall's brief and outwardly simple comments there were first of all explanations, for domestic consumption, of how the 'entire fabric of European economy' had been disrupted by the war and its aftermath, how confidence in currencies had been lost, the division of labour between the farmer and the city-dweller − 'the basis of modern civilisation' − broken down and of how Europe's immediate requirements were far greater than her ability to pay. Hence the task was above all to 'restore the confidence of the European people in the economic future of their own countries and of Europe as a whole'.

For the foreign audience there were warnings right away for all who sought 'to perpetuate human misery in order to profit therefrom politically or otherwise'. But the Secretary of State was very clear: 'Our policy', he said in a famous passage, 'is directed not against any country or doctrine but against hunger, poverty, desperation and chaos. Any government that is willing to assist in the task of recovery will find full cooperation ... on the part of the United States Government.' The Soviet Union, in other words, would not be barred from participation in the scheme.

Then came the crux of the speech: a short paragraph inviting the Europeans to agree among themselves on 'the requirements of the situation', and on the part each nation would take 'in order to give proper effect to whatever action might be undertaken by this government'. Marshall discreetly but clearly invited the Europeans to take the initiative, while the US role, he said 'should consist of friendly aid in the drafting of a European program and of later support of such a program so far as it may be practical for us to do so. The program should be a joint one, agreed to by a number, if not all, European nations'. The Secretary of State concluded with an exhortation to his public to eschew 'political passion and prejudice', and 'face up to the vast responsibility which history has clearly placed upon our country'.[13]

'Something between a hint and suggestion', was how Marshall himself later characterised his speech, adding that he was embarrassed that it should have been dubbed a Plan by the president and the press, with his name 'tagged to it'.[14]

THE RESPONSES IN EUROPE

'We expected them to jump two inches and they've jumped six feet' – the European response to the new initiative was almost instantaneous and the American press was taken aback. Ernest Bevin in person had been among the first to grasp the significance of Marshall's words:

> Within a few days of receiving the text of the speech, Mr Bevin had flown to Paris, made certain of France's willingness to become joint sponsor of a conference on European recovery, issued an invitation to Russia to concert an agenda and fixed the preliminary Three Power talks for the next weekend.[15]

Ernest Bevin was enthusiastic, but the instinctive Whitehall reaction to the Marshall speech was defensive: Britain 'was not economically a part of Europe' (said a Ministerial committee) and did not wish to be 'lumped in' with the Continental indigents – only recovery on a world scale would get enough dollars flowing to solve Britain's problems. The French worried at first that the American vision would cut across the Monnet designs and, above all, wreck their scheme for cutting off the Ruhr and placing Germany's recovery at their mercy. So when Bevin and his French colleague Georges Bidault came together to discuss a first reply (17–18 June), their purposes were not simply to organise a chorus of approval. They set the terms for a sixteen-nation conference which would create a Committee on European Economic Cooperation (CEEC). This committee would begin assembling a comprehensive list of reconstruction needs for American support, and deal with the more controversial American demands on liberalisation and integration.[16]

When the Russians arrived in Paris (27 June) to deal with the apparent American offer to include them in the scheme, Molotov and his team found themselves given little choice. In this famous crisis of Cold War history they were confronted with the Western insistence on a jointly formulated and implemented recovery strategy treating the whole of Europe, including Germany, as a single economic entity. They walked out after three days, insisting that the Americans and their key allies had no other intention than to line up Europe's economies under their own control and impose a new world division of labour: traditional great power imperialism in its latest, American, guise. The method for dealing with the Marshall initiative suggested by Molotov was for each country to prepare its own estimates of its needs, submitting them by way of a coordinating committee to Washington. This proposal was embarrassing because, as the course of events was to reveal, its procedure – involving no commitment to integration or any other form of structural change – came very close to what the West Europeans themselves truly desired.[17]

Was the Marshall speech responsible then for 'splitting Europe', as its opponents have long charged, even before the 'Plan' was drawn up?[18] After the Soviet Union had rejected the new American proposition – an offer made in the first place to reassure West Europeans that America was *not* intent on dividing the Old World into two hostile blocs – both French and Italian Communist parties were called severely into line by Stalin. Henceforth they would be called upon to lead the struggle against the Marshall Plan behind the banner of the Soviet Union in the Cominform, a specially invented propaganda and policy coordination body with Europe-wide reach. A new Soviet command system was thereby created, one which ignored totally the local conditions each party operated under, and left them open to every sort of charge of being fifth columns or at least mouthpieces of the USSR. In the meantime the Russians made sure that the Poles and the Czechs would withdraw their declared interest in Marshall's initiative.[19]

When the British and French saw Molotov and his team stalk out of the Paris conference they were convinced that the division of Europe was now practically irreversible, and enjoyed a certain relief. The French, for instance, had long been urging the Americans to realise that

> ... present French policy is based not simply on fear of future German aggression but equally, if not more, on fear that the United States will lose interest, eventually withdraw from Germany, and that some fine morning they will wake up and find themselves face to face with the Russians on the Rhine.[20]

Although elements in the American occupation forces in Germany continued to press for German unity in the hope that the West would dominate the outcome, Clay, at the top of the military regime, and the British, were convinced by now that the Soviets would come to dominate a Germany reunited under any of the schemes available up until then. For them the Marshall Plan was the key to West Germany's security: it would allow them to build up the English–American–French zone into a viable economic and political entity, and finally convince the French that they should relinquish their claims on Germany's industrial resources.

But this was just one of the possible implications of Marshall's words.

THE PURPOSES OF THE PLAN

In his 1955 survey of the Marshall Plan effort, carried out for its official bureaucracy the ECA (European Cooperation Administration), Harry Bayard Price noted how from a one-paragraph 'suggestion', had sprung a programme which 'evolved swiftly into a vast spirited international adventure: as the enterprise unfolded, it became many things to many men'.

Indeed. Originally, the aim of the European Recovery Programme, as it was officially known, was 'to balance Europe's budget at a level of consumption – in other words, a standard of living – high enough to give political stability', according to one of the first commentaries on the plan, written by the economist Barbara Ward. The Programme's Congressional enactment spoke of creating in Western Europe 'a healthy economy independent of extraordinary outside assistance' by 1952. To this end, writes the economic historian Imanuel Wexler, 'the act stipulated a recovery plan based on four specific endeavours: (1) a strong production effort, (2) expansion of foreign trade, (3) the creation and maintenance of internal financial stability, and (4) the development of (European) economic cooperation'.[21]

But in the most recent large-scale analysis of its objectives, Michael Hogan explains how the grand overall thrust of 'remaking the Old World in the image of the New', first attempted in the 1920s but bankrupted by the upheavals of the 1930s, now broke through again in the evolution of the ERP.

Starting with the lessons of the depression era and incorporating the inventions of the New Deal, the Marshall Planners eventually arrived at a design which would aim at nothing less than a replacement of the old European state system in its entirety. They would do this by applying to the ruins of Europe the perceived benefits of America's historical experience. There 'a large internal economy integrated by free market forces and central institutions of co-ordination and control seemed to have laid the groundwork for a new era of economic growth and social stability'. A single market on a continental scale, established and run like the United States, promised to 'limit Communist inroads, dissolve class tensions through a shared abundance, and set the continental countries on the path to a multilateral system of world trade'.[22] In this way a framework would be created capable of reassuring the French, controlling the Germans and containing the Soviets. To substitute the fear-based security obsessions which had dragged Europe into the abyss in 1914 and 1939, the Marshall Plan offered individual Europeans and their families the promise of ever-greater prosperity. An 'economic United States of Europe' would emerge, in which the American dream could be dreamt without leaving home: 'You Too Can Be Like Us!' that was the promise of the Marshall Plan.

THE FIRST DESIGN

Nothing could have been further from the minds of the European diplomats and experts who were given the heavy work of meeting Marshall's challenge. The crucial meeting to turn the American initiative into a concrete recovery design opened in Paris on 12 July.

> The summer-long meeting of the CEEC in Paris was a labor of endless complexities turned up from every nook and cranny of sixteen different national economies in Europe [wrote an American commentator forty years afterwards]. In addition, no-one on either side of the Atlantic could know in advance how Congress would react to the program or how much money it would be willing to appropriate.

There were endless other difficulties. Many of the participants lacked the staff, the statistics or the mentality to do the kind of planning required, and in any case none had ever even thought of doing it on a collective basis. Then again, all recognised that everything depended on Germany, but the German economy was a collection of three devastated zones in the west run by the military, and so was not represented as such. As for the method of calculating what was required from the United States, there was none. When the rule-of-thumb device was invented of estimating, or guessing, the volumes of specific goods desirable *if* the dollars were available, the total requests added up to $28 billion. The State Department made clear that $16 billion would be the outside limit, insisting that Congress would not even look at any higher figure (the final total authorised by 1951 was in fact just over $13bn, negotiated in portions, year by year).[23]

By the end of September the sixteen participating nations had drawn up – with much American prodding and assistance – a specific set of economic targets to be achieved by 1952. In reluctant deference to the United States vision of the entire process as the first step on the road to Europe economic integration, they had promised the Americans to create an Organisation for European Economic Cooperation (OEEC) to supervise and coordinate the realisation of the targets. After severe criticism by the State Department in the persons of Will Clayton and George Kennan, who rejected the original CEEC submission to Washington as a shopping-list compilation of each country's trade deficit, the Committee set the West European nations common objectives of industrial production, financial stabilisation and trade liberalisation. In the short term the production targets were the most urgent and important:

(1) Restoration of prewar bread-grain production and of an intensive livestock economy.
(2) Increase of coal production to 584 million tons yearly, an increase of thirty-two million tons above the 1938 level.
(3) Expansion of electricity output by nearly seventy billion kilowatt-hours and an increase of generating capacity by twenty-five million kilowatts . . . two-thirds above prewar.
(4) Development of oil-refining capacity to two and one-half times prewar.
(5) Increase in crude-steel production to fifty-five million tons yearly or 20 per cent above prewar.
(6) Expansion of inland transport to carry 25 per cent more than prewar.
(7) Rehabilitation and restoration of the merchant fleets of the participating countries.
(8) Supply from European production of most of the capital equipment for these expansions.

The plan depended on doubling exports to the United States and to the rest of the Western hemisphere, while increasing them to the rest of the world by a third. Of the total import cost of the programme of $57.4 billion, the US was to be asked to supply just over $19 billion. Even if all the forecasts turned out to be true, however, there would still be a $1 billion trade deficit – or 'dollar gap' – between Europe and America at the end of the programme, thus risking the defeat of the major financial objective of the entire effort. As Barbara Ward commented shortly after the start of operations: 'The goal which the Sixteen Nations propose to achieve before 1952 can best be summed up by saying that they seek an industrial and agricultural expansion equal to the tremendous increase in the American economy between 1940 and 1944.'[24] In this vast undertaking, said President Truman's special new committee on 'European Recovery and American Aid', the US contribution 'must be viewed not as a means of supporting Europe, but as a spark which can fire the engine'.[25]

THE MARSHALL PLAN AS HISTORICAL MONUMENT

Perspectives forty years on

The meaning of the Marshall Plan has been extolled, condemned and otherwise endlessly debated ever since the General made his speech. In the anniversary year of 1987, leading Europeans who had witnessed the birth of the Plan celebrated its conception, its methods and above all its impact. The Italian statesman and former Ambassador to the United States, Egidio Ortona, spoke of 'an ideal inspiration on how to maintain security and welfare wherever need be'. Monnet's collaborator, Pierre Uri, recalled how on the morrow of the speech the great man had exclaimed to him 'Now how are we going to use that to finance our investments?'. Dennis Healey, later British Minister of Defence and Chancellor of the Exchequer, but at the time International Secretary of the Labour Party, recalled the pattern of peacetime international cooperation between states that the Plan inaugurated.[26]

In a British survey of 1987 Lord Franks, the eminent civil servant who chaired the CEEC conference in Paris, spoke as follows:

[Marshall] was afraid that in social and economic disintegration, the strong Communist parties of France and Italy might take over. He wanted to prevent that. He wanted to be sure that western Germany and western Europe – the one couldn't recover without the other – did recover. And this required the infusion of goods – food, steel, machine tools – which only American dollars could buy. The Marshall Plan was about putting American dollars in the hands of Europeans to buy the tools of recovery.

In this view the Marshall initiative contained a shrewd mix of morality, self-interest and political farsightedness:

I think the Americans did this quite largely from humanitarian reasons. General Marshall was deeply moved by the millions of people from east Germany sculling about in western Germany without the means of subsistence, supported by food brought in at the cost of dollars by Britain and America; deeply scared about the plight of people in western Europe. By the spring of 1947 the French farmers, the Italian farmers were hoarding their grain, not sending it to the cities, using it to feed their cattle ... Remember, food grains ran out in Italy by November, 1947. They ran out in France in March–April 1948. There was a crisis. It was this that America stepped into. And it stepped into it both to save the people of Europe, and to preserve western Europe as a land of democratic, freedom-loving people, and prosperous, *on the side of the United States*. That is when the American commitment to western Europe was made, in my view.[27]

The American veterans of the Marshall Plan interviewed at the same time as Lord Franks took a slightly less high-minded stance. Paul Nitze, a very senior statesman of postwar American diplomacy, underlined the size of America's balance-of-payments overhang at the time – $5 to $7 billion a year – and the progressive breakdown of the international economy it threatened. But Alger Hiss, a former State Department professional, preferred to emphasize the role of the Plan in fighting the Left – not the threat of Soviet invasion, but the strength of national Communist and socialist parties, (a distinction however which the Administration did not care to dwell on in public). Acheson himself is quoted as, in his own words, the individual who 'probably made as many speeches and answered as many questions about the Marshall Plan as any man alive: ... and what citizens and the representatives in the Congress always wanted to learn in the last analysis was how Marshall Aid operated to block the extension of Soviet power and the acceptance of Communist economic and political organization and alignment'.[28]

The psychological objects of the Plan

In spite of these words the Marshall speech had explicitly declared that the proposal was 'directed not against any country or doctrine but against hunger, poverty, desperation and chaos'. While George Kennan wrote in *Foreign Affairs* that 'the palsied decrepitude of the capitalist world is the keystone of Communist philosophy', the ERP was intended to have long and short term effects which would go well beyond the neutralisation of Communism. Kennan's planners spoke of Europe's difficulties as stemming from 'a profound exhaustion of physical plant and spiritual vigor', coming on top of a historical 'maladjustment' of economic nature, 'which makes European society vulnerable to exploitation by any and all totalitarian movements and which Russian communism is now exploiting'.[29]

From this reasoning the men who launched the Marshall Plan saw that a massive injection of confidence was required in Europe along with all the relief goods, and from the beginning the symbolic and psychological dimensions of their action were as high among their priorities as its economic effects. The Planning Staff proposed an immediate gesture on as large a scale as possible to tackle an obvious industrial bottleneck, and singled out the rapid restoration of the coal mining system in the Rhine valley as their target operation. The purpose was first of all 'psychological':

> . . . to put us on the offensive instead of the defensive, to convince the European peoples that we mean business, to serve as a catalyst for their hope and confidence, and to dramatize for our people the nature of Europe's problems and the importance of American assistance.[30]

Although nothing was to come of the idea, the surviving outline of this scheme bears a striking resemblance to the methods used by the ERP men in their great mobilisation of public opinion in favour of the Marshall Plan in Europe in the years between 1948 and 1952. 'Maximum publicity and public dramatisation' were called for, aiming to show the US and its allies rushing every means available to increase coal production in the chosen area. Involving non-governmental organizations such as the labour unions, the action would be portrayed as as an effort from 'the US *public* to the peoples of those areas'. Above all it should be specially characterised as an undertaking to highlight 'every possible way in which the United States could help to boost production'.[31]

Production and integration: the two imperatives

At the time and often still today, Marshall Plan money and supplies were seen above all as a great boost to European production, especially in the critical commodities of coal and food. The CEEC conference of European leaders and experts was told:

> The program must be designed to bring about the greatest practicable increase . . . in production of materials needed to fill their basic requirements and to limit requests for supplies from the US to those necessary to fill deficits which those countries cannot . . . themselves satisfy.
> Further, the production program of a participating country should not be based only on its own needs but rather on the contribution that can be made to filling the needs of all participating countries.[32]

The supreme emphasis on increased production remained at the heart of ERP efforts from the first day to the last, and its achievements in this direction are still applauded and celebrated to this day. A semi-official American account declared on the thirtieth anniversary of the Plan:

It was a magnificent effort despite all the problems, and the effects on Europe's economic vitality were striking. By 1952, European industry was churning out goods at the rate of 200 per cent above that of 1938. Perhaps even more important was the increase in agricultural output, up 15 per cent over '38.[33]

But today's historians, like its admirers and detractors at the time, see in the Marshall Plan a wide variety of priorities and emphases. In bringing to light the ERP idea of European integration Michael Hogan has made clear that in many ways this was the great string attached to Marshall Aid. The concept was supported by informed opinion, Congress and throughout the top levels of the State Department. Eisenhower endorsed it even before he became President in 1953, while Congress acknowledged, when the new Atlantic security system came into being in the early 1950s, that European 'economic unification', even 'political federation', remained cardinal goals of American diplomacy.[34]

In the final analysis integration for the Europeans was the right solution to their problems because it had worked in America. In this sense the abstract, Wilson–Roosevelt impulse to bring America's unique answers to the world's problems of conflict and development had left behind the utopias of the United Nations and Bretton Woods and had now found a new incarnation. Although not simply a ploy, it was at best unrealistic to suggest that the Russians should embrace the great scheme as originally envisaged. They could never subscribe to a design which included a revitalized Germany in a system of continent-wide planning or a European customs union, all to be constructed within three or four years. The British and French were to fight as hard as they dared for years against just such a notion.

But there was to be even more than production and integration in the ERP. Based on the perceived lessons of the American experience, the Marshall Plan evolved into a complete model of investment, production and consumption. Because it provided the means, *productivity* would eventually emerge as the key concept for getting results. Ever more efficient and cheaper production would be managed scientifically by forward-looking industrialists, and guided on rational economic lines by the state. This would transform the ancient battle between reactionary capitalists and revolutionary workers into a constructive, dynamic relationship, uniting enlightened producers and contented consumers. *Growth* would resolve all the difficulties, overcome all the challenges, just as in America.

Pointing out that the word 'growth' first appeared in its contemporary guise within Truman's Council of Economic Advisers in 1949,

Charles Maier calls this epochal development 'the politics of productivity'. He suggests it underlay not only the 'consensual hegemony' enjoyed by America *vis à vis* Western Europe in the 1950s and 60s, but finally guaranteed the stabilisation of European societies. The legitimacy of liberal democractic politics was renewed: 'productivity meant collaboration of parties, countries and classes'. To the radical alternatives of redistribution proposed by the Left, the Marshall Plan 'made economic growth under conditions of welfare-state capitalism a plausible alternative'.[35]

THE EFFECTS OF THE COLD WAR ON THE MARSHALL PLAN

But in 1947 'economic growth' and 'welfare-state capitalism' were still strangers to each other, separated ideally and politically by a vast array of circumstances, including the Atlantic Ocean. More than any other factor, however, it was the escalation of the Cold War between 1947 and 1948 which distorted and delayed the prescriptions of the Marshall Plan. These the Europeans were in theory happy to embrace. But for reasons not hard to identify, the American idea of economic integration between them remained an important exception. In the words of the distinguished Italian diplomat and historian Sergio Romano: 'the European states wanted only to restore their own economies and to reacquire and strengthen their national sovereignty'. Events however intervened. As Romano recalls:

> ... within months they had to pay for the defense of their economic sovereignty by giving up their military sovereignty, accepting what turned out to be a much more important link with the US in another field. This was the truth of 1948, when the debate on the economic future of Europe, the predominant debate in 1947, came up against the 1948 confrontation on the security of Europe. There is no doubt that most European countries would have preferred not to go into any link, political or military, with the US.[36]

NOTES

1. Cf *New York Times* Index 1947 p 649; Lippmann cit in Hogan MJ *The Marshall Plan: America, Britain, and the reconstruction of Western Europe, 1947–52* Cambridge 1987 p 39

2. Excerpts of Acheson speech in DAFR 1947 pp 159–63
3. Freeland RM *The Truman Doctrine and the Origins of McCarthyism* NY 1972 Ch IV/4 (cit at p 183); Holt RT and van de Velde RW *Strategic Psychological Operations and American Foreign Policy* Chicago 1960 p 167
4. USWA 1945–47 pp 379–83
5. Ibid p 430
6. FRUS 1947 vol III pp 216–17
7. Roll op cit p 92; USWA 1945–47 pp 383–90; Freeland op cit p 160
8. Calleo DP and Rowland BM *America and the World Political Economy* Bloomington 1973 pp 42–3; Roll op cit p 98; Van Buren Cleveland H Reflections on the Marshall Plan: Then and Now. In Ellwood DW (ed) *The Marshall Plan Forty Years After: Lessons for the International System Today* Bologna 1989 pp 4–5
9. Cleveland op cit pp 5–8; Kindleberger CP *Marshall Plan Days* Boston 1987 Chs 1, 2; Wexler I *The Marshall Plan Revisited. The European Recovery Program in Economic Perspective* Westport 1983 p 18. The economic historian Alan Milward has suggested however that the 1947 crisis was essentially a balance of payments upheaval brought on by the success of industrial investment and production since the war: Milward *The Reconstruction of Western Europe 1945–51* 1984 Ch 1. Discussion in Bibliographical Essay
10. Rostow *The Division of Europe* op cit pp 73–4 (State Department cit in FRUS 1947 vol III p 233 n 5)
11. Kennan and Clayton documents reproduced in FRUS 1947 vol III pp 220–32
12. Summary of discussion in ibid pp 234–6
13. Text in DAFR 1947 pp 9–11
14. Conversation British Ambassador–Secretary of State, 30 June 1947; text in NA RG 59 Office of European Affairs
15. Ward B *The West at Bay* NY 1948 p 146
16. Milward *The Reconstruction* op cit p 63
17. Milward *The Reconstruction* op cit pp 61–6; Hogan op cit p 45–53; Wexler op cit pp 10–12
18. Cf Miller op cit pp 227–8; FRUS 1947 vol III pp 889–92
19. The founding of the Comintern and the 1947 crisis of the Communist parties is examined in Spriano P *The European Communists and Stalin* 1985 Ch 23 and in Agosti A Il partito comunista italiano e la svolta del 1947. In *Studi storici* n 1 1990 (both are archive-based works sympathetic to the Communist point of view); cf Galante S *La fine di un compromesso storico. PCI e DC nella crisi del 1947* Milan 1980 Chs 4, 5; for the French case Wall IM *French Communism in the Era of Stalin* Westport 1983 pp 54–8, Ch 3
20. Mortimer op cit pp 57–8; Rostow *The Division of Europe* op cit p 44
21. Price HB *The Marshall Plan and its Meaning* Ithaca 1955 p 4; Ward B op cit p 158; Wexler I op cit p 5
22. Hogan op cit pp 18, 27
23. Donovan RJ *The Second Victory. The Marshall Plan and the Postwar Revival of Europe* NY 1987 p 41; Milward *The Reconstruction* op cit Ch II; Hogan op cit pp 61–82
24. Ward op cit Ch X (cits at p 159); cf Wexler op cit Ch 2

25. *European Recovery and American Aid* A Report by the President's Committee on Foreign Aid Washington DC Nov 1947 p 3
26. Remarks collected in Ellwood *The Marshall Plan Forty Years After* op cit
27. Mortimer op cit p 55, emphasis in original
28. Ibid pp 85, 56–7
29. FRUS 1947 vol III p 225
30. Ibid pp 225, 222
31. Ibid p 222
32. Ibid p 352
33. Wilson TA *The Marshall Plan* Foreign Policy Association NY 1977 p 47
34. Hogan op cit pp 424–6; cf Kindleberger CP *Marshall Plan Days* op cit Ch 4
35. Maier CS The Politics of Productivity op cit; The Two Postwar Eras op cit; Why Was the Marshall Plan Successful? In *Transatlantic Perspectives* Winter 1988
36. Comments in Ellwood *The Marshall Plan Forty Years After* op cit p 104

CHAPTER SIX
Interdependence and Defence: the Start of the Cold War

A NEW KIND OF CONFLICT

In a few months between the end of 1947 and the middle of 1948 the ever-increasing tensions between the West and the Soviet Union broke out into flagrant confrontation. Surrogate conflicts for war erupted in Greece, in Italy, France and Germany. The 'Cold War' was authoritatively proclaimed by the journalist Walter Lippmann in July 1947 and defined by the French philosopher and sociologist Raymond Aron as 'paix impossible, guerre improbable'. In the very same number of *Foreign Affairs* which Fish Armstrong had used to paint his fresco of European misery, George Kennan launched the concept of 'containment' on its fateful progress. It meant, he said: 'the adroit and vigilant application of counter-force at a series of constantly shifting geographical and political points . . . wher[ever] they [the Soviets] show signs of encroaching upon the interests of a peaceful and stable world'.[1]

Forty years later Kennan asserted that what he had had in mind was a political 'response' to the dangers then prevailing throughout Europe, not a military response to a military danger ('I saw, in fact, no such danger'). Neither he nor anyone else had ever expected that the need for 'containment' would last so long. As Kennan told a Marshall Plan fortieth anniversary audience in Berlin:

> What I did hope was that it would create a species of provisional stability in East–West relationships and that this stability would make possible the negotiation of a general European political settlement – a settlement that would correct the imbalances flowing from the outcome of the war and would place the continent on a hopeful path of peaceful development. Such a settlement, needless to say, would have made unnecessary and unthinkable anything like the division of Europe that now exists.[2]

As for Russian behaviour, the great British historian Arnold Toynbee asked retrospectively:

> Why was it . . . that, even before the Second World War had been won, the Soviet Union began to make a series of moves that progressively wore out the goodwill of her Western allies? Why did she provocatively deprive them of any effective voice in the postwar realignment of those East European countries in which the German occupation or ascendancy was liquidated by Russian arms? . . . Why did the Soviet Government choose to flaunt their hostility to the United States so frankly in American faces? If the foremost aim of Russian policy had been to put the Americans on their guard against the Soviet Union and to goad them into militantly opposing Russian designs, the Russians could not have achieved this aim more successfully than by behaving as they did. Yet it was impossible to believe that this could really have been their purpose.[3]

Decades later the Cold War years would be seen as an era in which the atom bomb had made traditional war unthinkable while peace was impossible because of irreconcilable ideological hostility, the 'clash of the principles of legitimacy', identified by the French commentator Pierre Hassner. It proved well-nigh impossible to explain why or how such a situation had developed, even been allowed to take the world to the brink of war on a number of rare but terrifying occasions – 'it seems to me a miracle that we are all here . . . and still alive', an American analyst exclaimed at a Cold War study conference in 1967.

But the characterisation of the conflict offered on that occasion by a French expert had come over the years to be generally accepted. It was, said Jean Laloy, an 'unending and irreconcilable rivalry, a battle to which there can be no conclusion . . . a conflict incapable of resolution', in which psychological, moral and intellectual – i.e. ideological – forces proved just as dangerous and unpredictable as armed power or political interests: 'I remember [Laloy went on] that in France the Archbishop of Toulouse, a man of considerable importance, prepared those in his diocese to face the fact that communism would inevitably come, that it could not be avoided, that they would have to live through that troublesome phase'. But the question still remained: what could possibly explain the appearance in so short a space of years of 'so crude and widespread a state of affairs'?[4]

TOWARDS CONFRONTATION

Steps in the crisis

Between the end of 1947 and the middle of 1948 the world witnessed:

- The breakdown on the 15 December of the fifth meeting of the Council of Foreign Ministers in London, adjourned *sine die*.
- The beginning, in January, of the London conference on Germany including only the powers of the Western zones plus the Benelux countries; the conference would proceed until June and would set in motion the foundation of the Federal Republic. On the 26 January the French franc was devalued 80 per cent.
- In February a *coup d'état* in Czechoslovakia and the consolidation of Communist power in the country.
- In March the death, in suspicious circumstances, of the Czech Foreign Minister, the distinguished liberal Jan Masaryk. Suspicion persists that the death, which caused great international controversy, was a murder plot organised by Kremlin agents. In the same month the Finnish government received an invitation from Stalin to sign a pact of 'friendship' and military collaboration similar to those in force between the USSR and Hungary and Romania.
- On 17 March the establishment by Bevin and his continental allies (France and the Benelux) of the Western European Union, a step towards a common defence system; the United States was invited to participate. Truman promised US help for European defence and called for universal military training with the temporary reintroduction of the draft. The ERP was finally ratified by Congress. America, France and Britain requested the return of Trieste to full Italian sovereignty.
- In April the Soviets' refusal of the Western request on Trieste; a general election in Italy took place in an atmosphere of total Left–Right confrontation with each side financed and armed clandestinely by its respective superpower sponsor. The Organisation for European Economic Cooperation (OEEC) was set up in Paris to supervise the European management of the Marshall Plan.
- From the 7th to the 10th of May the European Congress, a private meeting of the new European federalist movement at the Hague which saw the pronouncement of a new future for European integration.
- In June the beginning of the operations of the Marshall Plan on the ground. Currency reform by the Western powers in Germany promised to transform the economic prospects in their zones of occupation; Berlin was blockaded by the Soviet army. The Yugoslavia of Tito was expelled from the Cominform for foreign and economic policies differing from the Soviet model.

Meanwhile in the background a new and still more bitter phase of the civil war in Greece was opening. The rebels proclaimed the establishment of the provisional Greek Democratic Government on

Christmas Eve 1947 in a move widely – but almost certainly wrongly – seen outside as the Kremlin's response to the breakdown of the Council of Foreign Ministers. By February Communist forces were beginning to put pressure on the capital. Command of the army passed effectively into American hands with the arrival in Athens of a general from the Pentagon in the same month.

In France an extremely weak coalition held power after a political crisis in November. It faced violent Communist opposition in parliament, in the public services and in the docks and factories. By July 1948 it had collapsed, leaving the country without an authoritative government for two months.

In Germany the third winter of occupation passed by without a minimum of recovery evident in terms of improved rations, a shrinking black market or renewed faith of the Germans in their future. As Alan Bullock commented:

> Indeed, materially, at the end of 1947 it was hard to say that Britain or West Europe were any better off than they had been [at the beginning]. The British, plunging into financial crisis, had had to swallow their pride and eventually devalue sterling. France and Italy could only get through the winter if they received interim aid from the USA and that was not certain until the day after the London CFM broke up. There had been much discussion of the Marshall Plan but not a dollar had yet been allocated to it; there had been much discussion of the reorganisation of Western Germany but it is doubtful if it had yet led to a ton more coal being mined.[5]

The British intervene: the idea of European defence

At the beginning of the New Year the British Foreign Minister prepared a series of key documents on the European situation in the prospect of some kind of critical show-down with the Soviets at some point in the coming months. It was not war the Soviets sought, Bevin insisted, but the obstruction with any means available of West European reconstruction, in particular of the Marshall Plan. This could lead to a coup in a country like Italy, while in its own sphere of influence a definitive consolidation of Soviet power in Czechoslovakia was foreseeable.

In the face of all this Bevin proposed that the British 'as Europeans and as a Social Democratic Government' – and not the Americans – should lead a spiritual, moral and political offensive in favour of all those 'believing in freedom, planning and social justice – what one might call the "Third Force"'. Bevin hoped to see 'some form of union in Western Europe', taking off from the Anglo-French Treaty of Dunkirk which had been signed in March 1947. In the background too was a new proposal of Anglo-French union which Bevin himself had left in Paris in November – echoing Churchill's legendary appeal of 1940 – in order to reinforce the government of the centrist Robert Schuman in its struggle with the Communists. The gesture served too to demonstrate Bevin's conviction that Anglo-French cooperation should be the backbone of Europe's resurgence.

The Treaty of Dunkirk had been aimed against the possibility of German aggression. Members of the new scheme would bind themselves to give 'all the military and other aid in their power' to any of their number attacked in Europe. There was talk of steps towards economic cooperation and of coordination of social services. Beyond France and the Low Countries, Scandinavia, Italy, Greece and 'possibly Portugal' might eventually be included, as would Germany and Spain once democracy was guaranteed there. Organised in this manner, and with the addition of their colonial possessions, the Europeans would be able to face both the Western hemisphere and the Soviet bloc on a basis of parity. Attlee's Cabinet supported the project, which produced its first and only act of significance in the Brussels Pact (17 March 1948), signed under the strong impulse of the events in Prague.[6]

But an even stronger emotion in the British and French governments who sponsored the pact was the fundamental doubt persisting over the readiness of the Americans to come to Europe in its new hour of need, especially in the form which now looked likely to count most – military aid. Their contacts in Washington reminded the Europeans that 1948 was an election year, and with a Democratic victory looking less and less certain, the administration would be most unlikely to give comfort to its opponents by proposing yet another aid package to Congress. While the endless Congressional battle proceeded over the ERP, Truman had encountered serious difficulties in obtaining the much smaller tide-over funds known as 'Interim Aid'. Then again, no certainty existed on how or even whether the Marshall Plan would work: its aims were in any case explicitly long-term, and no one now believed it could achieve its stated financial objectives as soon as 1952. Even in the Greece and Turkey favoured by the Truman Doctrine, it was the scarcity of the American presence on the ground rather than its abundance which struck observers at the beginning of 1948.[7]

The impact of Prague: insecurity deepens

But the events in Prague in February galvanised everybody: Prague was decisive. In later years the leading figures of the Truman administration declared repeatedly that without Stalin's 'errors', their battles with the isolationists and protectionists in Congress would never have been won.[8] It was only after Prague that the passage of the ERP became finally assured. Truman made a solemn and emotional plea to the Congressmen in this sense at the beginning of March, suggesting that the forthcoming elections in Italy would be the next test. By 2 April the president was able to sign the legislative act of the ERP 'at a special ceremony organized to have maximum impact on the Europeans', says James Miller.[9]

Less than three weeks after Prague, Bevin and Marshall made the first tentative moves going beyond the Brussels Pact and towards a system of 'Atlantic' security based on full American involvement. Likewise the outline of a new defence system for the Mediterranean began to emerge, with particular reference to the delicate situation prevailing in Italy.[10]

Alan Bullock credits Ernest Bevin with the key initiatives which led finally to full American involvement in West Europe's security by way of the Marshall Plan and NATO. But the French foreign ministers, first Bidault then Schuman, were no less ardent in their pursuit of American protection. They feared, writes John Young, 'that, as in the Truman Doctrine a year before, the US was willing to antagonise Russia without making effective preparations for war'. Even after the Brussels Pact there was encouragement from Washington but no practical commitment, and at the end of April the French military representative at the United Nations delivered a letter from Schuman to Marshall 'begging for a strategic agreement on the use of forces in a future war'.[11]

The French pressures on the United States continued throughout 1948, and grew 'ever more desperate'. Berlin was the obvious pressure-point, but what was needed in general, in the view of the permanent head of the French Foreign Ministry, Chauvel, was 'the establishment of a "trip-wire", over which the Red Army could not step without provoking a Third World War'. More specifically, the French hoped to join the Combined Chiefs of Staff machinery – the joint Anglo-American set-up in Washington created in wartime – to receive immediately means to equip twenty-five French divisions, and to see a united Western command under an American general based in Germany.

But the French and their supporters were disappointed. While the US Senate passed in June the so-called 'Vandenberg resolution', which suggested for the first time the possibilities of regional military guarantees, there was still no automatic commitment to go to war in Europe's defence. Instead there was a great deal of exhortation to Europeans to look to their own resources.[12] Beyond the political background to this stance, in 1948 the Pentagon itself had little else to offer.

THE MILITARY IN AMERICA AND WESTERN EUROPE: STRATEGIC VISIONS AND CAPABILITIES

The world seen from the Pentagon

A certain number of parallels can be detected between the evolution of American military plans for the postwar world and those produced by the other key elements of the US government's wartime structure. Grand over-arching visions drawn up in the war years were rapidly forced to come to terms with the outcome of the war itself on the ground in Europe and in Asia, and with the political realities of postwar America: what domestic opinion would bear in terms of taxes and conscription. After a tumultuous phase of internal confrontation and rethinking, new plans would emerge with more limited ambitions but with much greater practical applicability. Yet the original frame of reference would remain in many ways largely intact.

This original framework revolved round such assumptions as the inevitably global nature of future wars and the inescapability of America's involvement in them. From this conviction sprang the need to acquire a world-wide network of bases and air-transit rights in order to project American power as closely as possible to would-be aggressors, and to secure access to vital raw materials. Other easily identifiable priorities included: US control of both the Atlantic and Pacific oceans; Latin America as a zone of exclusive US influence; the prevention of any hostile power's domination of the 'Eurasian land mass'; the pursuit as intensely as budgets would permit of development of the atomic bomb and other innovations in the technology of warfare; the necessity for a permanently high level of 'preparedness'. With or without significant allies, with or without the United Nations system, with or without conscription, these desiderata were considered funda-

104

mental by all the services, each seeking to enhance its own role in relation to them.[13]

The military were of course perfectly aware of the decline in British capabilities and the rise of Soviet power potential as a result of the war, but they tended not to frame their plans in terms of specific situations. On the significance of the bomb, they were vague as to how it could be adapted to other types of conflict, how it affected strategic planning or even the balance of power between the forces. The air force was clearly up and the navy down, but the business of prediction and war planning now seemed far more difficult than before. The military dismissed the UN vision as a typical utopian notion of politicians and refused to concede a minimum of their jealous sovereignty to the Security Council.

When the end of war came it quickly emerged that beyond the air force's faith in strategic air power, none of the services possessed plans for their responsibilities in the postwar period, not even for the occupation of Germany and Japan. Meanwhile the stampede to demobilise and dismantle made mockery of ideas that the armed forces might show America the way to a mature assumption of the responsibilities of world leadership. The defence budget dropped from $81 billion to $13 billion between 1945 and 1947, the numbers of men and women under arms from 12.1 million to 1.6 million in the same years.[14]

Hence the key problems for the US military after the war were all internal: what kind of armed forces did the country really want? How did it intend to maintain and pay for them? Such was the impact of the Bomb on public opinion that this weapon alone looked like the solution to all imaginable threats, yet another good reason for Congressional cuts in defence spending. In the words of a specialist study of 1986:

> ... though anti-Communist and anti-Soviet feeling ran high, neither public not Congress showed enthusiasm for the painful measures required to maintain trained reserves and a mobilisation base. The public and Congress did seem willing, however, to spend money for long-range bombers and atomic bombs.[15]

The birth of the new American security system

In the comprehensive National Security Act of July 1947 the questions of organisation were tackled first. It was under this legislation that the system of strategic coordination still functioning in the United States was born. A presidentially-appointed Secretary for Defense, located in the Pentagon, came into being. He would oversee the Chiefs of Staff of the three major services – the air force now attaining the status of a separate arm on a par with the navy and the army. Old and new intelligence services were consolidated in the Central Intelligence Agency, responsible to the president by way of a civilian political appointee at its head. Overall research and policy coordination would be guided henceforth by the National Security Council (NSC), containing the Chiefs of Staff, heads of the intelligence services, the topmost figures of the State Department and other key agencies, with the president himself in the chair.[16]

In this way unification of command was achieved and the supremacy of civilian power over the military re-established and recognised. But there was intense debate over the substance and disposition of the armed forces. While few enthused over the prospect of conscript armies, sentiment in the Pentagon ran strongly in favour of 'universal military training', involving a form of well-prepared, large-scale reserve. But this idea found few political supporters, so that by the end of 1947 the small-scale professional force left over from the war was able to count on a reserve of only about 1 million men engaged in active training. The army later claimed that in the depths of the 1948 crises, its effective combat forces consisted of two divisions immediately available, plus one in reserve.[17]

Defence planners were agreed of course by this point that preparing to oppose some form of Soviet domination of the 'Eurasian land mass' would be their most vital operational priority in the coming years, even though they remained convinced that the Russians were neither capable of war nor desirous of it. Like everyone else, including the CIA, they felt that if Europe fell under Soviet control, this would happen as a result of economic breakdown and misery and its exploitation by local communist parties. The leading military men on the ground – General Clay in Germany, General MacArthur in Japan, Admiral Stone in Italy – all declared that Communism was spreading in the ruins, and that the Soviets were expanding their influence, and it was in these terms that they lent their weight to assistance programmes of all sorts.

With the collapse of the traditional European empires in the Middle East and South-East Asia, there appeared to the military mind to be little to halt the Russian takeover of 'Eurasia'. As the American historian Melvin Leffler summarises this outlook: 'With [Eurasia's] resources, the Soviet Union would be able to overcome its chronic economic weaknesses, achieve defense in depth, and challenge American power – perhaps even by military force'.[18]

Aware that this was a far-fetched possibility, the Defense Department insisted on putting economic recovery before military aid in the division of resources to be applied to specific areas. Meanwhile long-range programmes to develop and multiply the existing handful of atom bombs were set in hand, together with planes to deliver them. But such was the inadequacy of long-range bomber design that forward runways would be essential for their operation, giving new impulse to the long-standing schemes aimed at establishing a world-wide network of American bases. Besides Britain, Turkey would be a favoured nation in this area once the Truman Doctrine measures began to turn into specific operations during 1948. Henceforth the United States possessed the means to penetrate immediately key areas within the Soviet Union itself. Aware of the provocative nature of such moves, army planners were less surprised than most when the Soviet blockade of Berlin began.[19]

By mid-1948 Western Europe had become the key area in the world view of the strategic experts. They too believed in European unity, in the economic revitalisation of West Germany and the founding of the Federal Republic. But they were divided on what to do in case of war. Defending its own corner without an enemy fleet to take into consideration, the navy insisted that lines of communication from the Mediterranean and across the Atlantic and Pacific remained the key priorities. The air force declared that massive strategic bombardment in front of an invading Soviet army would be the only way to stop its advance. The army disagreed, feeling that Allied ground forces would have no option but to retire from Western Europe and gather strength for an eventual counter-attack, which could only come from outside. But there were no concrete plans for such a scenario in 1948, simply convictions that the Soviets could not possibly contemplate such an attack before 1954 at the earliest, and hopes that allies, particularly the British, would be able to do much to defend themselves.[20]

The greatest risk was war by accident, or as the NSC put it somewhat contortedly, by 'Soviet miscalculation of the determination of the United States to use all the means at its command to safeguard its security, through Soviet misinterpretation of our intentions, and through US miscalculation of Soviet reactions to measures which we might take.' But this view did not challenge the very low $15 billion budget limit set by the president for 1949–50. Inevitably, the military began to point to the new gap emerging between the nation's overseas responsibilities and its practical capacity to defend them in the short term. The Joint Chiefs of Staff declared in November 1948: 'current United States commitments involving the use or distinctly possible use of armed forces are very greatly in excess of our present ability to fulfil them either promptly or effectively'.[21]

The threat of war in European eyes

In Europe a very similar range of sentiments was to be found in the hierarchies of the armed services. The British thought the Russians unable to make war before 1956 at the earliest, while Whitehall's warplans put 1957 as the most optimistic date for their own readiness. In Britain, too, commands were now unified under a civilian Minister of Defence, and the Labour government had quickly decided to maintain a conscript army. Even before decisions had been taken on the construction of a British atom bomb, three separate designs had been commissioned for long-range bombers (these were the Vulcans, Victors and Valiants of the 'V Bomber' force which eventually went into service at the end of the 1950s). But British forces had been reduced from just over 5.5 million on VE Day to 1.1 million by 1947, and the sense of permanent financial crisis brought hard choices between the consolidation and the projection of British power. Alan Bullock reports:

> . . . at the end of 1947 there were only 91 active infantry battalions, 50 fewer than at the outbreak of war in 1939. Conscription had been retained but the cut from 18 to 12 months service, in face of a Labour back-bench revolt earlier in the year, had robbed it of much of its value. The War Office was warned in July 1948 that the strength of the army must be reduced to 305,000 (many of them twelve month conscripts by 1950) and the last of the armoured divisions was threatened with disbandment. So short was the Home Fleet of trained men that only a handful of ships could be kept on active service and the autumn manoeuvres had been cancelled to save oil.[22]

So while the Foreign Office talked of a 'Third Force' and of strengthening Western European security, there was ambiguity on what armed power the British would actually commit to the Continent. Should war break out by accident or miscalculation, said the British Chiefs of Staff after the Berlin blockade had begun, there was no hope: 'Our forces . . . are not in a position to fight with what we've got. If the UK is committed to war there will be complete disorganisation, leading to disaster.'[23]

The French military thought the Russians could get to the Pyrenees in twenty days if they were so minded.[24] In spite of de Gaulle's determination to rebuild the armed forces as a key source of national power, lack of equipment and arms factories, the overhang of 1940 and

Vichy, but especially budget restraints, all led to chaos and impotence. Officially charged with defending the empire as well as occupying a part of Germany, with participating in UN security schemes as well as providing a rapid deployment force, by 1948 the French armed forces were hard pressed to offer anything more than a symbolic presence anywhere. Little more than 600,000 service men (with about 400,000 in the army alone, mostly twelve-month conscripts) constituted the entire armed services. The fleet was reduced to half its prewar size and appeared negligible compared to the British and American navies. Unable to find its way in the new world of high-technology weapons and ideological warfare, the military establishment hoped the politicians would provide neutralism, the empire a reliable fall-back position and the Americans any real fighting capacity that might be needed.[25] The French air force was 'unfortunately in no state to participate' in the Berlin airlift, the French government was told by its air commanders.[26]

By this time the French armed forces had acquired, in addition to all their other troubles, a responsibility for helping to maintain order in the case of social or political upheaval. In Italy this task was understood as the army's principle *raison d'être*, confirming a tradition going back at least as far as unification. After the ignominious collapse of 1943, the Italian army and air force were still almost non-existent by the end of the war, though the navy had maintained a minimum of dignity at the side of the Allies. While desultory efforts were made by the Americans and the British in the years after the war to pass on surplus equipment to these forces, there could be no illusions about what would happen if, for example, the Yugoslavs decided to make a fight out of the Trieste question. The Peace Treaty put effective ceilings on all the services and obliged the navy to hand over no less than half the ships as war booty – not even as reparations – to be divided out among the victor powers (though in the end all but the Russians renounced their claims on the fleet).

However, the *carabinieri* – the branch of the army with specific internal police functions – were back up to strength, reequipped by Allied military government. In 1948 the British and Americans were willing to break the Peace Treaty ceilings to allow the *carabinieri* to expand further. Adding in other specialised police forces, a situation soon developed in which the armed power available for internal use outnumbered and outweighed that effectively dedicated to external defence. Although the Left insisted on maintaining a conscript army and on a clear commitment by the armed services to respect the norms of the new Republican Constitution, the military caste remained largely unreformed and beyond the reach of parliamentary control. With the addition of new agencies of intelligence and counter-espionage created in these years, the role of the military in defending the institutions and legitimacy of the first Italian Republic would emerge in future years as debatable but little debated.[27]

Count Sforza, the venerable Minister of Foreign Affairs, told parliament in March 1949: 'We do not possess the instruments for a power policy, nor do we wish to possess them.' Simply to regain acceptance as a legitimate member of the international community of nations proved a slow and depressing task, and notable efforts were made to maintain distinct relations with Moscow. Until America was rearmed and ready to act – in some distant future – no other posture could be contemplated.[28]

In reality the United States was not as far away as appearances suggested.

NOTES

1. Lippmann W *The Cold War* NY 1947; Aron cited by P Hassner at symposium 'Origins of the Postwar Crisis', London Oct 1967 proceedings in *Journal of Contemporary History* April 1968; cf. Gardner LC Lost Empires. In *Diplomatic History* Winter 1989 p 3; 'X' (George Kennan) The Sources of Soviet Conduct. In *Foreign Affairs* July 1947 especially pp 576, 581
2. Kennan G The Marshall Plan and the Future of Europe. In *Transatlantic Perspectives* Winter 1988 p 7
3. *Survey,1939–46* cit pp 20–1
4. 'Origins of the Postwar Crisis' cit p 225,226
5.   Bullock op cit pp 502–3
6. Ibid pp 513–17; Warner G The Labour Governments and the unity of Western Europe. In Ovendale R ed. *The Foreign Policy of the British Labour Governments, 1945–1951* Leicester 1984 pp 65–6
7. Jones H *'A New Kind of War'. America's Global Strategy and the Truman Doctrine in Greece* NY 1989 p 121
8. Eg Acheson D *Present at the Creation. My Years in the State Department* NY 1969 Chs 12, 21, 22
9. Miller JE Taking Off the Gloves: The United States and the Italian Elections of 1948. In *Diplomatic History* Winter 1983 p 48
10. Bullock op cit pp 528–30
11. Young JW *France, the Cold War and the Western Alliance, 1944–49* Leicester 1990 pp 180–1
12. Ibid pp 183–4
13. Sherry MJ *Preparing for the Next War. American Plans for Postwar Defense 1941–45* New Haven 1977 Chs 2, 4, 5

14. Ibid Chs 6, 7
15. Bull and Louis *The 'Special Relationship'* op cit p 167
16. Rearden SL *History of the Office of the Secretary of Defense. Vol.1. The Formative Years 1947–1950* Historical Office, Office of the Secretary of Defense, Washington DC 1984 p 21
17. Baldwin HW The Recruitment and Training of the New Armed Forces. In Kerwin JG (ed) *Civil–Military Relationships in American Life* Chicago 1948 pp 42–61; Matloff M (ed) *American Military History* Office of the Chief of Military History Washington DC 1969 pp 540–2
18. Leffler MP The American Conception of National Security and the Beginnings of the Cold War, 1945–48. In *American Historical Review* April 1984 pp 358–65
19. Ibid pp 372–3
20. Ibid pp 374, 379; cf Osgood RE *Limited War. The Challenge to American Strategy* Chicago 1957 pp 155–6
21. Leffler op cit pp 374, 376–8
22. Bullock op cit p 523
23. Watt DC British Military Perceptions of the Soviet Union as a Strategic Threat, 1945–1950. In *Power in Europe?* op cit pp 332–3
24. Young J op cit p 171
25. Ibid pp 125–6, 171–2; Delmas J Reflections on the Notion of Military Power through the French Example (1945–1948). In *Power in Europe?* op cit p 341
26. Young J op cit p 199; Delmas op cit p 347
27. These paragraphs are based on: Cerquetti E *Le forze armate italiane dal 1945 al 1975* Milan 1975; Rochat G L'esercito. In *Storia d'Italia* vol V Florence 1976; Boldrini A and D'Alessio A *Esercito e politica in Italia* Rome 1974; Ilari V Le forze armate italiane dal Trattato di Pace al Patto Atlantico. In *Strategia globale* n 3 1985
28. Cf: Vigezzi B Italy: the End of a 'Great Power' and the Birth of a 'Democratic Power'; Varsori A de Gasperi, Nenni, Sforza and their Role in Post-War Italian Foreign Policy both in *Power in Europe?* op cit; Romano S La guerra fredda. In *La Stampa* 3 July 1987

CHAPTER SEVEN
The Road to Containment

DEFENCE AND ECONOMICS IN SOUTHERN EUROPE

Because it was on the Continent's southern flank, in Greece, Turkey and Italy, that political and strategic situations were most compromised, it was here that the Americans were first forced by their local allies to follow through in military and economic terms the logic of the Truman Doctrine and the concept of containment. In the course of 1948 it became clear that the commitments established in stages in Greece, Turkey and Italy since 1944 made it essential to reinforce the strategic unity and internal stability of the entire region.[1] Only in this way could the Mediterranean as a whole become an effective link in the projected American global security system. Only with this approach could the Soviets be prevented from moving out of the Black Sea and towards the Middle East and North Africa, and the economic recovery of all of Europe west and south of the Iron Curtain be guaranteed.[2]

Greece and Turkey after the Truman Doctrine

In Turkey '90 per cent of the American aid was in army equipment, aircraft and ships; the remainder was devoted to the improvement of arsenals and highways', according to a semi-official report of the time. Even though there was no particular Soviet pressure on the country in 1948, nor any threat of internal subversion, the overall heightening of East–West tension ensured the deepening of American interest in Turkey, and attracted a new injection of $275 million in 'Truman Doctrine' funds, as well as automatic inclusion in the ERP. Endorsing

Secretary Marshall's judgement that compared to the moment of the original Truman pronouncement, 'the hour is far more fateful now', the Senate Foreign Relations Committee declared that any reduction in aid would only encourage totalitarianism and would represent a 'catastrophic blow to the forces of freedom and independence'.[3]

Turkey's true importance lay in its strategic location. Greece by comparison was considered crucial because of its 'high symbolic value [in] the global framework of the Cold War', according to the American historian Howard Jones. By spring 1948 the Americans had spent $1.1 billion in aid to Greece and were facing the possibility that even extreme generosity under the ERP would be unable to set the country up on a self-sustaining basis. But more significantly for the future, the US mission on the spot had already shifted the greatest part of its funds from the economic to the military side of its efforts, and besides supplying equipment was now, 'at the request of the Greek government', sending military advisers into the field to assist directly in operations.[4] It was 'a new kind of war', a 'test of staying power', said the redoubtable *New York Times* correspondent in Athens, Anne O'Hare McCormick: 'a preview of the frontless, almost faceless, war of tomorrow – a war of Trojan horses pointing the way for machine guns. The battle-line is everywhere and nowhere (for the Kremlin's central directive is) rule or ruin.' With the atom bomb useless in such a situation and economic processes too slow, new ways had to be found to project American power into Greek politics, not simply to bring a satisfactory result in that country, but to demonstrate to friends and enemies alike America's endurance, will and strength: what would in the Vietnam era be termed 'credibility'.[5]

All the key ingredients of the Western Cold War mentality can be seen taking shape in the American experience in Greece: the conviction that the opposition's every move corresponded to a fully elaborated game-plan manoeuvred from Moscow (an element mirrored by the Communist version of the same mentality); the belief in the need to 'carry through . . . no matter how long it takes nor how much money it costs', in the words of a State Department expert; the judgement that the country was a test case watched by the entire world; the certainty that should Communism triumph with its unique methods of subversion, neighbouring countries would fall to it in rapid succession; the faith in ideological campaigning of all sorts, open and clandestine.[6]

Yet in practical terms reality was far harder to grasp than this scheme suggested. Knowing little of their enemy – its ferocious internal rifts, its conflicts with the Kremlin, least of all the distinctive nature of Greek Communism and its relation to national history and politics –

the Americans remained convinced that economic reforms and modernisation would solve all the underlying problems. But the balance between economic action and military intervention turned out to be extraordinarily hard to strike in Greece, as it would be in all of Western Europe.[7] The United States could break Greek governments and armies but learned that it could not make them. Moreover, the United States could never match the relentless, even desperate, pressures of its local political allies to be given constantly increasing quantities of economic and military aid, even combat troops. With tension rising in France, Italy and Germany in the European theatre, in Palestine in the Middle East, and in China, the Pentagon was all too aware of how limited its deployable resources really were, and that neither Congress nor the public would ever tolerate the despatch of troops to Greece, even to fight Russia there. By mid-1948 the Americans and their Greek allies were arguing over 'whose war' it really was.[8]

The Italian elections

But the greatest challenge to the US to clarify its intentions and actions in Europe in the early part of 1948 emerged in Italy, on the occasion of the first general elections to the new republican parliament. Vividly remembered, celebrated and excoriated to this day, 18 April 1948 inaugurated the era of perpetual Christian Democrat rule in Italy, and the country was said to have 'chosen sides' once and for all.

At the end of 1947, in fulfilment of their Peace Treaty obligations, the remaining British and American soldiers of the wartime occupation regime left Italian soil, to the open consternation of right-wing forces convinced that the Left awaited just this day to unleash the revolution. The US government – unlike any of the other Peace Treaty signatories – gave a warning for the occasion that threats to democracy would be met by force. For their part the Americans knew that behind the constant industrial and social upheaval, there was not just left-wing militancy but also the deliberate deflationary policies and the efforts by the employers to 'shake out' surplus workers. The American Ambassador worried as a result that the Communists might even be strong enough to come to power by *legal* means.

But seen from within the Left did not appear so strong. The right-wing socialists had already split away from the Left bloc while the Communists found their position between the pressures of their membership, the dictates of the Cominform and the impulses of their socialist partners increasingly uncomfortable. The American historian John Harper observes that prime minister De Gasperi:

... understood the left's position well enough and did not really fear an open insurrection. He and Tarchiani [the Italian Ambassador in Washington] continued to exploit America's by now acute sensibility, but their goal was less military aid than a new 'emergency response' to relieve deflation and the desperate payments crisis.[9]

When the US government finally obtained 'interim aid' for Italy, it immediately set about reflating the Italian economy, promoting projects in agriculture, for the development of the South, for the reconstruction of railways and the merchant marine.[10] But this was just one dimension of what turned out to be 'the most hectically fought political campaign that ever took place in Europe', according to the leading CBS journalist in Europe, Howard K. Smith, writing a year later. And it was Smith who identified the most important and unprecedented factor in the battle as 'the frank, open entrance of America' into it.[11]

When the National Security Council had started work in November 1947 its first paper concerned Italy, the 'prerevolutionary' conditions said to exist there, the possibility that the Communists could come to power by legal or extra-legal means and the impression that Italy had first priority in Cominform strategy. The NSC was convinced that: 'the majority of the Italian people ... are ideologically inclined towards the Western democracies, friendly to the United States and conscious of the fact that US aid is vital to Italian recovery'. The Council was also clear that 'the prevailing economic distress' was what gave the Communists their mass support.[12]

But as the elections came nearer, the emphasis in NSC deliberations changed. With a parliamentary victory appearing ever more probable, a vast propaganda mobilisation was set in motion with a significant new 'black' or clandestine dimension supplied by the CIA and a part of the American trade union movement. The official campaign included the promise of revision of the Peace Treaty, an appeal – signed also by Britain and France – to return Trieste to Italy, and a host of publicity-winning minor gestures. The State Department made clear that Communist voters would be banned from emigration to the United States, and Marshall himself declared that should the Left win, the country would be excluded from the benefits of the ERP.

American experts in 'counter-insurgency' looked back ten years later on the Italian campaign of 1948 as opening a new era of 'psychological warfare'. They make clear that no overall propaganda strategy existed: whatever it took to stop the Left was allowed. A pattern of action emerged based on 'explanation, terror and reassurance'. Covert funding of the Christian Democrats and the right-wing socialists began to the extent of $1 million and there was a great effort (though not as great as Washington would have liked) to supply the forces of law and order with the equipment to face down an insurrection. The use of military forces was 'never completely ruled out', writes James Miller; in fact a number of situations were envisaged which 'would compel American military intervention'. While the US air force had already indicated its requirements for bases in southern Italy, the navy proved adept at showing its presence at moments considered appropriate.[13]

The private campaign set in motion by the Italian–American community was even more remarkable, not least for its originality. Ten million letters and cables were sent from individual Italian-Americans 'to relatives and acquaintances in Italy begging them to vote against the Communists'. Famous stars such as Sinatra and Gary Cooper recorded radio programmes; the Vatican and the American propaganda agencies, USIS and Voice of America, ran campaigns in parallel. 'Freedom flights' carrying airmail from America were organised with the cooperation of the US Post Office and TWA, and the red, white and blue 'Friendship Train' distributed piles of gifts gathered on its tour of America.

When the uproar died down and the true impact of the conservative victory of 18 April 1948 could be measured, it became clear that not all the plans had worked. The DC victory – for the first and so far only time the Christian Democrats secured an absolute majority – was based on the mobilisation of the Vatican more than on outside aid, while the American money and support lavished on right-wing socialists disappeared almost without trace. In terms of international politics, the event demonstrated that the USSR had done nothing to aid the PCI – refusing to surrender Trieste, renegotiate the Peace Treaty or aid Italy's admission to the United Nations – while the West Europeans, specifically the British and French, though willing to recognise that Italy was of one of their weaker brethren, had proved powerless to come to the country's aid in its hour of need. The Americans for their part had demonstrated a quite new and infinitely ingenious capacity for projecting their power into such situations. But the long-term implications of the effort did not look encouraging to thoughtful commentators.

The influential economic counsellor in the American Embassy in Rome, Henry Tasca, complained that the industrialists, large land-owners and other elements of the ruling groups were 'disorganized or disoriented and incapable of realizing their social responsibilities'. Tasca thought their only concerns were for their own immediate short-term interests, and that they were capable of any compromise rather than recognising the need for long-term reform and social modernisation.[14] The CBS commentator Smith went further, denouncing America's alliance 'with social elements in Italy whose aims have nothing to do with democracy'. By such methods the United States had compromised its long-held faith in self-determination and plunged into an open-ended commitment to the Christian Democrats. Foretelling the future with accuracy, Smith declared that without its own self-sustaining reform process, the country would be 'an object of our charity for many years to come.'[15]

The new American commitment in Southern Europe

It was in terms of these preoccupations that the United States placed so much hope for the peaceful future development of countries such as Greece and Italy in the Marshall Plan, the most brilliant of the new inventions for projecting American power into Europe. But the choice between the hopeful politics of growth it represented and the baleful Cold War logic of military mobilisation turned out to be far harder to make than even the pessimists could foresee in the spring of 1948.

One reason was to be found in the new kind of interdependence which had emerged between those exposed to the Communist menace and their American defenders. In Greece, said a State Department observer: 'The Greeks in power will use us for all we are worth. We think we are doing them a favour; they know they are doing us a bigger one.' As Howard Jones notes, it was generally assumed that America 'had the leverage to dictate policy in Greece because of the aid program'. But whether Greeks carried out the conditions of this programme or not, the aid would continue given the nature and symbolic importance of the American commitment.[16] Hence it was America's 'clients' who determined the use the aid was put to in the last instance, in Greece as in the rest of Europe. All concerned could make a virtue of this situation in terms of respect for national sovereignty and the principles of 'non-interference'. But the whole effort would have failed if it did not bring radical change. Ideally, said a Brookings Institution study of 1948, US policy should: 'seek out and strengthen those local political elements that are judged most able, not necessarily to maintain the status quo, but to provide the basis for a more stable regional equilibrium'.[17]

But the less the pleas from Washington for reform, modernisation and economic openness were heeded, so the more inextricable became America's position, since the Left continued to grow almost everywhere. As the Cold War was escalated by both sides, this unhealthy paradox would condition European reconstruction and America's role

117

in it for years to come, wherever a militant left-wing opposition appeared capable of upsetting the precarious patterns of stabilisation which had emerged in the various nations by the end of the 1940s.

DEFENDING GERMANY

Consolidating the Western zones

In early 1946 the Chairman of of the Christian Democratic Union (CDU) Konrad Adenauer had written to a political friend who had recently emigrated to the United States:

> Asia stands on the Elbe. Only an economically and spiritually regenerated Europe . . . can check the further advance of the Asian spirit and power, a Western Europe to which belongs, as an integral element, the part of Germany that is not occupied by Russia . . . Europe could only be saved with the help of the USA.[18]

This was not a particularly popular view in 1946. While the Germans in all zones took it for granted that national unity would be restored at some point in the not far distant future, the Americans in Washington and on the spot were looking for ways to restore as much of Germany as they controlled to a state of economic independence based on whatever degree of industrial restoration necessary. The first German economic council was created in the Anglo-American Bi-Zone in May 1947. In July the sixteen Marshall Plan countries declared at the CEEC meeting in Paris that: 'the German economy should be integrated into the economy of Europe in such a way as to contribute to a raising of the general standard of life'.[19] In February 1948 the so-called 'Frankfurt Charter' created a shadow government for economic policy with executive and legislative organs. The informal London conference on Germany of February–June 1948 prepared for the merger of the three Western zones, authorised the convocation of a constituent assembly to give them a common framework of law, and pushed forward with the final stages of preparation for the crucial currency reform of the 21 June.

The Western Allies, in other words, continued to place supreme emphasis on rebuilding Western Germany's economic strength as its principal line of defence. The Americans in particular – who had taken over the financial and import responsibilities for the British zone at the end of 1947 – looked for means not just to build up production, but to devolve responsibility onto reliable German agencies and men. In this way they would teach democracy by practice and hasten the day when their forces of occupation could leave.

The Russian reaction: the blockade of Berlin

This approach was dramatically thrust into the background by the blockade of Berlin which began in the last days of June. The Russians soon made clear that this was their response to the variety of moves strengthening the Western zones, in particular the reform of currency in these zones only (since the Soviet authorities could not be trusted to print the same money and use it responsibly in their zone). After a series of increasingly unpleasant skirmishes in the four-power control organs in Berlin, electricity and coal supplies were cut off, then land and water transport along the corridor from the West was brought by stages to a complete halt. While those on the spot noted a certain caution in the Soviet build-up of pressure on the city, from outside it looked as though the Third World War was about to break out.

General Clay, ever more robust commander of the American forces in Germany, had been using the Berlin situation at that time to boost the army's rebuilding campaign at home, aimed at persuading Congress to reverse the effects of the very rapid postwar demobilisation. Now he pressed for breaking the blockade by force. But Clay was overruled by Truman and Marshall, and so fell back on the British idea of an improvised airlift of supplies. This famous Cold War effort began on 26 June 1948, and went on – against all odds and forecasts – until May of the following year.

In its early months the airlift was seen 'as a desperate means of staving off disaster while a more or less humiliating agreement was found with the Russians', write the latest historians of the great crisis, Ann and John Tusa.[20] The Russians seemed to hold all the cards on the ground, and could count on 300,000 troops in their zone around Berlin. They had no hesitation in breaking up the four-power system of military control in the city, as well as all the organs of municipal government, from transport management to electricity supply, from food distribution to the city assembly. The physical division of the city began in these months: by April 1949 fifty-three streets were closed and controls on those still open ever more arbitrary.

Only gradually did it become clear that the Russians did not want war over Berlin. They wished to harass the Allies out and to convince the starving population, by fair means and foul, that salvation could only be found on their side. While the behaviour of Stalin and Molotov oscillated unpredictably between violent hostility and sudden spasms of willingness to talk, the airlift went on without serious interference. By closing the air corridors into the city, refusing to take part in air traffic control or even putting up barrage balloons, the Soviet side could have stopped the effort in hours. But they did not, even when it became evident that the airlift had survived the winter and began to be reorganised on a permanent basis in February 1949.

Wings and prayers had kept it going until then. The American and British air forces on the spot had begun with handfuls of two-engine DC3 type planes left over from the Second World War. While it was known that thousands of tons of supplies would need to be sent in every day, on the fourth day the RAF managed to lift forty-four tons of supplies using thirteen of its fleet; the Americans brought in 384 tons making use of about seventy planes. By the middle of July bigger British and American aircraft were available, and up to 1,500 tons could be delivered in a day. In September nearly a hundred big American transports were in service and fifty more were due. The British had begun to coopt craft from the variety of tiny companies making up their civil aviation industry at the time, and had to strive desperately to integrate them with the regular RAF operation. By the end of January there were 225 four-engined American transports capable of carrying up to ten tons each, working alongside 131 assorted RAF and civilian machines. Planes landed according to tight schedules every three minutes at one of the Berlin airports, every day for twenty-four hours a day, weather permitting.[21]

But the airlift was a miracle of improvisation not of organisation, at least in the first eight months. The physical difficulties of keeping crews, aircraft, loading and landing facilities operational in siege conditions showed that no one had ever foreseen such a challenge from the Russians. Unprepared for an effort lasting more than a few weeks, the difficulties of the air forces were aggravated by interservice rivalries, bureaucracy in Washington and London, and the sheer lack of any comparable experience. Some capacity had to be kept at home for any other crisis which might break out. There were never enough crews, planes, spare parts, maintenance facilities or clear flying days. The Russians might suddenly announce 'exercises' in or around the corridors; break-downs would happen in communications or ground operations, the civilian flyers would withdraw their cooperation. The physical difficulties of flying in thousands of tons of coal, petrol, flour or salt were beyond the grasp of imagination until they were actually faced. And these were just the bulk items, the biggest in the endless list needed to keep alive a major world city.[22]

The planners discovered that the two-and-a-half million people of the Western sectors of Berlin had consumed 12,000 tons of goods a day before the blockade, at a standard of living still not substantially different from the months after the war. Just to stay alive, eat and keep warm required 5,500 tons of the basic necessities every day. But before spring 1949 this figure had been exceeded only on one occasion – US Air Force Day, 18 September 1948. By means of an extraordinary effort 144 British and 651 American sorties provided almost 7,000 tons in the twenty-four hours. In contrast the monthly average for September was 4,641 tons. With winter coming, flying would become far less certain and up to 40 per cent of this tonnage might be undelivered. As Ann and John Tusa point out:

> Berliners were in a parlous state to withstand the rigours of winter on diminishing supplies; they were already some 8.5lbs underweight, and nutritionists feared that on the present average ration of 1,600 calories a day they would soon be suffering from malnutrition. They were living in leaky, draughty, bomb-damaged homes, yet the allies would be hard-pushed to give them 3 cwt of coal for the worst months of the year. The chances were that the Berliners would have to endure hunger, cold and fear in the pitch dark.

Deliveries in the closing months of the year were all well below the targets, largely due to bad weather.[23]

But the disasters predicted never happened; once again freak weather conditions decisively influenced the politics and economics of a postwar crisis. In January came a 'meteorological miracle': the winter was far milder than could ever have been predicted and stayed so through most of February. Both months saw record deliveries; the corner was turned. A completely new organisation was set in motion which would give the city stand-by emergency transport guaranteed by the Western forces, a permanent safeguard against blockade.[24]

The Berliners were never told how perilously close the airlift had come to failure: 'they only got news of remarkable cargoes or cheery official pronouncements, and assumed that everything was going smoothly', say Ann and John Tusa.[25] In reality many inhabitants of the Western sectors privately doubted the good faith of the Allies and dismissed contemptuously their willingness to appease the Russians over many daily issues on the ground – by allowing both Western and Eastern zone currencies to circulate in their own sectors, for instance. But the West Berliners displayed great resolution in public. On 9 September 250,000 demonstrated openly denouncing Soviet behaviour and appealing to the West not to barter away their rights. Nine out of ten of those interviewed in an American official poll in October

121

insisted that they preferred living under blockade conditions to those produced by communism in the Eastern zone.[26]

'If we mean that we are to hold Europe against Communism, we must not budge', said Clay. 'I believe the future of democracy requires us to stay here until forced out.' No one was firmer than Bevin, whose whole approach was framed in terms of the so-called lessons of the Munich crisis and appeasement, ten years previously. It was on this basis, writes the historian Avi Shlaim, that he stiffened American resolve and 'from beginning to end . . . consistently resisted the basic solution proposed by the Russians for lifting the blockade of Berlin in exchange for a Western suspension of the London Programme'.[27]

All concerned were well aware of the symbolic importance of a stand at this juncture in the Cold War for the city, for the Germans – whose apathy and cynicism were widely reported – and for the rest of Western Europe. Appalled, even overwhelmed, in the case of the French, by their inability to mount anything like serious military opposition to any form of Soviet push, the western Allies used the language of symbols to state their intentions when nothing else was available. So when sixty B29 bombers were sent in from the United States to Britain and Germany in the middle of July 1948 they apparently included a number armed with A Bombs. Years afterwards they were revealed to have contained none. But in deterrence, if nowhere else, the medium is the message, and the combined effect of the B29s' arrival, together with the material and propaganda success of the airlift throughout the winter of 1948–49, eventually returned the political initiative to Western hands. The Federal Republic of Germany was established on 23 May 1949, two weeks after the end of the blockade.[28]

Towards a transatlantic military pact

With the French government in crisis in mid-1948, Bevin felt he was taking over the leadership of Europe as he renewed his campaign for an Atlantic pact in July against the background of the Berlin crisis. In response, under a new resolution offered by the leader of the Senate Republicans, Vandenberg, Congress authorised the American government to explore the possibilities for strengthening national security by means of regional schemes of mutual assistance. But the language of this new Congressional policy position framed action cautiously, in terms of the UN charter. Indeed, it soon appeared that the Berlin airlift notwithstanding, the United States was not willing to start despatching large quantities of military equipment to Europe to build up a permanent war-making capacity. Substantial military guarantees were not on offer, let alone an automatic commitment to go to war in support of an ally as the Brussels pact provided.

To the great consternation of the French and the Belgians, and to the astonishment of everyone aware of the continually rising tide of anti-Communist hysteria in American public opinion, winning over official Washington to the war-danger of the situation seemed as difficult as ever. Influential figures such as George Kennan insisted that the Soviet Union did not intend an invasion, and that the West Europeans would do best to build up the structures suggested by the Brussels Pact.[29]

Even when the epochal North Atlantic Treaty was finally signed in April 1949, after a long winter of negotiations, the emphasis remained on the individual rights of each member to take 'such action as it deems necessary', and there were considerable restrictions on the specific responsibilities of the Pentagon. The point of the North Atlantic pact in its original, pre-Korea, form was still psychological and political reassurance first of all: 'The essential objective [said the Senate Foreign Affairs Committee] is increased security, not increased military strength', while the key to the capacity of treaty-signers to resist attack, 'depends primarily upon their basic economic health'. Specifically this meant increased industrial capacity and the development of labour resources – clearly fundamental objectives of the Marshall Plan.[30]

Atlantic security or German security?

As President of the constituent assembly (formally, the Parliamentary Council) set up after the London conference, Adenauer felt that by autumn 1948 questions of Germany's defence could be discussed in public among Germans themselves for the first time since the war. In private he talked with reliable survivors of the *Wehrmacht* officer class. In his official role Adenauer went far to placate the general impulse to neutralism and pacifism, in private he agreed with the conclusions of his military advisers: 'No Rapallo tactics* – clear pro-Western attitude, anti-communist'. In this view it would be impossible for the western allies to overlook for long the usefulness of an eventual German contribution to the North Atlantic alliance, a position which Adenauer

---

* During the 1922 Genoa economic conference the outcasts of the international system Germany and the Soviet Union, signed (at nearby Rapallo) a treaty of friendship which was followed by secret agreements for limited military collaboration.

first expressed in public in early 1949, drawing 'massive criticism' at home and abroad.[31]

The sense of horror which spread through Germany and Western Europe as the logic of the Cold War was seen to extend to German rearmament is almost impossible to recapture today. In his 1955 volume provocatively entitled 'The Colossus Again', the distinguished French expert on Germany, Alfred Grosser, pointed out that official occupation policy continued to insist on denazification and demilitarisation, and this was confirmed by Truman and the State Department as late as June 1950. Eisenhower too, military adviser to the president, emphatically excluded the possibility of a German presence in Atlantic community forces in 1950. Meanwhile in France neutralism remained a most powerful sentiment, so that 'when recommending the Atlantic Treaty to the General Assembly, M. René Mayer [Defence Minister] did not even mention German rearmament; and M. Robert Schuman repeated on several occasions that it would never happen'.[32]

While there were those inside Germany whose satisfaction at choosing the liberal over the totalitarian way of life released them from 'worry about the price the Germans would have to pay for the losing of the war', in the words of the historian Wilfried Loth, the dwindling of hopes for a reunited nation was a painful process for the great majority of citizens and politicians. Consequently they 'tended to leave the responsibility for the establishing of the division as far as possible to the occupying powers', says Loth. Thus, even as the Federal Republic was being founded in the spring of 1949, both Adenauer and the leader of the main opposition party, Schumacher of the Social Democrats, proclaimed that they intended to take the whole of Germany into the Marshall Plan and the North Atlantic pact.[33] But the speed of events, the endless disruption and demoralisation, the whole tenor of the Cold War and the atomic era, created much disorientation in Germany. Rudolph Augstein, editor of the already influential weekly magazine *Der Spiegel*, spoke of a 'military no man's land' corresponding to a 'political no man's land in the heads of the puzzled people'. As the first elections to the new federal parliament were held in August 1949, Augstein deplored 'a lack of power both in politics and elsewhere, which seemed for the time being to paralyse a whole people, the people at the centre of Europe'.[34] It was a condition felt not only in Germany.

THE DWINDLING OF THE IDEAL OF EUROPEAN UNITY

Ambiguities of the new federalism

As the 'consciousness of powerlessness' spread through Western Europe, said a German historian in 1986, so did the impulse to seek common solutions in some form of integrated political action to increase economic and strategic security. But how was a minimum of national and collective dignity to be saved when the Continent was ever more obviously split in two and the dependence on American power overwhelming? Hard choices would have to be made. The Italian commentator Sergio Romano recalled in 1987 how very quickly European nations decided 'to defend [their] economic sovereignty and pay the price of the loss of [their] military sovereignty': 'Of course we needed an alibi in order to do this. . . . And the alibi was Europe. We all told each other that we were going into the military political alliance of NATO because that was the first and necessary step to eventually arriving at a united Europe. Now that was only an alibi.'[35]

Enfeebled, distracted but supremely anxious to be involved in any push towards a unitary rebuilding of Europe, the Federal Republic should have been the easiest entity to integrate into a concerted scheme of limited sovereignty. As already mentioned, the preamble to the 'Basic Law' produced by the Parliamentary Council as the legal foundation for the new Federal Republic explicitly anticipated 'a united Europe'. 'But it was not to be', Alfred Grosser noted in 1955, 'and western Germany became a State with its own egocentric mission like the others.'[36]

By the end of the 1940s 'the European idea' had developed a two-fold character, said Grosser: 'It combined a constructive internationalism with fear-ridden anti-communism; the proportion of the two sentiments and their mode of expression varying in different men at different times, according to the world situation'.[37]

There was positive movement in a number of directions. On 1 January 1948 the Benelux customs union came into force and the French considered joining it. A French–Italian customs union was under active negotiation and there were talks between the French and British on coordinating economic plans, greatly spurred by Bevin's 'Western union' vision and the Brussels Pact. Elsewhere a northern grouping based on Sweden, Norway and Denmark was emerging, while in the Mediterranean Greece and Turkey were reported to be considering a tariff union.[38]

Sentiment at the highest levels in West European governments seemed to favour the cause of European integration and the main political blocs, the Christian Democrats and the socialists, had spawned specific movements to promote it. A more conservative current had been headed by Winston Churchill since his Zurich speech of September 1946. The symbolic high point of this wave came in the Hague Congress of May 1948, an unusual event in postwar Europe in terms of the weight of prestige and publicity attracted to a private political gathering.

'It was a heady occasion', writes a veteran of European integration, Richard Mayne, 'attended by 750 statesmen from all over western Europe.' Churchill was named honorary president. He attended, along with a future Conservative Defence Minister, Duncan Sandys. The Belgian prime minister and senior statesman, Paul Henri-Spaak, was prominent, while distinguished French ministers included Bidault and Schuman, both in the highest offices, together with Blum, Ramadier, Reynaud – all ex-prime ministers. In their company was François Mitterrand, the minister for War Veterans. The Italian prime minister, De Gasperi, was present, on a similar mission to the German delegation of fifty led by Adenauer, who saw the occasion as the first opportunity to launch a new German identity on the European stage. Mayne recalls how:

> Sitting together in the great Hall of the Knights of the Netherlands – the Ridderzaal, where the Dutch Parliament met – they seemed to many the embodiment of an historic dream: the first States-General of Europe, demanding on behalf of people so long divided, so recently reconciled, a political and economic union, a European Assembly, and a European Court of Human Rights.[39]

Intense lobbying by Spaak and others following this success concentrated on the French government and the mechanisms of the Brussels Pact. By May 1949 the Brussels Treaty nations (known formally as the Western European Union) and five others – Italy, Denmark, Sweden, Norway and Ireland – had drawn up a design for a Council of Europe, made up of a Consultative Assembly and a Committee of Ministers. After the Assembly's first meeting in Strasbourg in August 1949, its president, Spaak, said: 'I came to Strasbourg convinced of the necessity of a United States of Europe. I am leaving it with the certitude that union is possible.'[40]

The phase of disappointments

Yet in little over two years Spaak resigned, disgusted with the failure of the Council of Europe to push forward the grand objectives it had been created for. In a bitter valedictory speech, Spaak denounced the overwhelmingly negative attitudes he found all around him:

> Today everyone has his own good reasons why he should not make any move. Some Germans will not support a united Europe until the whole of Germany is united. Some Belgians will do so only if the United Kingdom joins in. Some Frenchmen are against a unification of Europe if it entails their being left to negotiate direct with the Germans. The British will not form part of a united Europe so long as they have not found a solution acceptable both to themselves and the Commonwealth. Our Scandinavian friends look on at all this in a somewhat disillusioned and disinterested [sic] manner.[41]

Particular scorn was reserved by Spaak for the British. To his astonishment, Churchill, back in power (since October 1951) had reaffirmed the Labour government's line on European integration: Britain's ties to the Commonwealth countries were far more important than any conceivable links with Europe, and there could be no derogation of national sovereignty in favour of over-arching bodies set up in such places as Paris or Brussels. Looking back at his Zurich speech, Spaak now realised that the united Europe favoured by Churchill was a regional construction befriended by the emerging superpowers: the United States, the USSR (hopefully) and Great Britain with her empire and Commonwealth.[42]

The British, it turned out, were not interested in the logic of interdependence, least of all in the form of supranational institutions with pan-European political ambitions; no time in London for theoretical reflections on the breakdown of the international system between the wars, on changes in the nature of sovereignty, or even on the sources of the Communist challenge. Inaugurating a tradition of official pronouncement on 'Europe' which continues to this day, Attlee told the Commons just before the Hague Congress that over the 'abstract' discussions of a constituent assembly, he preferred 'dealing with practical matters in a practical way'.[43] Although the British Foreign Minister had been sincere in his earlier visions of European solidarity, it now appeared to many that all Bevin's talk of a Western union had been little more than a manoeuvre: to create the conditions for consummating the longstanding British plan for getting the Americans 'well-embedded' in Europe.[44]

But the hopes embodied in the Council of Europe (like the Western European Union, still existing) did not subside solely due to the perfidy of the British. The logic of the Cold War was far stronger than that of European federation, and the great questions of Germany's future – and France's attitude to it – had become ever more pressing.

127

Above all there was the open-ended dependence on the United States, whose extremist vision of instant economic and political integration via the Marshall Plan (discussed in the following chapter) tended to discredit the whole idea. As the Russians exploded their atom bomb in August 1949, three years earlier than Western intelligence had predicted, so the West Europeans clung ever more fervently to the promises of the security system embodied in the North Atlantic pact.

For the longer term the French and British placed their hopes in independent nuclear defence projects which they now strained to set up. By so doing they demonstrated to history that in the longer view renewed national power remained the supreme objective. Meanwhile in comparison with the immediate anxieties of defence in the atomic age, quite different priorities and time-scales persisted in economic affairs. Proudly celebrating in the Marshall Plan their new marriage of convenience, the West Europeans were determined – each in its own way – that in this area America's power would be managed to suit the ends they considered important.

NOTES

1. Reitzel W op cit p 100
2. Ibid pp 168–9
3. USWA 1948 op cit pp 477–9
4. Ibid pp 473–4
5. Jones H op cit pp 4–5 (McCormick cit in ibid)
6. Ibid pp 118, 121, 130, 132, 148
7. Ibid pp 124, 173, 189; cf Stavrakis PJ *Moscow and Greek Communism, 1944–1949* Ithaca 1989
8. Ibid pp 137, 139, 157; cf Nachmani A op cit p 500
9. Harper JL *America and the Reconstructiuon of Italy 1943–1948* Cambridge 1986 p 148
10. Ibid p 156
11. Smith HK op cit pp 205–6
12. NSC 1/1, 1 Nov 1947, in FRUS 1948 vol III p 724; NSC 1/2 Feb 1948 in ibid p 766
13. These paragraphs are based on Holt and van de Velde, op cit Ch VI, and on Ellwood From 'Re-Education' to the Selling of the Marshall Plan in Italy. In Pronay N and Spring DW (eds) *The Political Re-Education of Germany and her Allies after World War II* 1985 pp 225–7; Miller JE Taking Off the Gloves cit, and Miller JE *The United States and Italy* op cit pp 236–49; Filipelli RL *American Labor and Postwar Italy, 1943–1953* Stanford 1989 Ch 6
14. Harper op cit p 157

15. Smith op cit pp 207–11
16. Jones op cit p 73
17. Reitzel op cit pp 171–2
18. Loth W German Conceptions of Europe during the Escalation of the East–West Conflict,1945–1949. In *Power in Europe?* op cit pp 322–3
19. Bullock op cit p 572 n 2
20. Tusa A and J *The Berlin Blockade* 1988 p 408
21. Ibid pp 198, 216, 231, 273, 306, 394
22. Ibid Ch 10
23. Ibid pp 190, 301–3 (cit at pp 302–3)
24. Ibid pp 391–2
25. Ibid p 389
26. Ibid pp 296, 340
27. Shlaim A Britain, the Berlin blockade and the Cold War. In *International Affairs* Winter 1983/4 pp 3–14; Clay cit in Ninkovich F op cit p 65
28. Shlaim op cit; Warner G The Division of Germany 1946–1948. In *International Affairs* Jan 1975, pp 69–70; Bullock op cit pp 571–80; Ninkovich op cit pp 64–5
29. Ibid pp 582–85; the Vandenberg Resolution is reproduced in *Documents on International Affairs* (henceforth DIA) 1947–1948 pp 233–4; Kennan's view described in Mortimer op cit pp 61–2
30. Grosser op cit p 45
31. Messerschmidt M et al West Germany's Strategic Position and her Role in Defence Policy as seen by the German Military, 1945–1949. In *Power in Europe?* op cit p 353–5.
32. Grosser op cit pp 45–6; position of Truman and State Department cit in Warner G The United States and the rearmament of Germany 1950–54. In *International Affairs* Spring 1985 p 280; French neutralism discussed in Rioux op cit pp 138–9.
33. Loth op cit pp 527–35
34. Hlürten H Farewell to the Power State? The Perception of the Political Environment and the Idea of the State in Public Opinion in the Western Occupation Zones of Germany between 1946 and 1948. In *Power in Europe?*. op cit p 436–7
35. Wendt B-J Europe between Power and Powerlessness. In *Power in Europe?* op cit p 552; Romano in Ellwood *The Marshall Plan* op cit pp 104–5
36. Grosser op cit p 40
37. Ibid
38. Cf *The World Today* March 1948 pp 93–5
39. Mayne op cit p 291
40. Ibid p 295
41. Cit in Jansen M and De Vree JK *The Ordeal of European Integration 1945–1985* Bilthoven 1985 p 92
42. Emerson B 'Paul-Henri Spaak and European Integration.' Paper presented at the conference, 'European Unity in Context' Hull 1989
43. Speech of 5 May 1948 reproduced in DIA 1947–1948 pp 237–40 (cf *The Independent* 20 April 1990)

44. Cf Bullock op cit pp 520–2; Warner G Britain and Europe in 1948: the View from the Cabinet. In *Power in Europe?* op cit pp 34–44; for a useful survey of the historical debate on this question Melissen J and Zeeman B Britain and Western Europe, 1945–51: opportunities lost? In *International Affairs* n 1 1987

CHAPTER EIGHT

Interdependence and Economics: the Limits of Reform

BETTING ON THE FUTURE

Today experts are agreed that the shape of the postwar economic order in Western Europe was discernible from 1949 onwards. It was the year when the fruits of continued high investment and of expanding production became visible at last to the long-suffering populations of the Old World. The American reporter Howard Smith described how from the autumn of 1948,

> ... continuing transfusions of American goods plus the first good harvest since the war brought material improvement and a perceptible return of color to the collective patient's cheeks. ... Britain felt able to relax austerity just enough to devote some labor to replanting her public squares; gray residential London became speckled with bright, freshly painted front doors.[1]

The turning point proved to be the decisive one. From those months 'the greatest and longest economic boom' in history was assured, an 'astonishing period of increasing output and incomes', opening up prospects of consumption and plenty undreamed of at any time in the past, least of all in the dire years just endured.

From the longer-term perspective, say economic historians such as Alan Milward (quoted above), 'Western Europe's greatest boom began with the end of the war and proceeded without interruption until 1967.' In this view 1949 was the year when the boom changed gear. So much momentum had been built up by the successful, more-or-less organised effort to rebuild after the war that a shift to rapid modernisation of structures and of consumption patterns became imaginable. With West German recovery at its heart, and American aid its underpinning, an unprecedented expansion in investment, trade and

131

industrial output took place which would set the pattern for the export-led affluence of the 1950s. In 1948 the average level of real earnings of West European workers was already around a fifth higher than in 1938.[2]

If governments seemed to lead the way in promoting renewal, the private sector in fact did most of the work right from the start, providing something like two-thirds of total investment in most countries. 'Evidently', argues Milward: 'private investors did not share the fears of some politicians in 1947 that the Russians would soon be in Calais banging away with their guns at Dover'.[3] Vera Zamagni characterises Italian politicians, experts and entrepreneurs as 'betting on the future' from the very end of the war (if not from the time of the 1943 armistice), with 'remarkable progress' evident by 1948 in engineering and textile exports, as well as in the rebuilding of infrastructure and the reorganisation of public industry. From that year until 1963 Italy enjoyed an 'uninterrupted boom', with manufacturing output increasing on average by 10.6 per cent and GDP by 6.3 per cent per year.[4] Seen in the same perspective France was on course for an average annual growth rate of 4.5 per cent, while industrial output was expanding by 'a steady and sustainable 7 per cent per annum'. The crucial early bottlenecks of transport and energy had been eliminated and unemployment neutralised. In 1949 agricultural production reached prewar level for the first time, and for the first time too prices stopped rising. Observers noted that relative industrial peace prevailed, that the Communist Party appeared weaker, and that large-scale strike movements comparable to those of earlier years seemed to have disappeared.[5]

After the exit of the Communists from the Belgian government, the Socialist and Catholic coalition, led for two-and-a-half years by Spaak, 'promoted and indeed witnessed the return of the economy to peace-time conditions', in the words of a contemporary admirer. Inflation ceased as a new 'social contract' was drawn up for wage-earners.[6] The Dutch economy had been ready to change gear as early as January 1948 when the government thrust 'recovery' firmly in the background in favour of what has been called 'the first true restructuring plan in Dutch history'. In Holland industrial production had overtaken its prewar level in the last quarter of 1947, a development, Richard Griffiths points out, which only fifteen months earlier had not been expected for another three years.[7]

Austria in contrast was still a 'study in inertia' in January 1948, in the eyes of a British commentator. The Austrians were said to be living 'under a deep cloud of self-pity, unrelieved by hope or incentive to do anything themselves to better their lot'. In the absence of a Peace Treaty and with the consequent need to obtain the approval of each of the four occupying powers for any sort of constructive action, the economy remained completely blocked.[8] Yet Austria had managed a successful currency reform and enjoyed industrial peace. By the end of 1948 the most ambitious investment plan presented to the OEEC was the Austrian one, with the change-up from reconstruction to development clearly in view: three-quarters of the sum sought was for 'new' investment, affirms Milward. A substantial portion was allocated to railway electrification, the rest divided between specific agricultural, industrial and power modernisation projects.[9]

The transformation in West Germany

But the most extraordinary transformation had come over West Germany. An eye-witness report describing Berlin at New Year time, 1949–50, listed all the outward signs of prosperity:

> In and near the Kurfurstendamm luxury shops are full of goods, and there are many new cafés, bars and restaurants. . . . The windows of the delicatessen shops and the menus of the more expensive restaurants show that there is plenty of food to be had. . . . Indeed one Berlin newspaper reported that this, the first real postwar Christmas, had resulted in extra work for the doctors because the return of the traditional goose to their menu had proved a diet too rich in fat for many Berliners.[10]

Intense debate surrounds the explanation for this metamorphosis, and indeed the origins of the entire phenomenon of Germany's postwar economic strength. According to the conventional wisdom, says Germany's most controversial economic historian, Werner Abelshauser, the origins of the country's economic 'miracle' were three-fold:

> *First*: recovery began on the 20 June 1948, the day when currency reform took place;
> *Second*: recovery was set off by foreign aid, particularly by the Marshall Plan; and
> *Third*: recovery was initiated by innovations in the economic system and in economic politics, well known as the 'Social Market Economy'.

But in his analysis, and in line with what has just been said about Italy, Holland, France and Western Europe as a whole, indigenous factors at work from the day the war ended, if not before, were more important:

> *First*: the deadlock of German industry was broken and a substantial beginning was made *before* currency reform took place in June 1948;

Second: foreign aid did not prove to be the crucial instrument in priming the German economy; and

Third: the 'free-market economy' or 'social market economy', based on the economic reforms initiated in 1948, had already been significantly modified and restrained by the early 1950s when the ultimate breakthrough occurred.[11]

Between 1945 and 1948 investment had been extremely low and the vast flow of refugees from the East, although potential members of a high-quality workforce, had been used with great inefficiency and waste due to the pervasive rationing system and the fact that money was worthless. But by 1950 the dismantling of industrial plant ordered by the first Allied postwar plans had finally come to a stop. At most, says Abelshauser, 5 per cent of the country's prewar capital stock in industry had been destroyed, and the rest was in 'remarkably good' condition. The country was 'poor but not underdeveloped', and when the crucial transport, coal mining and steel bottlenecks were broken by a crash effort of the military government and its local partners in the summer and autumn of 1947, industrial output started to rise quickly. In turn this success guaranteed the effectiveness of the currency reform, and, together with the freeing of prices, finally convinced the public that the way to the future was open.

But critics of this view point out that before the mid-1948 reforms the West German economy was not a truly functioning market system at all and so cannot be judged by conventional standards of performance. Goods were produced for the survival of the individuals and companies producing them, not for profits at the best price they could get. Buying and selling was not a question of money but of barter: so much of the goods I happen to have in exchange for so many of the goods you happen to be offering. Physical need and haggling ability decided who got what, with the shortages in every direction and the heavy hand of military occupation ensuring that everyone was dissatisfied at the end of the deal. Wendy Carlin writes:

> Between 1945 and mid-1948 resource allocation in the western zones occurred through means of barter in large parts of the economy, an active black market, and military-government direction in a few sectors. These mechanisms operated in the shadow of an edifice of controls inherited from the Nazi war economy and maintained by the military authorities. The military governments kept the bulk of controls in place, including the general price and wage freeze of 1936.

But in the chaos left by the war the Allies could never run the economy as the Nazis had done, even if they had wanted to. The result was that currency was worthless, standard tables of prices and wages

134

were irrelevant. Physical shortage dominated every act of production and exchange: people and companies alike lived by what they could get hold of in the course of a day. Confidence was low and expectations even lower.[12]

So in this view the change which came with the June reforms was more than technical. The economy was set back on a foundation in which money, prices and profits began to play once again their normal roles. Savings and investment could be planned, production could be organised to guarantee work and look forward to the future. The change over from a situation in which 50 per cent of output was either hoarded or used in barter was noticed instantly, and industrial production rose another 50 per cent in the second half of 1948 alone. Barter and side-payments in kind instead of in wages disappeared. Two weeks after the reform the *Economist* described some of the results which would make it famous:

> Housewives strolled down the streets gazing in astonishment at shop-windows – at shoes, leather handbags, tools, perambulators, bicycles, cherries in baskets, young carrots tied in neat bundles. In the early morning, farmers had been seen making their unaccustomed way into town with produce for sale, a little uncertain what were the legal channels for selling it.

In other words confidence had returned overnight. By the time ERP goods and funds began arriving effectively in the country from the end of the year, investment had taken off and the trend of recovery was well established.[13]

The debate continues on the kind of recovery which had taken place before the reforms, on the usefulness of the removal of bottlenecks by the Allies, on the effects of freeing almost all prices, on the impact of Marshall Aid. But no one could doubt that the success of the reforms looked like a victory for economic planning and management as run by the Allies and their collaborators in the Bizonal Economic Council in Frankfurt, centre of the emerging political system and its bureaucracy.

From this background loomed the bulky figure of Ludwig Erhard, whose political and public relations skills enabled him to appear dominant in West German economic policy-making until his downfall in November of 1966, the year when the long postwar boom is generally reckoned to have come to an end. No other figure in postwar European history linked his name so powerfully to his country's economic fortunes, no other linked its fortunes so effectively to its status in the world as, among other features, the outstanding example of the American way emulated abroad. Erhard himself admitted in a moment of frankness that he could be seen as an 'American invention', and in this fashion the Economics Minister's views and policies complemented perfectly the Atlanticism of his fellow Christian Democrat, Chancellor Adenauer (whom he succeeded in 1963).

Yet Erhard had always recognised that 'a considerable dose of *Sozialpolitik* was necessary and inevitable', says a German commentator on his career, and from his installation in the Bizonia government as Director of Economics in March 1948, he sat in a Cabinet which made sure that crucial sections of the economy – including housing, agriculture, transport – and its basic mechanisms, such as investment and pricing in heavy industry, were carefully directed from above. The Economics Minister never underestimated 'the framework-setting task of the political authorities', reports Volker Berghahn. In this view there was more of a 'planner' in Erhard than is generally remembered.[14]

By the standards of the first postwar period, everyone looked like a planner in Europe's second, successful reconstruction.

ATTEMPTING TO FULFIL THE PROMISES

Performance so far

Of all the topics covered in a comprehensive survey of the recovery published in 1953 by the severe experts of the UN Commission on Europe resident in Geneva, none received more attention than the great wartime slogan of 'full employment'. They were well aware of the achievements: 'In 1948, when industrial production in Europe as a whole regained its prewar level, European industry employed nearly 10 per cent more people than in 1938.' By the time of their report a rise of one-third or more in industrial employment was evident throughout Europe (East and West) over 1938, with Western Germany registering just under 30 per cent, the UK 20 per cent, France 15 per cent and Italy 'about 5 per cent'. Four out of the six million new jobs were in engineering, which the Commission thought a positive development, 'since engineering certainly provides the most promising outlet for the employment of manpower in Europe'.[15]

But there were great differences in performance between countries: there was no such thing as a 'general abolition of unemployment'. Besides the unemployment which continued to be hidden on a large-scale in agriculture almost everywhere, a wide gap had opened up between the north-west of Europe, where labour shortages were now widespread (particularly in Britain), and the Mediterranean countries.

In the latter a substantial increase in unemployment had taken place since the prewar years, particularly in the case of Italy. In 1950 27 per cent of the Italian industrial labour force was said to be unemployed, and the labour surplus in agriculture was somewhere between 40 and 75 per cent. In West Germany 16 per cent of the industrial labour force was without work in 1950: the industrial expansion was nowhere near enough to absorb the flood of refugees, while both fiscal and monetary policy at the time discouraged investment in human resources. In France employment was said to be 'almost stagnant', with numbers at work in industry still significantly below the 1929 level and much hidden unemployment in trade, services and agriculture. Only in Britain, Denmark and the Netherlands then did conditions in 1949–50 correspond in some fashion to the pledges of 'full employment'.[16]

Almost nowhere was there spare capacity for consumption, and no matter how certain the light at the end of the tunnel, rationing, scarcity, improvisation and the hope of CARE packages* from America were still very much the order of the day, even for those in regular work. Pre-war levels of total consumption were reached in France and the Netherlands in 1949, in Western Germany only two years later. With industrial output expanding, manufactured objects gradually returned to circulation. But food and housing – above all – remained as major grievances until well into the 1950s.

The CBS correspondent Howard Smith noted in mid–1949 how the currency reform in Germany had not only liberated prices – and inflation – but had brought tax reform 'benefiting mainly the wealthy'. The combined result was the 'gigantic bizonal general strike of November 1948'. The State Department consultant, Hans Speier, revisiting Germany in late 1950 was, like everyone, 'staggered' by the consumption revolution which had taken place, but he was quick to note a report that 10 per cent of the population was buying 30–40 per cent of the consumer goods. The Socialist opposition was significantly increasing its vote as social and economic inequalities widened:

> Much of the building effort seems to have gone into restaurants, night-clubs and similar installations . . . and yet immediately above the lighted windows of many of the most glamorous shops you still see nothing but sky. German exports are still only a fraction of German imports . . . and I was told, and could well believe from the evidence I saw, that a considerable part of these imports are luxury goods. You see Germans driving expensive American cars (with black-market gasoline). And the tourist traps in

---

* CARE – Cooperative for American Remittances to Europe – an American relief organisation founded in 1945.

Frankfurt are by no means frequented only by visiting Americans: many of the patrons are German postwar profiteers.[17]

In Britain the low-level profiteers and black-market operators of these years were given a new name: 'spivs'. But the controls to prevent their operations were probably resented even more than the men themselves. Although bread rationing had soon ended, the situation on the 'kitchen front', as the Ministry of Food called it, was scarcely better in 1949 than it had been in 1945. The Labour government had always envisaged a hard five-year transition period, and as the 1950 elections approached, political pressure on all sides – symbolised by such movements as the British Housewives League – demanded an end to the queuing and rampant officialdom. In November of 1949, with a general election approaching, a rising young Labour politician named Harold Wilson promised a 'bonfire of controls'.[18]

Labour Britain was no more egalitarian in substance than the society of 'the long weekend' had been between the wars. But the arrival of full employment was a great change, and involved significant gains for the working classes absolutely and in comparison with the white-collar sectors. Aided by rent control and price subsidies, real wages stood on average 20 per cent higher in 1949 than in 1938.[19]

Across Western Europe wages and prices generally rose in parallel, with gainers and losers differing marginally by phase, local situation and social class. But to maintain this linkage an unending struggle was necessary everywhere between the political authorities and both sides of industry. As new horizons of development opened, governments began to realise that inflation was the omnipresent risk in full employment strategies of all kinds, and sought as a first reaction to screw down personal consumption as far as they dared. Inviting Britons to 'submerge all thought of personal gain and personal ambition', the austere and high-minded Chancellor of the Exchequer Cripps reminded them of the vital priorities: 'First are exports . . . second is capital investment in industry; and last are the needs, comforts and amenities of the family.'[20]

BUILDING THE WELFARE STATE

Social security at last?

Except in West Germany, where Erhard placed 'tight money' ahead of full employment, the great emphasis was placed on collective consumption and the redemption of the wartime promises of housing, education and security in work, old age and ill health. To realise these aims and maintain economies in balance was the purpose of the 'social contracts' which emerged almost everywhere in these years. Involving permanent negotiation between governments, employers and trade unions of a distinctly 'corporatist' kind, these arrangements characterised the long boom throughout Western Europe and appeared an indispensable element in the foundations of the postwar 'mixed economies'.

Expressed in concepts such as 'universality' in Britain or 'solidarity' on the Continent, the new settlements were supposed to embody the inter-class consensus on renewal associated with the great expansion of left-wing parties and trade unions in the war era. Whatever the costs – which conservatives never failed to lament – governments containing strong socialist and/or Christian Social parties set about building the national welfare state with determination and vigour. In exchange they demanded the help of producers' groups in the search for stabilisation.

In Belgium, for example, a 'National Conference of Labour' composed of employers and trade unions met under the chairmanship of the prime minister every six months from 1944 to 1948. It then made way for a comprehensive system including a National Economic Council, 'Professional Councils' for each of the largest branches of industry and 'Works Councils' for factories and businesses employing at least fifty workers. In this framework governments restrained wage pressures while organising new measures of welfare: food and child allowances, housing programmes and support for poorer families. As one admiring Belgian observer commented: 'The Social Christians are definitely more interested in the family than are the Socialists, and they give a great place to family problems in their programme.'[21]

In this the Belgian Catholic party echoed developments in France, where their colleagues in the MRP had insisted on distinguishing family policy from social security and succeeded in hiving off the family allowance system in 1949. But this did little to diminish the extraordinary progress in reorganising and building anew which the Fourth Republic offered in the area of welfare. In Rioux's authoritative judgement:

> ... the main ambitions of 1945 had been realized. The new system was based on the principle of *solidarité* (that is contributions were not simply totalized to the credit of individuals but were immediately made available to all the members); it was on its way to becoming comprehensive; it was run democratically, with the State merely overseeing its operation and meeting the unavoidable early deficits. Finally, with contributions propor-

tional to incomes but payments the same for all, the system made significant social transfers possible: collective obligation thus became an element of a redistributive economic and social policy. By 1949 payments of one sort or another from the Social Security system represented 12 per cent of gross household incomes.[22]

Yet, as Richard Kuisel explains, this was one of the few major elements of 'liberation *élan*' to endure after the war: 'Socialist, syndicalist, egalitarian and moral fervour receded before the more potent desires for recovery, reconstruction, management, and national independence'.[23] An expanding public sector helped give substance and credibility to the French welfare state and reformism, yet the overall framework of collaboration was at this stage much looser than in Germany or Britain. While producers' groups of all sorts gradually acquired much more power than before the war, the influence of the major parties was greatly extended by means of their trade union wings. France too displayed a 'corporatist bias' in its politics.

Tripartite collaboration was envisaged in the Economic Council created in 1946. Yet suspicions were much too deep, interests too far apart to enable it to function effectively. Agricultural, industrial and civil service lobbies reconsolidated in traditional fashion after the Vichy corporations were dissolved, and by 1949 were directly involved in the political tumult generated by the struggle against inflation. While the 'battle for production' which had helped legitimise the industrial unions still went on, Cold War tensions had split the left unions and brought the *patronat* back to prominence. In the more exalted liberation visions in France democracy was to be extended to the work-place, and a law of February 1945 had created works councils in all enterprises with over a hundred employees. By the end of the 1940s there was little sign of the effects of this innovation, and even the burden of wage negotiations remained in the hands of the Ministry of Labour.[24]

In Germany, in contrast, one of the most distinctive features of the industrial scene had been produced by the drive for economic democracy: *Mitbestimmung*, or co-determination, by which enterprises with 1,000 or more employees would allow workers' representatives to sit on the supervisory council, and on the board of directors. The scheme as eventually worked out after much argument with conservative employers and sceptical occupation authorities 'fell short by a long way of the original ideas on economic democracy and "equal participation of capital and labour" as enunciated in the early post war years', in Berghahn's view. But a long-term judgement on it emphasises the system's contribution to the widely-spread peace on the industrial relations front which distinguished postwar Germany. Methods for managing conflict emerged which had proved far beyond the capacities of the unions of the Weimar era.[25]

But it was in their new constitutions (Basic Law in the West German case, pending reunification with the East) that the defeated nations made their most fundamental commitment to the social security and well-being of their citizens. Article 20 of the West German document states that 'The Federal Republic is a democratic and social federal state', meaning, says Berghahn, 'that there is no going back on the principles of democracy, social welfare and federalism, short of a breach of the constitution itself'. A specific article requires the state to protect marriage and the family.[26]

A similar provision is contained in Article 31 of the Italian document. By comparison, its very first line declares that 'Italy is a democratic Republic, based on work.' A significant number of its articles guarantee rights to work, social welfare and industrial democracy. Others anticipate the state's role in managing continuous social and economic reform, using such means as a tripartite National Economic and Labour Council.

The British model at work

In this way the 'revolution of rising expectations' was institutionalised in these countries (though with very different outcomes for the relations linking the state and its citizens between Germany and Italy). Elsewhere the wartime visions were already being scaled down by 1949, redefined in strictly economic terms or challenged by inflation, conservative opposition and American scepticism. This was clearly the case in the land where the most distinctive of the 'social contracts' had emerged, Great Britain.

Having popularised the concept of the 'welfare state' the British went further than most in the early years after the war in its realisation. They took the earliest opportunity to put a major effort into housing, and differed from the Continental nations in attaching so much weight to this priority. But by this time they had already reorganised their pensions and insurance schemes in a new national system, overhauled education and launched the National Health Service. The 'universality' principle linking these efforts differed from the Continental idea of 'solidarity' only in that under the British scheme there was no 'contracting out' – private arrangements would be an addition but not an alternative to the state system – and there was a more complete separation between the insurance element (very small compared to the burden on general taxation) and delivery of services.

For many years in fact the British welfare provision was more comprehensive and generous than anything comparable elsewhere, and whatever the worries about cost, no one doubted the sense and practical efficiency which had gone into setting it up. Speaking of the NHS in 1975, the historian Peter Calvocoressi judged it 'the most beneficial reform ever enacted in England'.[27]

With a unitary trade union movement solidly behind a unified government, the political authority for these changes seemed untouchable and social peace guaranteed. The whole was presented as a triumph for the voluntary methods of consultation and partnership characterising relations in Britain between the state and the producers' groups ever since the First World War. These the Second World War had evolved into a vast system of economic management. Bevin as Minister of Labour had exulted in March 1945: 'Voluntary in its nature, democratic in its functioning, united by law yet stronger than law because it rests on men's words, it stands stronger than anything else man has yet conceived.'[28]

It was naturally assumed that the system could be carried on into the postwar era, in spite of the great weakening of the employers' side caused by the Labour victory and full employment. There was to be no formalisation of it nor any extension of industrial democracy; moreover the wartime physical controls on the labour market were allowed to lapse, thereby removing a key function of the unions. Instead all efforts had to be bent to dealing with the immediate economic situation on a crisis footing, and here the unions proved indispensable – in the short term. The government was not prepared for the wages–prices spiral which set in and found itself thrashing around for a wages policy beyond the gentlemen's agreements on restraint of the war years. In fact the satisfaction of the unions on the welfare and employment front was such that voluntary wage restraint was agreed on again in 1948. But within a year the economy revealed much more of its fundamental fragility, and all concerned in the informal corporatist triangle were called back to the battle against inflation and the trade deficit.

A pattern was thereby created, says the political historian Keith Middlemas: not long-term accords for new industrial equilibria and modernisation, but short-term crisis-avoidance manoeuvres for the sake of peace at any price. So consolidation and 'subdued fanfares for the mixed economy' would be the Labour promises for the 1950 and 1951 elections, aimed at the white-collar employee, not the manual worker. Inevitably there was disappointment in some quarters: 'the activist saw the welfare state and the nationalisation measures of 1945–8 as the beginning of the social revolution to which he believed the Labour Party was dedicated; while his leaders took these achievements to *be* the social revolution'.[29]

SO FAR AND NO FURTHER: PLANNING AND NATIONALISATION

The Labour experience

Labour Party programmes in the years after the war did in fact hold out the prospect of planning the economic future, but as a means of promoting social security, rather than of modernising production and distribution. The extension of public ownership was a key element in this moderate, stabilising strategy. In fact, had the activist taken the trouble to read the Labour government's 1947 *Economic Survey* his illusions might have been removed much sooner than they were. Declaring coordinated planning to be well-nigh impossible, the document declaimed: 'The task of directing by democratic methods an economic system as large and complex as ours is far beyond the power of any government machine'.[30]

This pronouncement was made after the government had set up bodies on investment and capital and then allowed them to wither away under the pressures of daily events and Whitehall traditions. But as successive crises washed over the economy in 1947, planning efforts involving close consultation with employers and unions were stepped up. The redoubtable Cripps was made Minister of Economic Affairs and assigned an impressive-looking planning staff. When he became Chancellor, at the end of 1947, the mechanisms for elaborating and coordinating economic policy proliferated, and Cripps – an erstwhile pillar of radicalism – became an enthusiastic promoter of modernisation under the Marshall Plan.

By this time the government had either already carried out or planned nationalisation for the Bank of England, civil aviation, coal, cables and wireless, transport, electricity and gas. The iron and steel industries were expected to follow. Yet it soon emerged that neither party nor government had any particular ideas on how to develop or even run the new public sector. Very large amounts of compensation were handed over to acquire enterprises such as the coal mines and the railways which were dilapidated far beyond the interest of private enterprise: overall the 20 per cent of industry taken over was 'the unprofitable part'. Existing managements stayed in place and the familiar formula of the 'public corporation', brought back to define the legal status of the nationalized industries in the absence of anything new, ensured that government possessed less control over them rather than more. 'Socialist planning of this type was acceptable even to Conservatives', comment the British historians Sked and Cook.[31]

France

As already mentioned, French efforts were much more ambitious, in many ways the most ambitious of all. Developing the British wartime example of industrial working parties for tripartite analyses of ailing sectors, the planners round Jean Monnet had created a network of Modernisation Commissions. Their task was to elaborate the specific plans for raising production, productivity and competitiveness in the targeted industries. With coal, electricity and the railways fully nationalised after 1946, key sectors could be controlled and integrated technically into the overall effort.

Monnet and his men proved adept at using the institutional looseness of the new Republic to create their own alliance networks and mechanisms for managing the greatly increased power of the state. They took it for granted that there was wide consensus for the modernising purposes embodied in their highly concentrated planning drive, and they enjoyed a privileged relationship with the Marshall Planners, whose background Monnet knew well from his wartime experience in Washington.

But it was the urgency of the situation which had given Jean Monnet his authority, suggests Richard Kuisel, and when circumstances improved it was soon challenged by excluded lobbies and producers' groups, as well as by the Finance Ministry and the National Assembly. The basic lines of action remained: the government formally became the conductor of the *économie concertée*, and planning, including nation-alisation, was made to serve not the construction of socialism but the stimulation of competition and the technological conquest of economic growth.

By the time of the debate on the 1950 budget economic stability brought back more 'liberal' approaches: public investment declined as private investment rose and wartime controls disappeared. The state was now expected to 'cause things to be done' rather than doing them and a pattern of collaboration emerged which would last over a decade. A staff planner wrote in 1950 that the objectives were now: 'to achieve planning that is flexible in its methods and limited in its objectives while modifying as little as possible the existing social structure and accommodating itself to an accelerated return to a free economy'.[32]

Holland

Elsewhere in Western Europe similar trends had already emerged. The Dutch restructuring plan turned out to be 'a mixture of prediction and prescription', and not 'a centrally guided, interlocking set of complementary measures', writes Griffiths. Rapid industrialisation was the only substantial objective identified, while the treatment of agriculture was relegated to the budget. As for method, the 'plan socialism' ideas of the first postwar Minister for Trade and Industry, involving the institutionalisation of the relationship between government, employees and employers, were set aside when he was replaced by a Catholic Party politician. Government officials appointed by the socialists were removed, and all visions of the state 'leading' reconstruction were left behind. Official intervention in the economy was reduced to more traditional levels.[33]

West Germany

In West Germany the question of the state and the economy had come to a head as the key issue in the first election campaign to the new Bundestag, in the summer of 1949. As Konrad Adenauer recalled the campaign, there were two clear fronts. 'The CDU/CSU championed the freedom and welfare of the individual', and the 'social market economy' would be the arena in which these ideals would be reconciled. A campaign pamphlet maintained that

> The 'Social Market Economy' produces the maximum economic benefit and social justice for all by letting free individuals make an efficient contribution to an order that embodies a social conscience. It combines freedom and obligation, genuine competition and an independent control of monopolies. Genuine competition is possible where there is a system that rewards the better performance in a framework of equal chances and fair conditions of competition. The proper market price gives the right direction to the cooperation of all concerned.[34]

In contrast there stood the beliefs of the major opposition party, the Social Democrats: 'with its principles of the all-powerful state, the planned economy, nationalisation'.[35]

145

Adenauer took the CDU–CSU victory to be a ringing endorsement of the 'social market economy', and appointed Ludwig Erhard to realise it. His arrival represented a historical defeat for the 'strong anti-capitalist movement' which German historians have identified throughout the former Reich in the years after the war. As such it was also a great victory for the American occupation regime, which had made no secret of its ideological and practical preferences. After fending off impulses in some British quarters to project Labour nationalisation schemes onto the coal mines of the Ruhr, an effort strongly supported by the Social Democrats, Clay and his staff struggled to postpone any major choice between socialisation and self-determination. Their underlying strategy was simple: 'Time is on our side [Clay had said in October 1947]. If we can defer . . . the issue while free enterprise continues to operate and economic improvement results, it may never become an issue before the German people'.[36]

Italy

After the 18 April elections all talk of planning and nationalisation was considered beyond the pale in Italy, leaving government free to follow its own course. Only in recent years, however, have historians been able to trace the course of the economic action practised in reality by the centrist Cabinets of De Gasperi. The economic historian Bruno Bottiglieri talks of the emergence of a 'liberal protectionism', the fruit of 'a pragmatic impulse dictated by the double and often contrasting objectives of expanding the economy and establishing in the country a great Catholic party'.

Liberal was the philosophy and language of Giuseppe Pella, the powerful Treasury Minister of the key years 1948–53, ably reinforced by the outspoken head of the industrialists' association, Angelo Costa. Protectionist was not only the bias of the tariff regime (continuing a tradition which would endure until the late 1960s), but also the aid given in large and small doses to the sectors the Christian Democrats most wished to cultivate in society. Hence the financial support bills in favour of the big export industries, which soon turned into subsidies at the slightest sign of crisis. Hence too the income support measures to shelter the lower-middle classes and the agricultural workers. Specific state development initiatives, if necessary for the South, agricultural reform, or the public infrastructure, would be paid for by others, e.g. the Marshall Plan, and would not be allowed to interfere with the fundamental premise of monetary stabilisation and the defence of savings, thought to be above politics.[37]

What remained unclear for long was the choice of instruments to carry out this strategy. The public sector industries were reorganised to complement and support, not to compete with the private sector. For the governing party they would come to provide an additional industrial and financial power base, an inexhaustible supply of patronage. Yet they proved capable of launching significant strategic initiatives. Such were the historic decisions of 1948–49 to expand steel production and to develop the natural gas reserves of the Po valley, thereby demonstrating – in Vera Zamagni's view – a new ability to plan for the long term and ensure Italy's place among the advanced industrial nations.

Critics such as Bottiglieri, however, note how the Christian Democrats preferred to bestow their approval only when positive results were guaranteed. Where significant macroeconomic risk and innovation seemed involved, then the Marshall Plan might be considered useful, and it was under its auspices that the small band of planners in Italy found employment, particularly in the southern development fund, (the Cassa per il Mezzogiorno, inspired originally by the example of the Tennessee Valley Authority). But it too was soon called upon to play its role in the great Christian Democrat game of building clienteles and organising consensus.[38]

By the end of the 1940s the entire set of ideas revolving around the enlarged social responsibilities of the state, aiming to guarantee the individual security of its citizens and the solidarity of the whole, was running into increasing difficulties. The German election results in particular demonstrated that the country's grand reformist energies were spent, its legitimacy undermined by fears of inflation and impatience for the arrival of full prosperity. It was the ability to meet this concern – 'Recovery Now!' – that gave market-orientated, liberalising politics their new appeal, visible in Britain, France and Holland as well as in Germany.[39]

The turbulence of economic life and this scaling-down of political ambitions had obvious effects on official priorities. While not renouncing the ambition to control basic economic forces or wishing to dismantle the new welfare states, the more conservative forces now in the ascendancy tended to reduce the aims of policy and focus them much more narrowly. Wherever governments in Western Europe possessed the tools to do so, they sought to apply a strategy whose fundamental objective, stripped of all rhetorical and political pretence, was 'to achieve a high rate of expansion without (excessive) inflation and foreign deficits', in the words of the UN experts, who went on to say: 'The operation of such a policy presents the only really new experience in economic policy in the postwar period.'

While not 'entirely unsuccessful' in the years until 1950, such efforts had been confined to a few north-western countries, where national budgeting enabled macroeconomic aggregates – consumption, investment, savings – to be identified, forecast and discussed. The use of national budgets was 'the most significant sign of integrated planning' in the UN economists' view, and helped explain the notable tolerance for the comprehensive limits which persisted on wages and profits.

But the degree of control promised was often illusory. The so-called Keynesian revolution was still in its very early stages, and the vast shiftings of external forces were much too great for the transitional mechanisms of international and national coordination tried out in this phase. Trade deficits in particular always threatened to get out of hand. The biggest source of disruption, however, was always the internal one: 'Any wider aims of economic planning were gradually given up, as all policy efforts had to be increasingly concentrated upon the single goal of suppressing inflation.'[40] What had gone wrong?

THE PROMISES IN CRISIS

The British devaluation

On the 18 September 1949, after intense agonising, the British government devalued sterling by just over 30 per cent and set off the largest international monetary crisis of the postwar years. The Scandinavian countries very quickly devalued by the same amount, as did Holland, Egypt and Indonesia. Canada, France, Germany, Italy, Belgium and Portugal all devalued directly afterwards, though to lesser degrees. The republics of Latin America did likewise. After the dollar, sterling was by far the most important trading and reserve currency: countries accounting for four-fifths of world trade were involved in the upheaval.[41]

In France the government fell. Conservatives were already in the ascendancy, placing the confidence of the employers and competition in labour and capital markets far above 'the collectivist aspirations of the Liberation', which were now, writes Rioux, 'definitively repudiated'. A nationally imposed wage freeze proved impossible to maintain and free collective bargaining returned, bringing a rapid rise in wages. In Italy reactions to the devaluation were a key factor in the break-up of De Gasperi's latest coalition in November. Left-wing Christian Democrats complained of official indifference as unemployment worsened, of the absence of economic policy coordination, and of a simplistic insistence on a strict accounting balance in public finances as the sole objective of government action. But they gained little attention.[42]

The immediate cause of the British decision had been the collapse in sterling-area exports to the United States as America went into its long-predicted postwar recession. The downturn proved far less serious than expected and was weathered relatively well by most West European economies. But besides revealing the vulnerability of the British recovery and the inability of the British government to discover where its long-term interests lay between the sterling area, the Brussels alliance and the American connection, the devaluation saga brought to a head a long-developing crisis over trade, payments and internal development involving all the West European nations.

The West European economies at the crossroads

At stake was the future of the Western European countries' commercial and financial relations with the rest of the world, but above all with their new 'sponsor', the United States. None had been able to discover a way of achieving a balance between the needs of internal reconstruction and the dynamics of the international economy as it had developed since the war. The American economy dominated every calculation: it was by far the major source of primary products, of manufactured goods and – above all – of liquidity, for the Europeans and for their customers. As long as its productivity continued to grow faster than anyone else's these advantages would tend to increase, whatever the hopes otherwise of the ERP. This was the situation at the root of the continuing financial imbalance between Europe and the United States. The British view of the 'dollar gap' had been very bluntly expressed at the time of the original Marshall Plan announcement: 'the recovery of continental Europe would not itself solve our problem; we depend upon the rest of the world getting dollars (UK and Europe's deficits with USA are only half the world's dollar shortage)'.[43]

All took for granted that full employment and a rising standard of living implied a vast expansion of exports, especially in a world where invisible income had collapsed or dwindled in value as a result of war and inflation. The British looked to a 75 per cent increase between 1945 and 1950; the French linked the success of their Plan to a 10 per cent increase over the peak year of 1929 by 1949; the new West

German government thought they would have to double exports in two years if they were to stabilise living standards at the very low 1949 level without further American aid.

But until 1949 internal reconstruction priorities, determined separately within each country, always took precedence over the necessity of building commercial and financial mechanisms to realize the sought-after export revolution. Instead complex bilateral trade agreements protected currencies against external risks by means of detailed controls on the quantity and nature of goods to be exported or imported, and on the foreign exchange to be employed. These were the very barriers which had supposedly caused the disasters of the 1930s.[44]

Neither the proliferation of these accords nor, on the other hand, tentative steps towards European integration such as the Benelux arrangement were adequate in relation to the scale and urgency of the export challenge. Moreover, they could not contribute towards solving the question of the new Europe's dollar earnings or, more generally, of its place in the world economy.[45]

The 'simple arithmetic of the problem' – said the UN experts in Geneva in spring 1950 – 'is to eliminate . . . the dollar gap which amounted to just over $5 billion during the past year, or little less than in 1948, most of which was covered by extraordinary financial aid from the United States'. In practical terms this meant an enormous increase in exports from Europe, or from Europe's customers in the rest of the world, to the dollar area. Or else it meant the production of substitutes for imports from the dollar area. Otherwise, the Americans running the Marshall Plan were worried that borrowing would continue for ever, and it was in a frame of mind set to avoid this risk that they had begun their efforts in Europe.

By 1949 they too had become aware that the political economy of the problem was in reality even more challenging. First there was the need to develop a system which would allow the expansion of international trade across the board in Europe without American emergency aid and with respect for single national priorities and peculiarities. The second necessity was to accommodate – above all in French eyes – the resurgence of German competition, already widely noted in 1949. Finally came the promotion of Europe's part in global economic growth. In the opinion of the UN experts: 'Europe's problems can be satisfactorily solved only within the framework of an expanding economy, not merely in Europe itself but in the world at large'.[46]

The devaluations of 1949 took place at a time when physical recovery from the war as the basis of economic dynamism gave way to the search for new, market-orientated strategies of expansion, when the inflationary threat came no longer from unsatisfied demand but from unpredictable costs. Hence the devaluations, in Milward's words, 'forced to the forefront the serious issues about the unity of the western world and about the economic basis of that unity'.[47]

At this point it soon emerged that no group had clearer ideas on what these issues were than the Americans of the Marshall Plan. They spoke of

> ... our own belief that, over long term, attainment and maintenance of economic viability as well as political stability and military security require West European union or unions. As ECA aid declines in future, we will be less able to cushion shocks and ease adjustments of unification. Time is running out to accomplish this work in so many ways, not least of which is Soviet possession of the atomic bomb so much ahead of schedule.[48]

In the first year of Marshall Aid – from June 1948 – most of the goods imported into Europe had been food and raw materials. But the balance of payments impact of these materials, only emerging in significant fashion at the beginning of 1949, was looking distinctly inadequate by the autumn, and the Marshall Plan's political and institutional achievements in promoting European modernisation quite marginal. Now a new approach was tried, attempting to promote a major structural reconstruction of Western Europe in the light of a concept of security which was at the same time economic and strategic.

Without such a new conception, believed the Washington experts, there was a risk that the whole effort would fulfil none of its aims in the time allotted, or else 'would have to be continued in some form or another, perhaps indefinitely, if the United States were not to lose sight of its original global objectives for the postwar period'.[49]

NOTES

1. Smith HK op cit p 276
2. Milward AS op cit pp 477–89
3. Ibid p 484
4. Zamagni V op cit p 290; also Zamagni V The Italian 'Economic Miracle' Revisited: New Markets and American Technology. In E di Nolfo (ed) Power in Europe? II Berlin 1991
5. Rioux op cit pp 177–81; France's Prospects for 1950. In *The World Today* Feb 1950
6. Van der Bruggen C Belgium: A Survey of Recent Events. In *International Affairs* July 1950

Rebuilding Europe

7. Griffiths op cit p 11
8. Austria: A Study in Inertia. In *The World Today* Jan 1948
9. Reconstruction in Austria. In *The World Today* Feb 1948; Milward op cit p 481
10. Berlin, New Year 1950. In *The World Today* March 1950
11. Abelshauser W West German Economic Recovery, 1945–1951: A Reassessment. In *Three Banks Review* Sept 1982. An early view of the 'conventional wisdom' is to be found in the report written by the State Department economist Kindleberger in 1949 after three years of work on Germany and the Marshall Plan, reproduced in his *Marshall Plan Days* op cit Ch 3
12. Carlin op cit pp 48–53 (cit at p 49)
13. Ibid pp 53–7 (cit from *Economist* 3 July 1948 at p 56)
14. Berghahn VR *Modern Germany. Society, economy and politics in the twentieth century* Cambridge 1987 pp 184–5; Berghahn VR Ideas into Politics: The Case of Ludwig Erhard. In Bullen RJ et al (eds) *Ideas into Politics: Aspects of European History 1880–1950* 1984; cf Nicholls A The Other Germany – the 'Neo-Liberals'. In Bullen op cit, especially pp 170–4
15. United Nations Dept of Economic Affairs *Economic Survey of Europe Since The War* Geneva 1953 pp 145–7
16. Ibid pp 74, 77, 147–50, 159; Carlin op cit pp 58–9
17. Smith op cit pp 131–2; Speier op cit pp 96–7
18. Addison *Now the War is Over* cit Ch 2
19. Ibid pp 28–9
20. Cit in Sked A and Cook C *Post-War Britain. A Political History* Harmondsworth 1979 p 38
21. Van der Bruggen op cit pp 340–1
22. Rioux op cit p 79
23. Kuisel op cit p 217
24. Rioux op cit p 75
25. Berghahn VR *Modern Germany* cit pp 205–6
26. Ibid pp 198–9
27. Calvocoressi P *The British Experience 1945–75* Harmondsworth 1979 pp 35–6; cf Marwick A *British Society since 1945* Harmondsworth 1982 Ch 3
28. Cit in Middlemas K *Politics in Industrial Society. The experience of the British system since 1911* 1980 p 335
29. Ibid Ch 14, especially pp 393–415 (cit from Ralph Miliband, p 415)
30. Ibid p 412
31. Sked and Cook op cit pp 30–4 (cits at p 34); Lieberman S *The Growth of European Mixed Economies 1945–1970* Cambridge, Mass. 1977 pp 68–9
32. Kuisel op cit pp 237–47 (cit p 245); Frank R The French Dilemma: Modernization with Dependence or Independence and Decline. In *Power in Europe?* op cit p 269
33. Griffiths op cit p 15
34. Adenauer K *Memoirs 1945–53* 1966 p 165
35. Ibid pp 174–75
36. Schöder op cit pp 310–16 (cit p 316)
37. Bottiglieri B *La politica economica dell'Italia centrista (1948–1958)* Milan 1984 pp 10–12, 107–17 (cit p 12); Zamagni op cit p 287, 97
38. Bottiglieri op cit pp 117–19; Salvati MA *Stato e industria nella ricostru-*

zione Milan 1982 pp 273–88, 372–82; Zamagni *Dalla periferia* op cit Ch 11

39. Cf Abelshauser W American Aid and West German Economic Recovery: A Macroeconomic Perspective. In Maier CS and Bischof G (eds) *The Marshall Plan and Germany* NY/Oxford 1991
40. *UN Economic Survey . . . 1953* cit pp 68–70, 72
41. Ibid pp 152–3
42. *Survey of International Affairs, 1949–50* 1953 p 109; Bottiglieri op cit p 52; Rioux op cit p 185
43. Milward *The Reconstruction* op cit p 63
44. Ibid pp 220–1, 256–8
45. Ibid p 282; *UN Economic Survey of Europe in 1949* Geneva 1950 p v
46. *UN Economic Survey . . . 1949* cit p iii, 173
47. Milward *The Reconstruction* op cit p 280
48. Cit in ibid p 284
49. Ibid p 285

CHAPTER NINE

Filling the Dollar Gap: the Evolution of the Marshall Plan

AMERICAN PRESSURE STEPS UP

The challenge to rebuild European security on the basis of the ERP was 'one of the most difficult ever to be faced by the western world', according to a leading Washington economist, Harlan Cleveland. Cleveland, an archetypal New Deal technocrat who had moved up from the Economic Section of the Allied Commission in Italy via UNRRA to the highest levels of the European Cooperation Administration, was the man who first identified 'the revolution of rising expectations' under way in the world. The vision he expressed in an August, 1949 policy document sums up very effectively the state of thinking on Europe's future in the upper echelons of the Marshall Plan by this time. Cleveland complained of: 'the stifling effect on the process of economic growth, on competition and on the spirit of enterprise of the restrictive policies and practices of the participating countries, particularly economic nationalism.' To combat these practices a vast new sweep of integration was essential. Under the control of a European equivalent of the American Interstate Commerce Commission, all trade and payments barriers would be eliminated. Then a single currency and a harmonised banking system would organise the grand unified market.[1]

In this way new 'free trade areas' could be created, said Cleveland's colleagues in the ECA, areas in which 'mass production for mass consumption and intensive internal competition can restore the dynamic of enterprise and economic growth'. In one vast market 'increased possibilities of specialisation' would boost competition and lower costs. The results, in the space of ten to twenty-five years, would 'transform the economic face of Europe, European productivity, and European living standards'.[2]

All paid lip-service to the question of productivity, but none insisted on it as the key to greater prosperity so effectively as the Marshall Planners. The experts of the UN Economic Commission for Europe were just as clear as the Americans on what was at stake:

> A solution of Europe's balance of payments problems is essential if the present standards of living of Europe's populations are to be maintained. In itself, however, the restoration of equilibrium in foreign payments will not contribute to the raising of living standards; it is even possible that in the process of restoring financial solvency, standards of living might have to be lowered. The more fundamental problem of the European economy is the increase in the productivity of European industry and agriculture which alone could satisfy the universal desire for better standards of living.

Everyone involved understood that at the heart of increased productivity was increased capital investment. Thus the UN experts were dismayed to note in 1949 that while such investment in the previous year had been about one-quarter larger in Europe than before the war, it was still far lower than in the United States: at best $30 to $50 per head compared with $65. Furthermore tendencies to look after the national investment picture and the national payments balance prevailed over all the impulses to transnational cooperation and integration.[3]

The results of the Marshall Plan up to the end of 1949

Only the ECA possessed the combination of political, financial and propaganda power, applicable across sixteen European countries simultaneously, to face up to this network of problems with anything like the means equal to the scale of the task. By the end of 1949 the programme was moving towards its half-way point. Just under $6 billion had been spent by the American ECA managers on goods and services for the participating countries; 86 per cent of the costs had been awarded in the form of direct grants. In order of proportion, the major recipients were:

Britain $1.822 million
France $1.297 million
West Germany $601 million
Italy $ 577 million

The principal items of expenditure had been:

Food, feed and fertiliser $2.126 million
Raw materials and semi-finished products $1.673 million

Fuel $894 million
Machinery and vehicles $562 million
Shipping and services $ 463 million

In addition the ERP countries had built up the equivalent of over $4.3 billion in 'counterpart' funds, the proceeds in local currency from the sale of ERP goods on national markets.[4] These sums went into a national account, and under joint government – ECA approval were being used for financial stabilisation purposes, or, more typically, for the rebuilding of infrastructure and the modernisation of productive capital. They also paid for the great propaganda effort which, as we shall see, accompanied the Marshall Plan throughout Europe.

The effects on business confidence were celebrated everywhere. They had been 'of inestimable value', said a Dutch official commentator retrospectively, because they influenced 'the development of investments which in no small measure are dependent on the future expectations of profit.' Expectations of large flows of goods and investment funds from America had played their part in releasing stocks in Germany at the time of the currency reform.[5]

'Few could doubt that the money had been well spent' declared the Council on Foreign Relations in 1950, in a comment on the ERP's results after the first year. They pointed to the rise of nearly a quarter in the total output of goods and services which the ERP countries had enjoyed between 1947 and 1949, and asserted that the 'over-all index of production, based on 1938, rose to 115 in 1949, as compared with 77 in 1946 and 87 in 1947'. Agriculture too had recovered, and progress on the inflation front was considered 'uneven but definitely encouraging'.

The foreign trade of the member states was back to its prewar levels, but its most remarkable feature was the increase of 50 per cent over the previous two years on trade between them. In contrast, against all hopes, exports to the United States had stagnated. Counting the ERP participants and their overseas territories together, exports to the US were just over $1.5 billion in 1949, 'a year in which US exports (mostly ECA financed) to the metropolitan countries alone totalled over $4bn', noted the New York commentators.[6] The fundamental Marshall Plan aim of 'viability', overall balance of payments equilibrium between the participating countries and the rest of the world, particularly with the dollar area, seemed as far away as ever.

The clash over Europe's future economic management

But much greater difficulties had spread at the institutional and political levels. The new 1949 proposals looking forward to a common currency and banking system represented one of the many responses to the fundamental fact that the West European powers would not swallow the American idea of integration between them, which stood as the great reforming condition of Marshall Aid.

This refusal was of course led by the British, who went to extraordinary lengths in order not to be treated on a par with France, Germany, Italy, etc., not to support even modest regional associations such as the France–Italy–Benelux combination ('Fritalux') proposed in autumn 1949, and not to concede even minimal alterations in the sterling area's arrangements. Even if this meant wrecking the chances of building a new European payments scheme which would – among other benefits – help bring West Germany into the emerging European trade pattern, the British remained unmoved. Above all they fought to deny authority of any sort to the ERP coordinating bodies in Europe, particularly the Organisation for European Economic Cooperation (OEEC), which had been created by the Europeans to manage the use of American aid.[7]

But the fate of the OEEC shows how reluctant all the participants were to surrender economic sovereignty to American designs. A newborn agency conjured up by the European foreign ministries to satisfy the technocrats and businessmen sitting in the ECA in Washington, the OEEC was seen by the latter as the embryo of a West European government.[8] Its first President was Paul-Henri Spaak, and its Secretary-General a rising collaborator of Monnet's, Robert Marjolin. Europe's foreign ministers were expected to be the members of its governing council. In the short term it was expected to question national authorities on their import and investment programmes, develop a comprehensive plan of production to submit for American approval and financing, and open the way for a new payments system in Europe, thereby enabling this plan to function in favour of trade expansion.[9]

But the French insisted on keeping Germany out of the original OEEC, accepting only the representatives of the military zones. More seriously, the methods used took no account of the vast differences in economic situations, policy traditions and priorities of the member-states; very few possessed development programmes for the coming years, or even the means to construct them. The responsibility for allocating the aid proved an 'intolerable burden' (said the British), so divisive that only recommendations – not decisions – came from the organisation. In spite of American wishes, it lacked the political power to promote coordinated planning, let alone integration.

The first OEEC long-term plan bore little relation to the hopes placed in it. There had been almost no connection between the size of its requests and the sums likely to be available. It admitted that the dollar gap would not be closed even after four years, and stressed that 'this report is not a joint European recovery programme'. The 1949 devaluations were made without reference to the OEEC and immediately 'made nonsense of the forecast deficits and the programmes of aid to finance them which had taken the OEEC nine months to hammer out', says Milward.[10]

The British, the French and General Clay saw to the neutralisation of the OEEC, aided on differing occasions by the smaller nations who invariably attempted to go to the Americans directly when their immediate interests were involved. Hence the ECA, with its missions in each national capital, its field headquarters in Paris and its directors in Washington, was always far more important than the OEEC in the management of the Marshall Plan.

Yet veterans and historians agree that the agency furnished an important pioneering experience in the measurement and management of interdependence. As an example, the eminent British civil servant Lord Roberthall recalled the unforeseen effects of differing full employment policies:

> ... states with less full employment will tend to import less and export more than those more ambitious. Some will have a surplus and an increase in reserves, others a deficit and a reserve loss. Thus the double commitment, on employment and on freedom of trade, means that each member has a *legitimate* interest in the employment policies of all the others.[11]

With the dwindling of the Bretton Woods institutions and the UN, followed by the fading of the ITO project, a gap had opened up in the general structure of international economic relations. The OEEC helped to fill this gap, providing a forum for the expert confrontation of trends, issues and policies. An eminent American veteran has recalled how it also:

> ... instituted one of the major innovations of postwar international cooperation, the systematic country review, in which the responsible national authorities are cross-examined by a group of their peers together with a high-quality international staff. In those reviews, questions are raised which in prewar days would have been considered a gross and unacceptable foreign interference in domestic affairs.[12]

The Americans demand a European single market

It was to the OEEC Ministerial Council that Paul Hoffman, the ECA Administrator, addressed his critical speech of 31 October, 1949 which launched the new integrationist push developed in Washington. Action had already been taken in the new phase to negotiate a first multilateral payments scheme, and to promote the general removal of quantitative restrictions on imports. But now the Administrator, in a formal intervention billed as no less significant than Marshall's original Harvard address, called for 'nothing less than an integration of the West European economy'. He went on: 'The substance of such integration would be the formation of a single large market within which quantitative restrictions on the movement of goods, monetary barriers to the flow of payments, and, eventually, all tariffs are permanently swept away.'

America's historical experience of creating just such a market taught very clear lessons on how to 'accelerate the development of large-scale, low-cost production industries', declared Hoffman. To enjoy such benefits Europeans would have to promote trade liberalisation, push for currency convertibility, and coordinate their national economic policies, either by improvements to existing bodies or by creating 'new central institutions'. Such developments would not come overnight: 'But the massive change in the economic environment would, I am convinced, set in motion a rapid growth in productivity. This would make it possible for Europe to improve its competitive position in the world and thus more clearly satisfy the expectations and needs of its people.'[13]

At the time, American observers doubted if any official US representative had 'ever spoken more bluntly to a European official audience', and there was surprise at Hoffman's urgency and his demand that facts and projects be ready for inspection by early 1950. Within weeks the ECA itself produced designs for 'a fully automatic multilateral clearing union and . . . effective machinery for direct coordination and review of monetary and exchange rate policies of the participating countries', writes Immanuel Wexler. In this way were set in motion the processes which would lead to the birth in September 1950 of the European Payments Union (EPU), seen henceforth as the key to the reform and integration push.[14]

THE EUROPEAN PAYMENTS UNION

The EPU, which started operations after September 1950 as an agency of the OEEC, was the historical link between the Marshall Plan and the Common Market. A remarkable compromise between American utopianism and European historical interests, it was the most highly developed of the devices for organising the transition to a world of free, intra-European trade where quotas and tariff barriers would be things of the past and currencies freely convertible one to another. The United States intended it as a key means to integration and even unification in Western Europe, and as such a step towards global multilateralism.

The EPU's functions resembled those of a bank of international settlements: the currencies of the members were fully transferable between each other and trade-offs were managed between countries with perennial balance of payments surpluses and those usually in deficit. With its own unit of account based on a mixture of gold and credit supplied largely by the United States, it acted as a European bank coordinating and funding the external operations of each national central bank. Its resources preserved the delicate gold and dollar reserves of each member from the oscillations of everyday trading and did away with the need for continuous deals and adjustments between the single nations and each one of its partners. 'With one stroke, the EPU created a currency area in which bilateral balances no longer mattered', say its historians.[15]

Marshall Plan capital to the tune of $600 million, as well as contributions from each member state, set the system in motion. In fact the EPU contained more 'American ingredients' than any of the other measures of European economic cooperation created in these years, according to a US witness of the time: 'ECA officials urged European governments to undertake discussions of the payments problems, they participated actively in the negotiations, and they were strong proponents of particular ways of doing the job.' Above all they were the ones who reconciled the British to the scheme, convincing them that they could participate in it without detriment to their arrangements in the sterling area.[16] The resulting compromise has been called 'the most successful example in practice of international economic cooperation in the postwar period'. The former Secretary-General of the OEEC has confirmed his belief in it as an 'ideal design' leading the way from the 'conservative bilateralism of immediate postwar Europe [to] the broader inter-dependence of the industrial democracies which marked the decade of the 1960s'. The European Monetary System can also be seen as one of its descendants.[17]

BUILDING CONFIDENCE: THE MESSAGE OF THE MARSHALL PLAN

The ideological dimension

But the EPU design was only one of the range of instruments the United States disposed of for projecting its power abroad in these years, and its capacity to invent new ones repeatedly took the Europeans by surprise. America expected its political, social, economic and cultural values to be taken up along with Marshall Aid, so the ERP gradually added to its equipment a remarkable set of tools for broadcasting the lessons of the American way to the Old World, a dimension of the Marshall Plan which has always been neglected.

The ERP was clearly a mighty weapon in the Cold War: Ambassador Harriman, its head in Europe, went as far as to characterise it in 1949 as a 'fire-fighting operation'. Consequently there was always a sharp tension in its activities between the short-term anti-Communist objectives and the long-term strategy of eradicating the presumed causes of war and revolution, bringing the force of the American example to bear on European chaos and backwardness.

But together these pressures guaranteed that when it began work on the ground the ideological and psychological features of the effort would be just as significant as its economic inputs. These additional facets of the Plan would aim to change attitudes and outlooks, aspirations and mentalities – for the sake of votes first: to stop the rise in support for communist parties and left-wing trade unions; but in the longer term to bring about that renewal of Europe's 'spiritual vigour' talked of by the State Department planners in 1947. As the effort evolved, this goal came to mean a radical shift in the priorities of individuals, towards new ideals of personal progress which could be defined in the language of income and consumption.

None of the West European nations was in a condition to challenge this kind of ideological power openly, or to develop alternatives; the only government which tried, the British, failed miserably.[18] So the Europeans were expected to get on the team as quickly as possible, leaving them barely time to wonder why they had had to exert themselves so in 1945–6 to alert America to the challenges ahead. Opposite stood the Cominform, the Soviet bloc bureau set up with the explicit aim of generating a massive propaganda counter-offensive against the Marshall Plan, in Western Europe as well as in the eastern sphere.

The ERP campaign for the American way

The outcome of this confrontation and of the whole Marshall Plan emphasis on building confidence was the largest international propaganda operation ever seen in peacetime. The planners in the ECA sought initially 'an effective means for countering Communist propaganda against us and at the same time building positive support for us and our policies throughout the world'. Giving assistance alone would not automatically produce good-will, they noted, referring to the experience of the Greek-Turkish aid effort. Instead:

> The aim would be to help the people of Racine and Muncie know where the things they produce have gone, what use is being made of them and what the people are like who are on the receiving end of their help. Vice-versa the workers of France and the farmers of Denmark must be told where the goods they receive come from, what the people are like behind the aid provided and what their motives are in providing help.[19]

To this end the European Cooperation Masterplan signed by each participating country contained a special section entitled 'Publicity', authorising 'that wide dissemination of information on the progress of the program . . . desirable in order to develop the sense of common effort and mutual aid which are essential to the accomplishment of the objectives of the program'.[20]

The key countries were considered to be France, the bi-zone and Italy, followed by a second band containing Greece, Turkey, Austria, Trieste and the French zone of Germany. A third included England and Sweden, and a fourth grouped the rest.[21] But it was in Italy that the largest campaign emerged, the one considered 'tops' in the Paris headquarters of ERP. The operating principles arrived at there changed little up to the outbreak of the Korean War. They were similar to the methods used in the other ERP countries but were probably applied more intensively, taking their cue from the frantic propaganda battle of the April 1948 elections. A January 1950 report from the Rome mission insisted: 'Carry the message of the Marshall Plan to the people. Carry it to them directly – it won't permeate down. And give it to them so that they can understand it.'[22] The basic thrust then was for a truly mass programme using 'every method possible . . . to reach Giuseppe in the factory and Giovanni in the fields', or as the Paris office put it, 'slugging it out way down among the masses'.[23] This came to mean tens of documentary films, hundreds of radio programmes, thousands of mobile cinema shows, millions of copies of ERP pamphlets, tens of millions of spectators for ERP exhibitions and films.

When applied on the ground these methods proved extremely flexible and no idea seemed too large or too daring for the Information Program in its heyday. Concepts such as Counterpart, the dollar gap, productivity and European integration were not only quite new to European ears but difficult to communicate in the best of circumstances. Little wonder that the ERP information directors in Washington felt that 'we have become in surprising measure . . . the principal fount for education about the big economic problems and developments disturbing the world today'.[24]

Opening up an ERP pamphlet or visiting a Marshall Plan exhibition in the months down to June 1950, what were the themes one would always find? What was 'the message'? A booklet distributed at the Venice exhibition on ERP in summer 1949 opens with a dramatic quantification of the dimensions of American aid: three ships a day, $1,000 a minute, two weeks' salary from every worker. The goals?:

> By utilising American free supplies of foodstuffs and raw materials, Italy and the other nations included in the ERP plan hope to attain by the year 1952:
> – A higher standard of living for the entire nation,
> – Maximum employment for workers and farmers,
> – Greater production,
> through exploiting all their energies and by a close economic collaboration with all the other ERP countries.

The essential mechanisms of the Plan are then outlined: how supplies of wheat and raw materials from the United States turn into lira deposited in a special fund at the Bank of Italy, which is then used for public works and other 'productive improvements aiming to diminish unemployment'. The details follow, underlining how work has been restored to lifeless industries, how new machinery has modernised factories and how greater output needed to be integrated Europe-wide to facilitate emigration and stabilise economic life on a continental scale. The concluding message states that:

> ERP is a unique chance offered to European nations toward reconstructing their economy, raising the standard of living among the masses, and attaining by the year 1952 an economic stability which is the foundation of political independence . . . Every worker, every citizen is bound up in this rebirth. The future and the peace of Italy and of Europe, the general well-being of all, depend on the will and the work of each single one of us.[25]

The reference to the masses and to workers illustrates the crucial importance the ERP as a whole attached to changing the balance of power, the structures and above all the attitudes prevalent in the world of trade unionism. Here information activities were only part of a vast operation directly aided by the American trade unions which actively sought to organise non-Communist unions where, as in France and Italy, hardly any existed before.

Without entering into the merits of this still controversial undertaking, which was largely part of the ERP as fire-fighting operation, it is worth noting that the entire thrust of the effort was to create trade unions with different ideological objectives to those dominated by the left-wing parties which had emerged since the war. The creation of a single 'non-political organisation devoted to the economic improvement of the job-holder' was to be the aim and a furious propaganda and political battle developed on this front from 1949 onwards, above all in France and Italy.[26]

In Britain too a major campaign was launched to modernise union practices and attitudes, involving the Labour government, the TUC and the leadership of the major industrial unions. With conferences, seminars, publications and team visits to the United States, the specially created Anglo-American Productivity Council worked on the conviction that while British industrial methods left much to be desired, it was the negative outlook of the workforce which more than any other factor blocked productivity improvements.[27]

Whether directed at workers or employers the key words everywhere were always mass production, scientific management and above all productivity. In each country there were specialised reviews on the subject, joint committees, trips to inspect American factories, conferences and eventually in some countries, even 'productivity villages' where model factories and workers' communities could be seen in action.[28]

Judging the results

For the first anniversary of the Marshall Plan Raymond Aron paid eloquent tribute in *Le Figaro* and over the radio to the results of the American gesture, and it was the psychological effects which the eminent French philosopher chose to emphasise. He spoke of the return of 'a sense of hope and confidence', of 'restored courage and reawakened energy', transforming, 'almost at once, the psychological atmosphere of the "cold war" '. A new sense of solidarity had emerged, said Aron, providing 'an occasion without precedent to bring about what has been the centuries-old dream of philosophers, and what is today an imperious necessity of history – the unity of Europe'. It was up to the Europeans themselves, he concluded, 'not to lose this unique opportunity'.[29]

But the Americans were not satisfied with the progress achieved in these directions. The great information effort itself had been set up in part because, as its director Al Friendly – one of America's best-known journalists and broadcasters – put it in April 1948, not only did the Europeans not know about American aid, 'they don't even know their own countries are cooperating with each other'.[30] Yet the ERP was intended especially to promote European self-help, stimulating cooperation and coordination without outside interference: that was the whole point of the OEEC, in which the United States did not sit. Thus a basic tension emerged in the effort which sometimes worked creatively, usually not, especially as this weak point was exploited ceaselessly by the Cominform campaign. The director of the Industrial Division in Holland said pithily: 'the United States was paying the piper and it was always a great problem how loudly we could call the tune'.[31]

The self-evident rightness of the Marshall Plan's goals and methods turned out to be harder to project than expected, and gradually awareness spread of the difficulties of applying abstract principles and concepts to complex and chaotic local situations. The outcome was disappointment with the short-term results, especially when measured in terms of the rise or fall of support for Left parties and unions. '[T]he European workman listens listlessly while we tell him we are saving Europe, unconvinced that it is *his* Europe we are saving', complained a senior staff member in Paris in February 1949.[32]

In the early days it was possible to believe that the working man of Europe was not particularly interested in the Marshall Plan battle against Communism, but sought rather 'a promise of a larger stake in his country's economy – enough income to enjoy better food, a new suit, a picnic or the movies, less cramped living quarters, a chance to retire when he is old'.[33] But by the end of 1949 experience and extensive opinion polling had brought a significant shift in outlook, to the point that the strategists felt obliged to realise ' the underlying concern of the majority of Europeans today is security . . . [meaning] employment, health and old-age benefits . . . [or further] that a man's life, when begun, contains the reasonable assurance and expectation of a rational progress toward a reasonable conclusion'.

The concept of higher standards of living was 'rapidly becoming anathematic [sic] to Europeans', said an expert in the Paris headquarters. But the basic ERP objectives of higher productivity and European 'economic unification [sic]' would not be affected in any way, since only by these means, felt the writer, could the Europeans in fact achieve the social security they so anxiously sought. In the meantime the Marshall Plan would have to recognise the legitimacy of welfare capitalism, insisting simply that it be applied, as doctrine and reality, without restriction in all Europe.[34]

POLITICAL FAILURE, ECONOMIC SUCCESS?

The limits of American power

Among European governments and bureaucracies there was also significant resistance. The British were the ones who had been most dismayed in 1949 by the new demands of Hoffman and his planners, 'burning with missionary zeal', and there was widespread anxiety in the OEEC countries as the new integration onslaught was launched.[35] Reflecting the worries of many contemporaries, it is this crusading dimension of the American effort, indeed of the entire ERP, which has attracted the most sceptical comments from today's historians.

Hoffman's standard, says the American scholar Michael Hogan, 'was nothing less than the total reorganization of Western Europe in an American mold', the newest expression of the most basic Marshall Plan impulses to project a 'New Deal synthesis for a European neo-capitalism'. Not surprisingly, suggests Hogan, the Europeans resisted: 'they refused to engage in joint programming [or] adapt national production plans to European needs'; they sought to 'preserve the greatest degree of national self-sufficiency and autonomy'. Undeterred, the ECA men simply stepped up the political pressure.[36]

Some historians have seen hubris and presumption at work:

> Underlying policy formulation was a sort of puritanical, missionary zeal to put the Old World to rights. The basis was a deeply held liberal persuasion that in some way the development of the Old World had been blocked while still in a state of sinful imperfection and thus had not reached, yet, the competitive heaven of high productivity which the United States had now attained.

These 'quasi-religious, quasi-nationalist assumptions', most common in Congress, simplified America's own history drastically and revealed policy choices to be based not on a realistic calculation of power and its limits, but 'just over-vaulting ambitions', writes Milward.[37]

Historical research has now demonstrated just how comprehensively the barriers erected by the European states in these years blunted such ambitions. Intent on defending their national security aims – above all in the decisions on Germany – their internal and external economic arrangements and their new social contracts, the West Europeans insisted on a marriage settlement with the United States whose substance was simple to state, difficult to live by: 'we want to be dominated, but on our own terms'.

At this point it would be easy to portray the Marshall Plan in deep political crisis by 1950, unable to bring about the sought-for shifts in attitudes, expectations and behaviour. Even in Italy, where so much effort was spent, government, industry and labour 'persist in taking a very dim view of productivity', a Labor Division inspector from Paris reported in June. According to this observer the fundamental economic and political context of the Marshall Plan effort there had to be changed, since it was up against 'the prime flaw of Italian industry . . . its parasitic nature, its monopolistic structure, practices and outlook', and its distribution system, 'an heirloom of the 13th century'.[38]

But to depict the fate of the ERP as a failure by its own lights would be to ignore the contradiction mentioned earlier between the short- and long-term aims of the plan. The ERP men were under immense pressure to get instant results, overnight jumps in production, immediately visible improvements in housing, transport, energy, industry, agriculture, downturns in communist votes by the next election, enthusiastic endorsement of everything America stood for by the next Congressional budget hearing. What happened was of course rather different.

At the time it was quite impossible to demand a drop in support for the Italian Communist Party in the 1951 elections when not a penny had been spent of the 1949 investment budget by the beginning of 1950, and equally idle to expect a quantum leap in British exports to America when US trade barriers remained unchanged and the UK was unable to satisfy demand at home or in the rest of the world.[39]

The new European economy

But considerations such as these hide the crucial structural shift taking place in Europe's economic situation as the 1950s opened. Milward highlights how:

> . . . in 1947 the exports of West Germany, Italy and the Netherlands were each less than those of Switzerland. By 1950 the countries of 'Little Europe' were the five largest West European exporters after Britain. In 1947 the total value of their combined exports was less than that of British exports, while in 1950 it was 30 per cent more. Their exports went very largely to

West European markets and such markets dominated the export trade of three of them, Belgium, the Netherlands and West Germany.[40]

If production grew fast, exports grew faster; in both categories West Germany's efforts outdistanced all others. At the beginning of 1949 it produced 80 per cent of the goods turned out by the prewar nation; at the end of the year it surpassed that level, and in 'the miracle year' of 1950 left it behind by over a third. The value of West Germany's most rapidly growing manufactured exports increased by almost $1.4 billion between 1948 and 1951 from a level of no more than $26.9 million. Meanwhile French and Dutch exports also doubled between 1948 and 1950, though starting from a much higher base.[41]

But it was the destination of these exports which was most striking. The largest part of the export increase was in trade between the West Europeans: intra-European exports grew by 90 per cent between 1948 and 1950. Again a pattern was set which would become characteristic of the new decade and would provide the substantial foundation for the road to the Common Market. The intuitions of the integrationists and the worth of the mechanisms set up by the Marshall Plan and the OEEC, particularly their more liberal payments systems, were confirmed.

A FRAMEWORK FOR INTERDEPENDENCE

The beginnings of Franco-German reconciliation

Among those most encouraged by these developments were Jean Monnet and his collaborators in Paris. But their faith in France's future and Europe's was sorely tested by the Cold War. Monnet told his diary in spring, 1950:

> Whichever way we turn, in the present world situation we see nothing but deadlock – whether it be the increasing acceptance of a war that is thought to be inevitable, the problem of Germany, the continuation of France's recovery, or the place of France in Europe and the world.

The anxiety that weighed on Europe, Monnet explained later, was that 'if we did nothing we should soon face war again':

> . . . Germany would not be its instigator this time, but its prize. So Germany must cease to be a potential prize, and instead become a link. At that moment only France could take the initiative . . . [But] in the confused state of Franco-German relations, the neurosis of the vanquished seemed to be shifting to the victor: France was beginning to feel inferior again as she realized that attempts to limit Germany's dynamism were bound to fail.[42]

Monnet predicted that unless West Germany's rediscovered competitive capacity was harnessed to a constructive project for the benefit of
the whole of Western Europe, the downward spiral of the '30's would
inevitably reappear. There were already signs that the total failure of
France's postwar diplomatic efforts to 'keep Germany in check' by
physical occupation of her territory and direct control of her industry
– attempting again the strategy which had failed in the 1920s – was
alienating her allies and disrupting French politics. Monnet's particular contribution was to bring his own version of 'lateral thinking' (his
words) to the problem. Looking back he explained:

> . . . if the problem of [German] sovereignty were approached with no desire
> to dominate or to take revenge – if on the contrary the victors and the
> vanquished agreed to exercise joint sovereignty over part of their joint
> resources – then, a solid link would be forged between them, the way would
> be wide open for further collective action, and a great example would be
> given to the other nations of Europe . . . It could, in fact, become the germ
> of European unity.[43]

Coal and steel were chosen as the vital resources to be shared
because they were 'at once the key to economic power and the raw
materials for forging weapons of war'. Long reflection on the questions
of supranational management and new analyses from the federalists in
the Council of Europe, together with the pressures of an economic
relationship with Germany which was changing to France's disadvantage by the day, led Monnet and his group to produce very quickly the
embryo of their scheme. It proclaimed:

> Europe must be organised on a federal basis. A Franco-German union is
> an essential element in it, and the French Government has decided to act
> to this end . . . the establishment of common bases for economic develop-
> ment must be the first stage in building Franco-German union. *The French
> Government proposes to place the whole of Franco-German coal and steel production
> under an international authority open to the participation of the other countries of
> Europe.*

Monnet declared grandiloquently in his memoirs: 'The aims and
methods of the European Community were now set.'[44]

The Schuman Plan

The new suggestion of the planners was immediately taken up by the
Foreign Minister Robert Schuman and launched with a great sense of
urgency as the 'Schuman Plan' in early May 1950. The Europe of 'the
Six' thus came into being when, besides Germany, Italy and the
Benelux countries all responded positively to the invitation. Observers

noted that these were the countries where federalist ideas had generally been strongest during and after the war, and where Christian Democrat politics were particularly well established. Among the British, however, there was talk of a 'black international', and they immediately took their distance. They were quite happy to see the Continentals reorganising their industries and removing barriers to trade. But only 5 per cent of their steel exports went to Western Europe, and the government insisted that a country which produced half the coal and one third of the steel of the seven countries combined was not going to 'accept the principle that the most vital economic forces of this country should be handed over to an authority that is utterly undemocratic and is responsible to nobody.'[45]

Whether the British made their great historical mistake over European integration at this point has been debated ever since. What seems certain is that their 'leadership' of Europe after the war, based on size, integrity and solidity of intent, was now cancelled out politically: '. . . at the bar of world opinion, the Schuman proposal has become a test', said the *Economist*, 'and the British government have failed it'.[46]

Adenauer's response made clear he placed his hopes for European integration before those of German reunification. He had already made several suggestions for Franco-German collaboration, even proposing at one point a confederation. Now he saw the Schuman scheme as a way of enlarging the Federal Republic's range of action, and going beyond the system of Allied tutelage under the High Commission and the International Ruhr Authority which still nominally – at French behest – controlled industry in that region. In their welcome for the scheme the Americans were also thinking of what would come after the High Commission arrangements. But their very strong approval, intensifying as the Cold War climate worsened, centred on the proof that only months after Hoffman's exhortations of October 1949, the Europeans were capable of generating their own proposals for liberalisation, integration and single markets in key areas of their economic life.

Was Washington deceived over the Schuman Plan? To their initial suspicions that a more sophisticated version of the prewar cartels prevailing in these industries was being proposed, Monnet replied that far from being discriminatory, restrictive or defensive, the new vision stood for 'the continuing increase of output and productivity by enlargement of markets and rationalisation of production'.[47] But by the time the treaty setting up the European Coal and Steel Community was signed in Paris in April 1951 the original design had almost been turned inside out. Each participating country sought to defend its own national priorities, traditions and practices in the final agreement, and so the outcome, says Milward, was not a triumph for the free market or for the technocrats but rather 'a set of complex regulations arising from the careful balancing and adjustment of the interests of the various nation states to allow them to achieve particular national objectives'.[48]

The concrete results were slow in coming and modest in proportion since the High Authority – presided over by Monnet – 'had constantly to struggle with national objections and intransigence', as another historian reports. But over the years it did generate among its members a 'European ambience and presence', an atmosphere of mutual confidence which came through the experience of 'tackling together a list of specific problems by stipulated deadlines' in a key economic sector.[49] However, seen in a longer-term historical perspective, the precedent it created appears extraordinarily significant. Bullock talks of 'as bold and imaginative an idea as any in European history', while Milward underlines how it opened the way to an enduring Franco-German alliance, 'the central tie in western European reconstruction which was so conspicuously missing in the 1920s'. The key to its enduring character in this view was the method it introduced: 'avoiding all major questions of war and peace and creating instead a formalized network of institutional economic interdependence'.[50]

So, says Milward, 'the terms on which European reconstruction was finally settled were more European than American . . . In the EPU it was the strength of Britain's position which had to be acknowledged, in the Schuman Plan that of France.' But by the end of 1950 the key question had become: who was truly ready to acknowledge the transformation of Germany's position? After Korea the United States re-exerted its power with new and overwhelming vigour to make sure the Europeans understood that reconstructing their defences was just as important as reconstructing their economies, and that this logic required the rearmament of Germany. Again the French launched an initiative to integrate West German power into a West European whole, in effect to force Germany to organise its own containment. But the contradictions were too many, even in France itself, and it was NATO, under its American Supreme Allied Commander, which would supervise the pooling of military sovereignty, not the proposed 'European Defence Community'.

Yet the fundamental reality of German reconciliation with the rest of Europe remained, if only a divided Germany in a divided Europe. Robert Marjolin, the Secretary of the OEEC, recalled in 1980:

In a way, it was the very extent of the German defeat, the quasi-annihilation of the country which made possible first coexistence, then tolerance, finally reconciliation. German imperialism had been finally destroyed, as French imperialism in Europe had been more than a century before. In a way, European history, the history of warring nation-states, had come to an end. Peace in Europe, based on a feeling of total exhaustion and on the hope of a better world, had become possible.[51]

But all these blessings were very heavily disguised at the time, and the short-term and long-term aims of reconstruction often seemed hopelessly irreconcilable to Americans and to Europeans. When the full-scale emergency of the Korean War broke out in June 1950 everything achieved up to that time seemed to be placed in jeopardy.

NOTES

1. Milward *The Reconstruction* op cit pp 284 n 2, 286
2. Hogan op cit pp 271–2
3. *UN Economic Survey of Europe in 1948* Geneva 1949 pp 224–7
4. USWA 1949 pp 118–19
5. Ministry of Foreign Affairs *Road to Recovery The Marshall Plan Its Importance for the Netherlands and European Co-operation* The Hague 1954 p 149; Abelshauser American Aid and West German Economic Recovery op cit p 406
6. USWA 1949 p 119
7. Milward *The Reconstruction* op cit p 168
8. Hogan op cit Ch 4
9. The Marshall Plan in Operation. In *The World Today* Oct 1948
10. Milward *The Reconstruction* op cit Ch 5 (cit at pp 206–7)
11. Lord Roberthall International Economic Cooperation after 1945. In *History Today* Sept 1983 (emphasis in original)
12. Lincoln Gordon in Ellwood *The Marshall Plan Forty Years After* (cit pp 48–9)
13. Hogan op cit pp 273–4; USWA 1949 pp 131–2
14. Wexler op cit p 159 and Ch 10 in general
15. Kaplan JJ and Schleiminger G *The European Payments Union. Financial Diplomacy in the 1950s* Oxford 1989 Ch 5
16. Milward op cit pp 320–34; Wm R Diebold Jr cit in Marjolin R *Europe in Search of its Identity* NY Council on Foreign Relations 1980 p 25. (I am grateful to Mr Diebold for bringing this pamphlet to my attention.)
17. Milward) op cit pp 325–8; Marjolin op cit p 26
18. Anstey C Foreign Office Publicity, American Aid and European Unity. Mobilising Public Opinion, 1947–1949. In *Power in Europe* op cit
19. Memo Waldemar A. Nielsen to Secretary Harriman 26 April 1948, in

NA RG 286, OSR Information Divn Office of Director, General Subject Files 1948–49 *Publicity & Information 1948* sub-file*

20. DAFR 1948 p 235*
21. *Principles on Guaranties for Information Media* 13 Sept 1948, in NA RG 286, OSR Information Divn, Office of Director, General Subject Files 1948–49, 'Huse (Personal File)'*
22. Notes dictated for use in Congressional presentation, 16 Sept 1950, in NA RG 286, OSR Information Divn, Information Subject File *Previous Testimony* sub-file*
23. Letter FR Shea, Chief, Field Branch, European Information Division to Berding 24 Feb 1949, in NA RG 286, OSR Administrative Services Divn, Communications and Records Section, Country Files 1948–49, Italy *Publicity and Information. Radio–Film* sub-file*
24. Comment by Robert Mullen (Director, Office of Information), in *Budget Estimate, Fiscal 1950*, in NA RG 286, ECA Washington, Information Divn, Information Subject File *Previous Testimony* sub-file*
25. Copy of pamphlet *ERP in Italy*, in NA RG 286, ECA Washington, Information Divn, Office of Director, Informational Country File *Italy* sub-file*
26. Memo on *Labor Information* 19 Dec 1949, in NA RG 286 OSR Information Divn, Mission files *Italy: Publicity and Information* sub-file*; Carew A *Labour Under the Marshall Plan* Manchester 1987
27. Carew op cit Ch 9; Addison *Now the War is Over* op cit pp 193–9
28. These were frequently portrayed in the monthly newsreels, *ERP in Action*, of which 13 editions were made, and in the documentary series *The Marshall Plan at Work*, dedicated to activities in 12 of the participating countries. A number of these films are visible in the National Archives, Washington DC, Motion Picture Branch
29. *Radio Address by M Raymond Aron of Le Figaro*, in NA RG 286, OSR Information Divn, Office of Director, General Subject Files 1948–49 *Publicity and Information 1949* sub-file*
30. Letter Friendly to C Houston, Director of Information, ECA Washington 31 Aug 1948, in NA RG 286, OSR Information Division, Office of Director, General Subject Files 1948–49, 'Huse (Personal File)'*
31. Report *ECA in Action* by Alexander S Keller 13 Oct 1950, in NA RG 286, ECA Washington, Office of Information, Office of Director, Country Subject Files *Netherlands*
32. Memo Henry S Reuss to A Friendly 25 Feb 1949, in NA RG 286, OSR Information Divn, Office of Director *Publicity and Information 1949* sub-file*
33. Ibid*
34. Memo Thomas K Hodges Editorial Research & Analysis Section, to R Drummond 19 Oct 1949, in NA RG 286, OSR Information Divn, Office of Director *Policy (1949)* sub-file*
35. Ibid pp 165–71; Milward *The Reconstruction* op cit pp 320–34; Hogan op cit pp 298–309

* These materials are examined further in Ellwood *The Marshall Plan and the politics of growth*. In Stirk PMR and Willis D (eds) *Shaping Post war Europe. European Unity and Disunity 1945–1957* 1991.

36. Hogan op cit pp 87, 210, 273–4
37. Milward *The Reconstruction* op cit p 211
38. Report *Productivity Trip to Italy (June 11–16, 1950)*, in NA RG 286, OSR Labor Information, Office of Economic Adviser, Country Subject Files 1949–50 *Italy-Productivity (General)* sub-file*
39. Italian case in ECA *Italy Country Study 1950**; for British experience Pelling *Britain and Marshall Plan* 1988 pp 34–7
40. Milward op cit p 360
41. Ibid pp 357–8
42. Monnet op cit pp 289–92
43. Ibid p 293
44. Ibid p 295 (emphasis in original)
45. Milward op cit Ch 12; Bullock op cit pp 769–83; Bullen R An Idea Enters Diplomacy: The Schuman Plan, May 1950. In Bullen et al op cit; Berghahn *The Americanisation of West German Industry 1945–1973* Leamington Spa 1986 p 132ff; Urwin DW *The Community of Europe: A History of European Integration since 1945* 1991 (a companion volume in this series) Ch 4 (cit, from Attlee, p 46)
46. Milward op cit pp 403–7; Bullock op cit pp 783–90; Warner The Labour Governments op cit pp 72–4; Acheson op cit Ch 42
47. Milward op cit p 398
48. Ibid p 418; Milward implies that as it eventually developed, the ECSC was in fact a cartel (at least in its external defences), and the Americans were thus forced to swallow 'a reversal of thirty years of American foreign policy' (p 400). But this dramatisation ignores the American assumption that the protectionist barriers maintained or put in place by the Coal and Steel Community (as by all its successors), would be temporary, part of their great illusion of instant unity.
49. Urwin op cit pp 51–7 (cits at pp 53, 55, 56); on the reservations of German industrialists, Berghahn op cit p 137–54
50. Bullock op cit p 769; Milward op cit p 418
51. Marjolin op cit p 19

CHAPTER TEN
From Korea to Recovery

In mid-summer 1950 Howard Smith of CBS was invited to give his views of the new Europe to a distinguished audience at the Royal Institute of International Affairs in London. He was lavish in his appreciation of the achievements:

> In France, the currency black market, which had become, with Notre Dame and the Eiffel Tower, almost a characteristic feature of French life, has died an ignominious death. That volatile symbol of all French life, the French franc, suddenly hardened, and there is no longer an advantage in dealing on the unofficial kerb exchange. Everywhere I have been, even in crushed Germany, the shop windows are filling up, life is perceptibly brighter, a certain abundance is beginning to grow evident.

Smith's eminent colleague, the American writer and broadcaster Theodore H. White, later confirmed the widespread sensation in the early months of the new decade that hope in the future at last was justified: 'Happy days seemed close at hand, and the individual triumphs of the Marshall Plan stood out crisp and brilliant.' In his eloquent volume on Europe at mid-century, *Fire in the Ashes*, White recalled how 'In every country in Europe there was some outstanding project to which a Congressman or visiting delegation of distinguished Americans could be taken and told, here is the Marshall Plan at work.'

In Sardinia there was malaria eradication, in Holland the reclamation of arable land from the Zuyder Zee, in Turkey 'Marshall Plan ploughs, tractors, railways, were changing an Asian way of life.' In France mechanisation of the coal-mines and electrification of the railways were going ahead, and the first continuous strip-steel mill in Europe was being built, promising goods most Europeans still lived without: 'cheap refrigerators, cheap automobiles, cheap tinned foods, cheap washbasins and sinks'.[1]

This was the prospect when the Cold War suddenly showed its full capacity to threaten the hopes and aspirations of Americans and Europeans alike from one day to the next. With no warning at all to the great majority of people in the Old World, a crisis sparked off by a small Communist regime in the Far East demonstrated in a single blow just how peace and prosperity were linked in the new era of American supremacy.

THE 1950 EMERGENCY

Looking back in 1953 on the relations between America and Europe since the outbreak of the Korean War in June 1950, Theodore White summed up the impact of events with his characteristic clarity:

> When the Communist armies of the Orient invaded South Korea in 1950, a tidal wave of panic swept the whole world and momentarily submerged the separate impulses of England, France and Germany. In that moment of peril nothing seemed more important to any of them than that their lives be defended. Thus, between 1950 and 1953, mighty achievements were written up in Europe as NATO took up arms and as the organs of European Unity [sic] were fashioned to protect one and all.

Among the Marshall Plan nations Britain, Belgium, France, the Netherlands, Greece and Turkey sent forces to participate in the campaign led by the United States under the United Nations banner.

Forty years after the start of the conflict commentators in Europe paid little attention to the anniversary. But in America there was reflection on how the war had come to be forgotten, swept away irretrievably by 'the "American High" of 1950s prosperity, domesticity and world power'. Historians and surviving protagonists, however, agreed on its extraordinary impact. The armed forces were transformed by it in size, quality and reach. Traditional isolationism was killed off, thrust aside by the impulses identified today as 'global unilateralism'. All the varieties of militant anti-Communism – temporarily even McCarthyism – were legitimised and amplified to a potency sufficient for them to echo through succeeding generations.[2]

Among its more or less immediate political results the conflict

- provoked the greatest internal convulsion in the United States since the pre-Second World War battles of 1939–40;
- hastened the end of the New Deal/Democratic hold on the White House, stretching back to 1932;
- killed off the Marshall Plan in its original, most well-known form;

176

– brought 'the largest military spending program in history';[3]
– transformed the North Atlantic Treaty into an effective defence system (NATO), and developed 'Atlanticism' as a pseudo-ideological cement for it;
– opened the way to German rearmament, and to proposals for the creation of a European army;
– split the Labour cabinet in Britain and greatly accelerated its demise.

Writing in 1951, the observers of the Council on Foreign Relations in New York struggled to maintain their calm and balance as they reflected on the course of events over the previous year. But in the aftermath of the escalation of October and November, as the US-led advance into North Korea was followed by Chinese intervention in the war, they clearly felt overwhelmed:

> In the last two months of 1950 the nations of the world suddenly found themselves engaged in an ordeal as darkly perilous as any in human history ... In its bearing upon the destinies of mankind it could be compared without presumption to the era of the Persian wars, the fall of Rome, or the pagan incursions into mediaeval Europe; in scale and universality of impact, if not of violence, it exceeded even the two global contests already recorded in the annals of the twentieth century.[4]

Already becoming harsher before Korea in response to a perceived new 'recklessness' in Soviet behaviour, American world policy had by now clearly changed in character. Policies were seen to be 'tough' and 'realistic' the more they concentrated on anti-Communism. Hostility towards the Soviet bloc was intensified at all levels; 'new and more exacting standards were set for the performance of nations already established in American friendship'.[5]

Reconstruction or defence?

As the logic of the NATO vision became clear, the long-developing tension between military and reconstruction priorities in each nation's economic policies burst into the open. After the North Atlantic Treaty had been ratified by Congress in July 1949 a number of West European nations had applied to the United States for military aid, and the Mutual Defense Assistance Program (MDAP) had come into being in October. Now, while a huge mobilisation began aimed at increasing the American armed forces from 1.5 million to 3.5 million by mid 1951, MDAP was expanded from a $1.2 billion effort to one costing over $5 billion. 'Clear priority' to economic recovery had been insisted on when MDAP was originally authorised. But in the new situation the ERP was completely eclipsed. Its funding receded to $2.25 billion for 1951 as intense debate broke out over the relative merits of military and economic aid.

In the confrontation on the 1952 budget, the 'guns first' lobby triumphed: Europe was assigned little more than $1 billion for economic aid, $4.8 billion for military support. The Marshall Plan itself was doomed. The ECA was ordered to close its doors not as scheduled in mid 1952 but at the end of 1951 to make way for a new Mutual Security Agency (MSA). When it had decided on much tougher stands in early 1950, the Administration still feared Congressional complacency and isolationism; Korea 'was what saved us', said the Secretary of State, Acheson, referring to the budget challenge. The global view of containment and the full Cold War mentality in Washington date from this time, say today's strategic experts. In the months between August and December 1950, the US defence budget passed from $15.5 billion to $42 billion; by the end of 1951 it had risen to just under $70 billion.[6]

On one level the Europeans were reassured by the instant and total American conviction that the South Korean invasion was part of a world-wide Soviet manoeuvre of aggression. They understood that West European defence was now more than ever a supreme strategic commitment for the United States, and saw that America was ready to go to war for such commitments, no matter how far away or how unprepared America's own forces. So there was satisfaction in Western Europe when Truman promised the dispatch of American divisions and when Eisenhower arrived early in 1951 to head the new NATO integrated military force (absorbing the one created up to then by the Brussels Pact powers).

But the Europeans were told by Washington in no uncertain terms in the following months and years that rearmament should henceforth be their key national priority, and that the United States would help most those who helped themselves. Neither the message nor its tone was welcome. As the Council on Foreign Relations commentators said:

> European governments were more interested in preserving their recent economic gains and keeping domestic tax rates and living standards within politically tolerable limits; thus they tended to expect more from the United States and proportionately less from their own peoples.[7]

The dilemma was particularly fraught in the case of Britain and France, the only powers of significant military weight on the scene, both already engaged militarily against 'insurgency' in Malaya and Indochina. 'For both of them . . . the task of rearmament presented problems much more serious than was apparent from hasty examination of the statistics on their economic recovery.' Output, standards of living and balance of payments situations were already strained to the limits in both countries, with the French burdened additionally by the tendency of fiscal policies (or the lack of them) to throw extra strain 'on the politically disaffected poorer classes', as the New York experts delicately identified them. In their view, France's 'special sensitivity to social disturbances ... exemplified the dangers that would be involved in any attempt to build military strength at the expense of popular welfare.'[8]

THE CRISIS OF THE MARSHALL PLAN

Rearmament

Throughout the ECA it was recognised that the strains of rearmament could produce 'internal security crises' in countries such as France and Italy, or at best sceptical neutralism of a kind evident in public opinion in a number of countries and articulated most effectively by *Le Monde*.[9] Nevertheless, said a Washington telegram to ECA Missions, 'We must recognise that goal of placing Europe in posture own immediate self-defence is an objective which over-rides in immediate importance any one of the economic goals we and European leaders have established in past two years.'[10]

But the ECA men on the ground had already decided that there was no conflict between the defence and the ERP objectives: it was just a matter of bending the existing policy goals to the new requirements. An August 1950 paper produced in Paris showed how, in order to increase European 'stability, self-confidence and, therefore, self-respect', the existing policy themes might be transposed:

(1) Marshall aid and military assistance are good for you because they give you – as Europeans – a fighting chance to make Europe strong enough to discourage any aggression.
(2) *But* – this strength can only be achieved through unity. As separate, rival powers, the nations of Free Europe *are* weak, *are* dangerously exposed.
(3) Productivity must increase because more food, more machines, more of nearly everything is needed to make Europe so strong it will be unassailable.[11]

The ECA's pollsters surveyed approximately 2,000 people in the middle of 1950, covering France, Norway, Denmark, Holland, Austria, Italy and Trieste. An average of 80 per cent of those polled knew of the ERP and 75 per cent approved of it (outside France, 55 per cent was the minimum), with 25–40 per cent having a detailed knowledge of how it worked. But as commentators remarked, it was among the minorities not 'on the team' that the key targets were to be found: the workers and peasants. They were the ones most seriously doubting America's motives, just as Communist propaganda prompted them to do.[12]

Realising that mobilisation for rearmament was a challenge to established attitudes and expectations as much as to economic goals, the Marshall Plan men on the ground intensified their propaganda offensive. Henceforth they openly referred to it in terms of 'psychological warfare', not least because it also embraced a large-scale 'black' or subversive dimension with a substantial intelligence gathering capacity.[13]

But the Americans were under no illusions as to the difficulties they faced. The start of the Korean War, far from being the propaganda boon that the United States and its European allies expected, was at first successfully construed by the Left to show that the ERP and NATO were, as they had always claimed, means to drag Europe into America's wars. In a top level analysis of two and a half years of effort carried out for the Paris headquarters, it was admitted that knowledge of the Marshall Plan and its popularity were by that time – November 1950 – stagnant. While the percentage of the population opposing the Plan in countries such as France and Italy was smaller than the Communist vote, still the doubts persisted in 'much too great a segment of the European population' round the question of 'whether US policy was aimed at progressive improvement in general living standards or was designed more to shore up economic and social systems which are not popular and to restore to power reactionary and conservative vested interests'.[14] The top Americans in Europe considered they had been 'led down the garden path' in countries such as France, Germany and Italy, where their investments showed so few signs of paying visible social or political dividends. They believed, said a British observer, 'that really strenuous efforts . . . from the masses cannot be expected unless "social justice" figured as part and parcel' of all future schemes to raise production for defence. The British version of welfare socialism, long regarded with suspicion, now acquired new favour in American eyes.[15]

But in the European ruling groups generally, morale and attitudes were considered unsatisfactory by the ECA, with 'neutralism, pacifism, we-don't-want-to-be-occupiedism' spreading, according to the London mission. Restoring self-esteem was the key priority in this view, which meant 'helping them regain dignity and influence in an [international] community which perhaps is changed but in which they can continue to play a useful part'. In this context 'European economic and political unification' (the phrase was standard) continued to play a key role, even if this meant running the risk of encouraging neutralism, and was in contrast with 'the drive for the military unification of the North Atlantic'.[16]

The politics of productivity after March 1950

In the years following, each of these themes received dramatic new emphasis, but none more than the productivity motif. Congressional amendments to the original ERP Act in 1951 and 1952 provided $400 million more for this purpose alone. Senator Benton, distinguished founder of the *Encyclopedia Britannica* in America and of the Benton and Bowles advertising agency, stumped the capitals of Europe himself as sponsor of one of the amendments. He aimed to demonstrate that while *Europeans believed in capital, Americans believed in capitalism*, and he explained that the difference was about untrammelled competition, or as a fellow believer in ECA put it, 'overcoming tariff barriers, restrictive trade practices and the other inhibiting forces to trade and a higher standard of living'.[17]

Most of the funds assigned under the Marshall Plan to 'technical assistance' – the great programme of exchanges, training centres, model factories, films, magazines and conferences, involving all levels of European industry – were spent after the Korean outbreak under a new 'Production Assistance Drive'. The point of exporting American engineering, production and marketing skills in this fashion, said the campaign's director, was to persuade participants to 'accept the American definition of the social and economic desirabilities [sic] of productivity'. This now meant guarantees that the benefits of new technology and methods would be shared equally 'amongst the three basic groups – labor, stockholders and the consumers', providing in this way, among other benefits, 'one of the underlying solutions to the Communist problem'.[18]

The culmination of this extraordinary effort, and in many ways of the entire Marshall Plan, was the European Manifesto signed by OEEC ministers (with American prompting and after many concessions to national sensibilities) in August 1951. While re-emphasising European cooperation and trade and payments liberalisation in particular, the declaration placed supreme emphasis on the goal of a 25 per cent production increase in five years. The means? Improved labour productivity with guaranteed redistribution of the proceeds: 'By this large increase in production, improvement in living standards and further social progress can in the course of this period be achieved while meeting defense requirements.' Such an increase had been achieved in the previous three years alone, said the Manifesto, 'by the hard work of [European] peoples and the generous help of the US'. Civilian and military requirements were assigned equal priority in the declaration, which repeatedly insisted that policies must be based on 'social justice' and assurances of 'continuous employment'. Sacrifices for defence were necessary but temporary, the Manifesto declared, so that 'progressively, a growing surplus will be available to raise supplies of consumers' goods'.[19]

GUNS AND BUTTER IN THE KOREAN PHASE: SIX COUNTRY STUDIES*

The setting

By the time the long boom was drawing to its close after the middle of the 1960s, the Korean War could be seen in Europe as little more than the final, decisive impulse which had set off the great expansion and proved that the European postwar economy was 'all-but depression-free'. Economists talked of a specific Korean boom, during which the European product as a whole expanded by an annual rate well above 4 per cent. This was the rate at which the national products of France, the Netherlands, and Norway expanded. Austria did even better, approaching 6 per cent, while West Germany outdid all the rest at 8.7 per cent per annum. This surge ended in 1952, but in 1953 the strongest of all the phases of expansion opened, with even higher annual growth rates and a clear, historical division emerging between the leaders – Germany, France and Italy – and the laggers, Britain, Belgium and Denmark. Naturally, suggested the economist Michael Postan, commenting on these figures in 1967, 'when followed step by step the upward movement of the European economy may well appear less smooth than it was'. Of no phase was Postan's magisterial understatement truer than that which began with the outbreak of the Korean conflict.[20]

---

* ERP Missions wrote yearly 'Country Studies' on the progress of their host nation in the light of the Plan.

The war's immediate economic impact has been summarised as follows by Michael Hogan:

> The European NATO countries increased their defense expenditures from $4.4 bn in 1949 to $8 bn in 1951. Partly because of this stimulus, industrial production in Western Europe climbed 62 per cent above the level of 1947. At the same time, however, the enormous expenditures for defense combined with the high price of commodity imports and the shortage of raw materials to generate inflation and erode Western Europe's overall trade balance. Between July 1950 and June 1951, the cost of living increased 20 per cent in France, and between 9 and 10 per cent in Great Britain, West Germany and Italy.

Exceptional pressures were put on world raw material supplies, and hence on their prices, by the expansion in the American defence effort. The short-term result was to undo much of the progress towards international financial equilibrium realised in the first years of the Marshall Plan:

> In the second quarter of 1951, Western Europe's commodity deficit averaged $650m. a month. The dollar gap started to widen again and the gold and dollar reserves of the participating countries began to decline, after having grown by $2.4 bn in the fifteen months following the devaluations of September, 1949. Industrial production also began to taper off in the summer of 1951, due in large part to raw material shortages.[21]

In no country was the destabilising effect of the Korean conflict felt more deeply than in the United Kingdom. Such was the surge in dollar earnings of the sterling area as America rearmed that the British had agreed with pride that they would receive no Marshall Aid in 1951. Within a year they were again in deep financial crisis and seeking renewed American support.

Britain

In spite of all that had happened in the Cold War and the start to winding down the Empire, the British armed forces were reduced by half between 1947 and 1950. In the government's 'Economic Survey for 1950', which came out in March of that year, defence was dealt with in a single paragraph which stated that the reduction would continue. But according to Winston Churchill speaking in July 1950, in Germany ten unarmoured and two armoured West European divisions faced over eighty Soviet divisions, of which twenty-five to thirty were tank formations. Under American prodding and the likes of Churchill's, the British immediately put rearmament at the top of the government's economic priorities. They raised conscription to two years and expressed their intention to create three new divisions, part of an overall effort which would lift defence spending from 8 to 10 per cent of GNP, but which was still explicitly dependent on new American support, estimated at £550 million 'payable in advance'.[22]

In the event none of this money was forthcoming and at the beginning of April 1951 yet another austerity budget was introduced. Income tax was increased by sixpence in the pound; purchase tax on cars, radios and domestic appliances was doubled; the tax on distributed profits went up from 30 to 50 per cent. Charges were introduced for the first time in certain sectors of the famous Health Service, over the vehement protests of its patron saint, the eloquent Welsh exponent of the Left Aneurin Bevan, who resigned, ridiculing the government's preoccupations and its devotion to American orders.

Less than a month after this Budget the Festival of Britain was officially opened by the King as 'an official celebration of Britain's recovery from the war'. It ran for five months and attracted 8 million people in London alone. Yet instead of reviving the government's popularity, if anything it stimulated appetites for the good times everyone assumed were just around the corner. With the British social contract firmly in place, 'there was nothing to shield the Labour government from the full force of the popular clamour for more consumer goods', comments Paul Addison.[23] The week after the Festival ended Attlee's exhausted team resigned. Churchill came back, narrowly winning the general election on a manifesto which held out hopes of talks with the Russians while insisting on building the British A-bomb. It also promised unprecedented numbers of new houses.

The American Ambassador to London commented:

> Brits are proud and sturdy people who have worked hard to recover from immense damage of two world wars. A year ago they were convinced they had achieved substantial success and were looking forward to further economic gains and hoped for an easing of international tension. This situation has been substantially altered and they have now been plunged back into serious economic difficulties which will affect their attitudes as well as their well being. Although often loath to admit it, thoughtful Brits realize that they are overextended economically, politically and militarily . . . There is no doubt that Churchill's principal objective is to re-emphasize close and intimate relationship between US and UK.[24]

In October 1950 the Cabinet Defence Committee had seen the Korean involvement as 'a useful demonstration of the United Kingdom's capacity to act as a world power with the support of the Commonwealth'. The Committee felt that 'we no longer had to rest content with the knowledge that we were a Great Power, but were becoming able, for the first time since the war, to sustain our world-wide commitments'. In particular the government hoped to show the Americans that Britain had regained her independent economic status and rejected the image of the UK as 'just another necessitous European nation'. In NATO, especially, the British thought that they could 'sit at the table on a basis of equality', as the Foreign Office put it after the new government arrived.[25]

But the Americans were never taken in. They recognised that a 'Special Relationship' existed with the UK and hoped that the NATO alliance would attain 'the moral quality of a partnership' for all its members. But when it came to 'burden sharing' – the great NATO bone of contention for the subsequent forty years – aid would always be aid, no matter what name was used.[26]

The last Labour Chancellor, Gaitskell, had thanked the Americans for their $2.7 billion of Marshall Aid, celebrating it as Britain's 'means to regain her economic independence and power'.[27] Although the largest beneficiary, the British Marshall Plan allotments in fact 'amounted to only 2½ per cent of Britain's national production and 12 per cent of her total imports', in the words of a contemporary account.

> More significant, they provided 57 per cent of her dollar imports and large fractions of essential foods and materials (aluminum 4/5; tobacco, sugar and petroleum 1/2; raw cotton 3/5; wheat 1/3). By the 'suspension' of Marshall Aid at the end of 1950, Britain was the first member of the ERP to attempt standing entirely on her own feet.

The Counterpart fund was employed to retire short-term public debt, rather than industrial renewal as elsewhere, to the dismay of the ECA men in London. It was another symptom of the fact that, as the ERP's semi-official historian recorded, 'American influence upon British economic thought and practice was less than in most of the other participating countries.'[28]

In public the Anglo-American Productivity Council's efforts in adult education reached a new pitch of intensity. One hundred and thirty-eight teams of managers, workers and technical specialists travelled to see at first hand in America 'the appreciation by workpeople of the need for higher productivity, the progressive attitude of management and the spirit of competition' prevailing there, as a report put it. The upper echelons of the TUC were enthusiastic, and the Fabian wing of the Labour Party, particularly the Chancellor Gaitskell, became deeply involved in the new American drive.

But elsewhere there was much scepticism. Industrialists and trade unionists were not slow to object to the idealised view of America being conveyed, and they pointed out, says Anthony Carew, that historically it was 'the high cost of labour in the US that had given rise to the high degree of mechanisation'. In Britain, 'the relation of wage costs to capital costs was the exact opposite'. In its final report in September 1952, the AAPC acknowledged how difficult it was to keep the productivity faith, 'in days when heavy taxation reduces incentives, when the steady supply of raw materials is uncertain, when limitations on capital expenditure restrict development, or when recessions in trade threaten employment. Yet there is no other way whereby the world can obtain a better standard of life.'[29]

The costs of over-extension soon became apparent to the Conservative government. The balance of payments situation appeared worse even than in 1947 or 1949; rationing still continued and in January 1952 the meat ration was actually reduced and the overseas travel allowance cut to £25. As the country strained under a rearmament effort bigger than all the other West European programmes put together, a condition of exhaustion and pessimism took hold of the Westminster establishment which would never be truly banished. Churchill's private secretary, John Colville, wrote in June 1952:

> It is foolish to continue living with illusions . . . the facts are stark. At the moment we are just paying our way. A trade recession in America will break us; the competition of German metallurgical industries and the industrialisation of countries which were once the market for our industrial products will ruin our trade sooner or later . . .
>
> What can we do? Increasing productivity is only a palliative in the face of foreign competition. We cannot till sufficient soil to feed 50 million people. We cannot emigrate fast enough to meet the danger, even if we were willing to face the consequent abdication of our position as a great power . . . Lord Cherwell [adviser to the prime minister on atomic energy] sees hope in the union of the English-Speaking World [*sic*; a Churchillian phrase] . . . . But now England, and Europe, distrust, dislike and despise the United States. Some pin their faith on the development of the Empire as a great economic unit . . . . We have left it too late . . . .[30]

A wide historical consensus now exists which states that the Korean armament effort set a pattern of gross over-spending on defence which caused permanent damage to Britain's economic prospects. At the end of 1953 the American Ambassador pointed out that the total tax burden was 'substantially heavier than in any other NATO country', including the United States.[31]

Yet by 1953 there were clear signs of a new kind of expansion. A dollar balance was struck for the first time since the war, while the country began to be drawn into the great West European trade boom. Certain industries, particularly motor vehicles, did very well out of the defence drive, and unemployment declined to a negligible 1.5 per cent.

As price and rationing controls were abolished on a wide range of items from white bread to building materials, the British version of the mixed economy would find itself on the verge of its greatest prosperity.[32]

France

France had come second only to Britain in the distribution of American aid and, says Rioux, enjoyed 'the largest share of free grants (23.8 per cent), a compensation no doubt for her diplomatic concessions over the German question and in recognition of her efforts in favour of European reconstruction'. Unlike scholars in other participating countries, Rioux does not tend to minimise the role of ERP support in national expansion:

> . . . not only did these dollars – which represented 48 per cent of the Fonds de modernisation et d'équipement for the period (April 1948 to January, 1952) – come at the critical moment to boost investment and planning, but American control of their distribution was minimal, left in fact to French officials to decide. With industrial output rising and trade reviving, the closing of the 'dollar gap', and the modernisation of production, the economic benefits directly attributable to Marshall Aid were incontestable.[33]

'This certainty', Rioux continues, 'makes even more surprising the French reluctance to acknowledge the advantages of American aid.'

In Paris in mid 1950 only 35 per cent declared they had even heard of the Marshall Plan and in France as a whole 64 per cent of those who had heard of it felt it was bad for the country.[34] But France was a special case, the only country with opposition on this scale, and the one in which the November 1950 ECA poll found the government's rating on economic policy down to 3 per cent in favour, (with two coalitions having already fallen in 1949 and 1950 on the issue of more money for lower-income groups). When French men and women were asked on this occasion 'which political party they felt was looking out for the interests of the working man 21 per cent named the Communist party and 13 per cent named the Socialists. In a sample of over 2000 people, no respondent ever mentioned any other party,' reported an appalled ECA man.[35]

So the party's total devotion to the twists and turns of Soviet policy, not to mention Stalinist methods and style, was effectively compensated by the persistently low standards of living to which the working classes were still confined. Widespread strikes in the spring of 1951 would be exploited by the Communists, said the American Ambassador, but were really due to the fact that the purchasing power of industrial workers was still below the 1938 levels. The 10 per cent inflation rate meant that in 1952 real wages remained 36 per cent below those of 1936. 'The infrastructure of industry had been rebuilt in the postwar years at the expense of the working class,' writes Carew, 'and inequality had increased.'[36]

None of the elements in the tripartite scheme of things favoured by the ECA responded well to Marshall Plan prescriptions. The government was menaced at one point with a threat to tie Counterpart funding to the development of a positive social programme, and was called on after Korea to spend more on low-cost housing for defence workers.[37] Industry and business were 'divided among themselves over the desirability of modernisation', and suspicious of Monnet's 'attempt to incorporate features of American industrial life in the planning process'. His exhortations to emulate the Americans in their emphasis on constant change and on positive states of mind were rarely welcome, not least as his efforts favoured in the first instance nationalised industries over the private sector.[38] Having been attacked, divided and weakened by the elements in the American power game fighting the Cold War in France, the unions were unlikely to be sympathetic to the ERP productivity drive, no matter how earnest its dedication to collective bargaining and redistribution.[39]

The immediate reaction of the government to Korea and the American demand for rearmament was 'to make a public commitment not to increase defence at the expense of living standards', reports Frances Lynch. In exchange for pledges of dollar support, it was agreed that the French should complete their air force programme in three not five years, and double their general rearmament effort over three years. For their part, the French were most anxious to see NATO reinforced, suggesting practical mechanisms to organise truly collective defence. But they were fundamentally hostile to any notion linking American aid to their acquiescence in German rearmament, hence their proposal for a semi-autonomous 'European Defence Community' to parallel the Schuman Plan.

Eleven per cent in deficit even including Counterpart and military support funds and various tax rises, the budget passed in May 1951 provided for a heavier defence expenditure proportionately than any other country: 10.52 per cent rising to 14–16 per cent in 1952–53. All agreed that only increased production – perhaps 4 per cent per annum – would square the circle so that consumption could be protected, but the fall-off in the ERP meant that the public investment to produce this growth actually declined. As the payments situation worsened and inflation soared to a level higher than anywhere else in Western Europe, the economy was subject to the inevitable squeeze: reduced credit, increased interest rates, tourist allowances cut, trade liberalisation suspended. Stagnation set in: while West German industrial production grew 39 per cent between 1951 and 1953, France's grew only 9 per cent. Today's analysts conclude that rearmament in France weakened the drive for modernisation, diverting resources from productive investment and undermining the franc.[40]

When the first general election since 1946 was fixed for June 1951, an atmosphere of intense political crisis prevailed. The causes were not immediately economic but a combination of conflicts: there were financial scandals, education arguments reminiscent of the Third Republic, and intense disputes over the Indochina war. Even more divisive were the efforts of the government to pass an electoral law which would minimise the impact of the two 'anti-parliamentary' forces, the Communists and the Gaullists. When the votes were counted the PCF and the RPF nevertheless emerged from the contest as the largest parties. Though losing almost half a million votes, the Communists still reached almost 5 million, or 25.6 per cent of the total (but under the special law it lost 42 per cent of its parliamentary seats). The Gaullists had taken more than 4 million, equivalent to 21.56 per cent. Only the manipulation of the electoral law prevented the Fourth Republic from destruction.

De Gaulle was thwarted and appalled by the outcome, but his impact had already been greatly reduced by the general Cold War mobilisation post-Korea. He now lost interest in his *Ralliement* movement, retiring to write his memoirs. Yet expert comment generally concurred with the State Department judgement that the outcome 'indicated a definite rightist and nationalist trend'.[41]

This was confirmed by the investiture as Prime Minister in March 1952 of a former member of the Vichy government. The centrist parties which dominated the game of coalition making and breaking proved 'patently incapable of producing durable majorities', comments Rioux. The foreign policy they pursued in Indochina, Algeria and elsewhere was almost entirely barren and futile. In contrast the contribution made by them to the organisation of Europe by the revolution in their policy towards Germany was, as we shall see, enormous. Above all they ensured that the fruits of sacrifice and planning for the long term would eventually be gathered. By spring 1951, whatever the immediate stresses and strains

> the long months of shortages were over and a new ease was in the air, a feeling that mass consumption was just around the corner . . . France could

begin to count her locomotives and babies, and appetites for the fruits of sustained economic growth were already being whetted. After the crisis, the war and the deprivations, a repaired economy was at last starting to offer fresh hopes and new horizons.[42]

West Germany

'In the years 1949–53 the Federal Republic spent more of its national income on social welfare than any other comparable state,' writes Anthony Nicholls.[43] Counting the homeless, the destitute, the war invalids and the refugees or 'expellees', many of them among the over 2 million unemployed, the figure of needy in 1950 is thought to have been close to 17 million. This in a country where the total number in work was 21.5 million. 'The most glaring [social] need, and the most complicated to meet quickly, was housing,' report West Germany's latest historians, the Americans Bark and Gress: 'In 1950, approximately 16 million households in the Federal Republic had 10.1 million housing units to share between them.' Of the 2.3 million housing units destroyed during the war, 1.6 million had been rendered usable again between 1945 and 1949. 'This was only half the problem. Many of those who did have housing in 1950 lived in squalid circumstances, under appalling conditions . . .'.[44]

Adenauer and his government touched the nadir of their popularity in 1950. As thirty points were added to the inflation index in a year, the percentage approving their policies fell in polls to 23 per cent. Ludwig Erhard commented retrospectively: 'It was self-evident that a people as experienced in inflation as the Germans should have reacted to an event such as Korea in so sensitive a manner. In other words, everyone went off the rails a little.'[45]

But the Social Market economy, say Bark and Gress, was never intended to deliver instant prosperity for all; its benefits would come in the medium term. Fortunately for Erhard, 'international conditions, in particular the Korean War, unleashed the full power of the German economy much more rapidly than anyone was able to anticipate in 1949'.[46]

Although Erhard denied that Korea was decisive, undoubtedly the great Western rearmament drive generated 'an insatiable demand for precisely the kind of industrial products that West Germany was permitted and encouraged to produce under agreements in force and under discussion' with the western allies':

They needed not only steel, including German steel, but also many products, including machinery and chemicals, that only Germany, because it was forbidden to produce armaments, could deliver in large quantities ... Beginning in February 1951, foreign currency began flowing into, instead of out of, West Germany. [47]

Yet in spite of Erhard's enthusiasm for the American way and the continuing special attention given to the country as the future motor of European expansion by the occupation authorities and the Marshall Planners, West Germany's development path emerged as a very special one: 'there was no immediate or easy transformation of industrial life along the lines desired by the Americans' writes the British industrial historian Anthony Carew. [48]

According to the earliest formulations, for instance that of Erhard in February 1948, investment would be 'financed by [Marshall] aid, while German incomes at the low, medium and high level can be used essentially for consumption'.[49] But General Clay and the ECA insisted that private capital formation would do most of the work, and that projects could not be launched without cast-iron guarantees on the German administration's dedication to financial and monetary stability. In the first ERP year no Counterpart funds were released for investment projects, apart from small quantities in the French zone. Even at its height in 1950, Counterpart financed no more than 12.8 per cent of net fixed capital investment; by 1951 the figure was down to 5 per cent. Although these sums were important – they broke bottlenecks in the coal, railway and energy sectors, then after Korea in steel – they fell foul of political conflict between the ECA and Erhard. There were very explicit limits to the amount of planning the Minister for Economic Affairs would accept from outside. The Americans in fact considered the Social Market vision risky and dogmatic, leaving too much to the market in very uncertain times and too long delaying the benefits to German consumers. In the reordering of priorities after the Korean crisis they attempted to have it completely suspended.[50]

Meanwhile, at the most basic aid level, military supplies would always count more quantitatively than those of the ERP. Only 17 per cent of the Bizone's imports in the first year arrived under the Marshall Plan and most of those were food, plus some raw materials. The order would soon be reversed, but there was never the level of capital goods imports seen in countries like France or Italy.[51]

When the Federal Government was set up, however, the whole thrust of the Marshall Plan in Germany had been changed. A special ERP Ministry under the Vice-Chancellor was created and it helped convert the American aid programme into an important form of 'risk insurance', easing the pains of an export-led expansion which was based on repressing home demand by deflation. At the same time West

Germany took a leading role in the EPU and in the whole liberalisation process. Policies were developed 'in full agreement with the ECA, [which] aimed at creating an integrated European economic area where the Federal Republic could make its full weight felt', as Abelshauser explains.[52]

The process was already well under way. Exports had grown by 58 per cent between 1948–49 and 1949–50 with the share of manufactures in them growing from 17 to 65 per cent in the same period. Although severely disturbed in the post-Korea upheavals, by October 1951 the country's international balances had recovered to the point where, under the auspices of the semi-liberalised trade and payments system already developed by ECA and EPU, West Germany was able to join the General Agreement on Tariffs and Trade. There the government chose a stance on liberalisation which 'held the middle line between the protectionist tariffs of Britain, France and Italy, and the free-trade policy of Belgium, Denmark and the Netherlands'.[53] The first balance of payments surplus came in 1951–52, and both imports and exports were higher than the levels predicted in the military governors' original submission for West Germany to the OEEC of 1948.

Yet viability was not attained with the dollar area; the great growth of the export trade came inside Western Europe and the surplus in this area was called upon to compensate a dollar deficit which was still substantial in spite of such measures as the creation of a significant German–American Trade Promotion Company. The result, says Gerd Hardach, a German economic historian, 'was exactly the trade triangle which the [1948 plan] had proposed, and which West Germany's OEEC neighbours had at that time criticized as the beginning of a German export offensive'. Again, a pattern had emerged, destined to endure, which could not have existed without American support, but which in certain of its essentials defied American designs.[54]

There were other, if less portentous, conflicts. In spite of their own insistence on monetary rigour, from 1949 the American authorities were complaining of excessive deflation, and, in spite of the figures on welfare spending, of passivity in the government's attitude to unemployment.[55] In the light of the large amount of food imports in Marshall Aid, they urged agricultural development, but at a time when the ERP itself 'made possible an early return to Germany's traditional pattern of production and trade', i.e. exporting manufactures and importing food. Together with the general push towards liberalisation, 'this structural effect was probably the most important contribution to West Germany's economic recovery', writes Hardach.[56]

The 'Americanisation of German industry' visible as a general phenomenon of the 1950s and 1960s, could hardly be said to have started before 1953.[57] This of course was not for lack of effort on the American side. Carew reports:

> Between 1949 and 1952 over 7,600 programmes, many of them study trips, were mounted by the State Department or the High Commission for Germany aimed at opinion formers active in politics, labour, business or the professions . . . the Germans borrowed readily from American industrial practice, especially in relation to methods of mass production, packing and shipping, advertising and marketing . . . the rapid absorption of American technology was a large factor in the rapid growth of the German economy.[58]

Even with the militant support of Erhard, however, the Americans were not able to stamp out the deep-rooted German tendency to create industrial cartels for the purpose of organising competition and managing large-scale wage bargaining. Seeing how efforts to pass an anti-trust law were repeatedly blocked by the major Ruhr industrialists, the *Wall Street Journal* predicted in August 1953 that the attempt 'to sell American-style capitalism to German big business' was likely to fail. Only in mid 1957, in a quite different economic atmosphere, was such a law passed.[59] (In Italy, by way of contrast, a basic anti-trust law was first passed in 1990.)

In a context of this kind the productivity message was likely to fall on stony ground. When the legal and political principle of co-determination was extended to the vital coal and steel industries in a key tripartite accord of 4 January 1951 – which saw the first large-scale wage increases since the war – it was clear that all sides had other priorities on their minds. Yet eventually, by the end of the decade, and after a change of generation at the head of industry, the American way would enjoy its triumph as a particular synthesis of American and German industrial cultures took hold. Management schools, work study associations, a massive national productivity centre, all gave the country 'a corps of trained production engineers which other European countries simply could not match', says Carew, an enduring result 'of years of endeavour and investment under the Marshall Plan'.[60]

But in the era of Adenauer's first government, from 1949 to September 1953 – when the CDU was re-elected with an increase of 50 per cent in its vote – the Chancellor needed more than the support of both sides of industry, and was concerned with much more than the working out of the Social Market theory. The history of this phase, say Bark and Gress, 'is in large part the history of how, by great effort, the Germans, led by "der Alte", restored confidence in themselves, and earned, step by step, the respect of their neighbours'.[61]

Denmark

'In the second half of 1950, the Danish economy more or less broke down,' reports Vibeke Sorensen, in the first full-length research study of the Marshall Plan in Denmark. The ECA Mission was a powerful influence in Copenhagen, but its efforts combined with those of the Social Democratic government failed to build a stable equilibrium between internal development and the new, very unstable world market. Yet however unsuccessful Marshall Plan policies were in Denmark, insists Sorensen, they 'forced through a broad recognition of the necessity of industrialisation and as such laid the foundation for a substantial change in the structure of the Danish economy'.

There were furious battles between the Social Democrats and the Liberal–Conservative opposition, between the believers in Keynesian-style macroeconomic management and the sound money-at-all-costs bankers, between the entrenched interests of agriculture and those who saw that only industrial investment would solve the country's long-term balance of payments problem. As elsewhere, the presence of the ECA and its demand for a four-year budget programme transformed the political weight of the planners. It helped reinforce the authority of the Social Democrat government as a whole, with its belief in full employment, social security and tripartite methods for developing policy and managing conflict. But this combination was not enough to convince the banking sector of the need for an expansionary policy of industrial development, nor could the dominant agricultural interests be persuaded to put the modernisation of the Danish economy as a whole before the defence of their position. As industry was exposed very sharply to the results of OEEC liberalisation investment actually declined as a percentage of GDP between 1948 and 1956.

ECA policy itself, however, was subject to shifts which had little to do with conditions in a country like Denmark. To reconcile the new integrationist push of late 1949 with measures to absorb the effects of the British devaluation – which hit Denmark particularly hard – meant putting monetary stabilisation above full employment and the defence of living standards. Meanwhile trade liberalisation – which excluded agricultural products – and the US insistence on the use of dollars to settle payments deficits between ERP countries aggravated the balance of payments problem even further. The Social Democrats proposed import restrictions, the opposition deflation. The result was an open political battle which brought down the Social Democrats in the autumn of 1950. To the dismay of the ECA men, politics had been allowed to interfere with the self-evidently correct strategies of Marshall Aid. Under the impact of rearmament and Korea the terms of trade deteriorated by a third between 1949 and 1951. Pressures for deflation became more intense, dominating the policy of the new Liberal government and opening a decade of slow growth. But the Americans insisted: the only way out depended on long-term improvements in agricultural and industrial productivity. These efforts eventually bore fruit, but only in the wake of the great boom of the rest of Europe at the end of the 1950s.[62]

Italy

The key question in Italy, according to a *New York Times* correspondent, Michael L. Hoffmann, writing in June 1949, was not the defeat of Communism but whether the country could develop its own authentic capitalism. A real capitalistic mentality, unafraid of risks, enthusiastically in favour of individual initiative, was 'as rare in Italy as a communist on Wall St', according to Hoffman's sources. The market was divided horizontally, a huge gap separating the luxury level and that of the workers and peasants:

Italian industrialists have never shown much interest in the job of adapting their products to the mass market, with the result that the scale of their operations remains small and their costs high. The idea of persuading the low income consumer to feel the need for something he's never had, using advertising, and then to give it to him at a price he can afford, could be the Marshall Plan's biggest contribution to Italy – if it gets anywhere.

Italian Conservatives were far too inclined to use force to hold Communism down, Hoffmann insisted, instead of trying the remedy of mass consumption and mass production. Italian industrialists rigged the feeble market there was and encouraged the unemployed to emigrate. If this mentality could be changed, Marshall Plan administrators expected other obstacles such as high interest rates and the obsession with frugality to disappear as a consequence, Hoffmann reported.[63]

The ECA Mission in Rome had been dismayed to discover that for lack of technical resources (e.g. reliable statistics), the government was 'simply not equipped to conduct a responsible monetary and investment policy'. But worse, the ever-present division between planners and *laissez-faire* believers passed not between government and opposition but through the middle of the local ECA coordinating committee, with the planners far weaker. There was constant American criticism of the government's inability to mount an 'aggressive' investment programme and its insistence on monetary stability above all. The two could be kept in balance, insisted the ECA, by reform and modernisation of the incredibly primitive tax system, and there was a special educational push aimed at the State administrators.[64]

But the Marshall Plan had another formidable adversary in Italy in the unexpected shape of the head of the industrialists, Angelo Costa. Weary of the preaching and prodding of the ECA men, which intensified significantly after Korea, Costa accused them of misunderstanding the context in which they were operating. The State in Italy, he insisted, did not enjoy the historical legitimacy of the US Constitution; instead its laws had long been seen as legalised exploitation and hence were systematically evaded. As for the planning of investment, financial targets and raw materials supplies, this could only cause harm, and in fact the country had already recovered from the war without them: 'In a country where time has created a delicate equilibrium between industry and agriculture, a dense network of relationships not only economic but social in character, innovative measures from above can only create disorder.'

Costa implicitly opposed the spread of large-scale industry and urbanisation, and now expressed his scepticism of the logic of productivity and rising wages. No matter how cheap synthetic textiles became, Italian women would choose to make their own clothes, he said; no matter how cheap tinned food, Italian culinary traditions would always be preferred. The small firm and the artisan tradition would be crucial to Italy's future just as in the past, while the concept of productivity ignored the most fundamental contrast between America and Italy: in the former capital was cheap, labour expensive, whereas in Italy the exact opposite was true.[65]

But this largely static view of Italy's industrial prospects, rooted in a timeless vision of frugality and personal savings as the fount of all riches, was belied by the aggressiveness with which private industry sought to break out of the autarchic patterns of the past and exploit the new opportunities offered by world markets. By 1953 industrial production had doubled since 1938 and annual productivity rises averaged 6.4 per cent, twice the British level. In FIAT output per worker quadrupled between 1948 and 1955 as a result of modernisation with American technology and ever more rigorous work discipline.[66]

The price paid was high. The years from 1948–53 were a period of extreme social tensions in Italy, greatly aggravated by more or less uncontrolled restructuring in industry and a controversial effort to carry through a land reform no longer postponable in view of the mass discontent surging in the South and other peasant areas. While industrial unemployment swelled to more than 2 million, widespread violence broke out in the rural regions. The large feudal land holdings were broken up but over eighty peasants died in the struggles, whose results seemed to leave all sides embittered. The 'southern question' took on its contemporary aspect from this failure, accelerating the need for some form of industrial development but without providing the wherewithal (except in subsidies) for the emergence of a new leadership class.[67]

In the cities wages improved but only slowly, with the result that two-thirds of the average income was still spent on food. The Communist Party increased its hold on Turin, Genoa and the Emilia region, but the limits of its power had been shown in the revolutionary outbreak which followed the attempted assassination of the Communist leader Togliatti in July 1948. Well aware of the strength of the government's power and the geographical and social narrowness of its own base, the party leadership quickly reined in the spontaneous outbreak and reasserted its established forms of mass mobilisation.

But in the harsh economic climate of the times these were not enough to prevent successive waves of violent confrontation on the streets between the unemployed and the police, whose methods aimed at repression at all costs. The evidence mounted that in the short term Christian Democrat techniques of prudence, mediation, clientelism and leaning on the Americans did not work. Strong pressures built up to expel trade unions from factories and to outlaw the PCI (Partito Communista Italiano) altogether. On the Right, as the CD vote plunged from 48.5 per cent (in 1948) to 35.1 per cent in the 1951 local elections, the neo-Fascist and monarchist elements each gathered 5–6 per cent.[68]

Yet, as elsewhere, a longer-term perspective reveals the gradual emergence of a distorted but true development pattern in these years. The emphasis in Marshall imports shifted from 'maccheroni' (i.e. foodstuffs) to 'macchinari' (machine tools), and the beneficiaries were not only FIAT and the steel industry but the electricity generating and chemical sectors. The way forward to Italy's remarkable emergence as a major oil refiner began here. The post–1949 intensification of the ERP brought a concrete initiative for land reform from De Gasperi, linked to the first major investment in the south from Counterpart funds. There was still no coordinated strategy of industrialisation; a variety of sector plans was accompanied by an ever-growing drizzle of money for public works to 'compensate' the weaker sectors of the nation for the success of the others. Again, a pattern had emerged by compromise and improvisation which was destined not just to endure but to prosper.[69]

The outbreak of the Korean War caused yet another escalation in the Left–Right battle, since the Communists and their allies succeeded in identifying a growing anti-war strain in the electorate and in convincing many that the conflict had nothing to do with Italy's essential interests. The financial strain of rearmament was also very great, pushing the government even further into dependence on the United States and on the Mutual Security programme in particular. By 1954 the sums spent by the Pentagon on military orders in Italy would exceed the industrial loans of the entire ERP.[70]

The government in fact 'was united only in its refusal to choose between guns and butter', says the historian D'Attorre, who points out that in spite of its inclinations, the state gradually acquired new planning and management functions, e.g. in the relaunching of the armaments industry. Foreign policy became ever more fervently pro-Atlanticist *and* pro-European, though the hybrid, dualistic development experience which eventually emerged in Italy had little to do with any of the strong models on offer in America and in north Europe. The working class went through more hard years in the early 1950s, and a new drift from the land towards emigration and the cities became evident; the mass of workers and peasants would have to wait some years before seeing the material fruits of their efforts.[71]

Greece

'Korea is the Greece of the Far East,' Truman reportedly told one of his collaborators shortly after the outbreak of hostilities; 'If we are tough enough now, if we stand up to them like we did in Greece three years ago, they won't take over the whole Far East.'[72]

When the 'Third Round' of the war between the Communists and the government ended in October 1949, the aid initiative passed to the civilians in the American Mission. They were then expected to carry out by 1952, in a war-torn land where non-military dollars had gone mostly into feeding refugees and propping up official finances, the ERP tasks more peaceable nations hoped to realise in four. The experts were undaunted. W.H. McNeill, one of their number, wrote soon afterwards:

. . . the Americans set out to reduce the relief rolls which had taken such a large proportion of aid funds in the war years; to restore communications; to expand industrial and agricultural production; and to reform the Greek government. Like Hercules of old, the American mission boldly undertook all these difficult enterprises, intending to sweep the Augean stables clean and erect a gleaming palace upon the battered structure of the Greek economy in no more than two and a half years.[73]

In reality the war, social reality and the primitive nature of the Greek official machine made impossible the kind of economic management taken for granted in other national reconstruction projects: 'the weight of effective opposition to the American program was as great as ever and support for it within the country was almost nonexistent'. This situation remained largely unchanged despite the fact that American money and expertise were applied there more intensively per capita than anywhere else. At its height almost 50 per cent of GNP was due to the ERP, which paid for 64 per cent of the total of civilian imports in 1950.[74]

The most successful modernisation projects were in agriculture, where individual peasants were persuaded by visible results achieved in the space of a few months. The arrival of fertilisers, high-yield wheats and irrigation with all its possibilities allowed the fragmented and backward agricultural sector to regain its prewar output by 1950, well before industry or mining. Largely under the impulse of military necessity, a heavy-duty road network was constructed for the first time, and a 'second wave of modernisation' was set off by the development of a national electricity grid between 1950 and 1955. Among the overall effects of this development 'a really radical change came to older geographical and social relations', wrote McNeill in a 1956 survey: 'urban attitudes and an orientation toward market farming began to penetrate regions formerly set apart by the primitive nature of the transportation system'.[75]

But this impulse to urbanisation was not matched by economic development in the towns, much less industrialisation. The ECA industry experts discovered that 89.6 per cent of 'firms' employed less than five workers in 1950, and 'outdated equipment, outmoded management practices, lack of capital' were the rule, not the exception. The greatest problem in organised change was always the political/ bureaucratic maze into which funds for investment disappeared. Anywhere between one third and over a half of the Counterpart funds remained 'unused', eventually re-emerging to help mitigate the budget deficit.[76]

Even by substituting governments with more reformist-looking

199

alternatives on their own initiative, as in 1950, the Americans failed to obtain a cabinet which had any 'idea of social reform or governmental modernisation *à l'américaine*', as McNeill reflected twenty years later. But by this time it was clear that not all the fault lay on the Greek side; no amount of money or bluster could cancel the original sin of 'naively assum[ing] that Greek society was essentially the same as American society, and needed only a few pointers to duplicate the American New Deal.'[77]

After insisting on scaling down the Greek armed forces and throwing all available resources into economic reconstruction, the reversal of American policy which came in the post-Korea upheaval was inevitably embarrassing. The logic of the new situation implied abandoning the idea that aid would be cut off at a predetermined date in 1952 and facing its indefinite continuation. Worries over cost were thrust aside as a new national mobilisation was ordered to prepare for possible Communist attacks from a number of points around the compass. The original concerns for autonomy and sovereignty faded as a structural relationship of dependence was built between the Greek and American armed services. On the basis of a shared ideology of anti-Communism and a mutual vision of 'preparedness', Greece (and Turkey) were admitted to NATO in February 1952. More significant for the future in McNeill's later view was the fact that 'the Greek army became a state within a state, having more important relations with the American armed forces and NATO planners than with other branches of the Greek government'.[78]

These developments, and the sense of urgency imposed by the new Cold War climax, changed American priorities *vis à vis* the Greek politicians: 'Not change, therefore, but stability and a firm assertion of traditional, national values were what defense against the communist danger seemed to require.' From this shift in perspective emerged the candidacy for the prime minister's position of Field Marshal Alexander Papagos, a de Gaulle-like figure who had commanded the army in the Albanian and anti-guerrilla wars. In the elections of November 1952 the Field Marshal's party, 'Greek Rally', won 49 per cent of the vote and 82 per cent of the seats in parliament, but not before a rejigging of the electoral system at American prompting. It was the first stable administration of the postwar era and 'set the style of public life for the next decade'.[79]

The Papagos era is also associated with the 'take-off' of the national economy into a new phase of expansion and development. Growth in GNP fluctuated wildly at first – 1.0 per cent in 1952, 13.5 per cent in 1953, 3.4 per cent in 1954 – but a more steady average of 6.0 per cent eventually appeared, accompanied by a decline in inflation to an average of 7.4 per cent. Tourism too took off in these years, passing from 16,500 arrivals in 1948 to over 100,000 in 1953, 200,000 in 1956, and so on, ever upwards.[80]

The exact contribution of official policies to these trends remains unclear. Greek social commentators point to the new middle class strata dependent on the state which emerged in these years. Already in evidence under the German occupation, they were greatly favoured by the partial development and internationalisation set off by American aid. More significant, suggest Greek economists, was the momentum given by the arrival of peace and the sheer quantity of US support in all its forms. But most important of all, they say, was the revolution in expectations: 'optimistic and rather constructive', the hopes of the majority were undeterred by the political travails of the various phases. Nothing, it seemed, could 'destroy the faith of the Greeks in their economy'.[81]

NOTES

1. Smith HK An American Looks At Europe. In *International Affairs* Oct 1950 pp 470–6 (speech of 18 July at Royal Institute of International Affairs; cit at p 470); White op cit p 247
2. Dionne EJ Jr Korean Conflict Profoundly Altered US Politics and World Role. In *The Washington Post/Guardian Weekly* 1 July 1990; cf Foot R Making Known the Unknown War: Policy Analysis of the Korean Conflict in the Last Decade. In *Diplomatic History* Summer 1991
3. Ibid
4. USWA 1950 p 395
5. Ibid p 251; cf Jervis R The Impact of the Korean War on the Cold War. In *Journal of Conflict Resolution* Dec 1980, 563–92
6. Jervis op cit pp 584–5; USWA 1950 pp 90–9, 123, 253, 437; Hogan op cit pp 389–93
7. USWA 1950 op cit pp 257–8
8. Ibid p 261
9. *Le Monde* 5 April 1950 (debate in France summarised in *Survey of International Affairs 1949–50* Oxford 1953 pp 145– 50)
10. Tel. OSR to ECA Rome 19 Aug 1950 in NA RG 469, Mission to Italy, Office of Director, Subject Files (Central Files), (1948–1952 *Program-Long Term* sub-file
11. Memo FV Norall to R Drummond 1 Aug 1950 in NA RG 286, OSR Information Divn, Retired Subject File (Information), *Mission Memoranda* sub-file
12. Minutes, Conference of Information Officers, Paris, 28 Aug 1950 in

NA RG 286, OSR Information Divn, Office of Director, General Subject Files 1949–50, *Information Officers* sub-file

13. Carew op cit pp 126–30
14. *Notes for Ambassador Katz Regarding Information* nd but end 1950, in NA RG 286, Central Secretariat, Subject Files 1948–1952, *Public Relations* sub-file
15. Hogan op cit p 411; Watt DC American Aid to Britain and the Problem of Socialism, 1945–51. In Watt (ed) *Personalities and Policies. Studies in the Formation of British Foreign Policy in the Twentieth Century* 1965 esp pp 76–80
16. *Some Notes on Information Policy* summary of comments by Tom Wilson, ECA London, 14 Nov 1950 in NA RG 286 OSR Central Secretariat, Subject Files 1948–1952 *Public Relations* sub-file; cf Hogan op cit pp 408–9
17. Benton speech, Rome, 28 Nov 1951 in NA RG 469, Mission to Italy, Office of Director, Subject Files (Central Files) 1948–1957 *Congress – Benton Visit* sub-file; cit in Hogan op cit p 418
18. Hogan op cit pp 415–18; Carew op cit pp 158–67
19. *European Manifesto* reproduced in final draft version in FRUS 1951 vol IV pp 54–7; cf Hogan op cit pp 411–14
20. Postan MM *An Economic History of Western Europe 1945–1964* 1967 pp 14–15
21. Hogan op cit p 393
22. Cairncross A *Years of Recovery. British Economic Policy 1945–51* 1985 pp 212–17; USWA 1950 p 260
23. Addison *Now the War is Over* cit Ch 8 (cit at p 200)
24. FRUS 1952–54 Vol VI p 720 (message of 28 Dec 1951)
25. Burnham P *The Political Economy of Postwar Reconstruction* 1990 Ch 6 (cits at p 151); Pelling H op cit p 106
26. Boyle PG Britain, America and the Transition from Economic to Military Assistance,1948–51. In *Journal of Contemporary History* July 1987 pp 533–4; FRUS 1951 Vol IV pp 966 (on 'burden sharing'); ibid p 980 (on 'Special Relationship'); but Acheson forcefully denied that a special relationship existed when the British tried to capitalise on it politically, Acheson op cit pp 387–8 cf Bullock op cit p 772
27. Pelling op cit pp 113–14
28. Mallalieu WC *British Reconstruction and American Foreign Policy* NY 1956 pp 70–3; Price op cit p 317
29. Carew op cit Ch 7 (cits at pp 139,140); Anglo-American Productivity Council, Final Report, Sept 1952 p 4
30. Adamthwaite A Overstretched and overstrung: Eden, the Foreign Office and the making of policy. In *International Affairs* Spring 1988 (Colville cit p 243); observations on British defence effort in FRUS 1952–54 Vol VI p 646
31. Debate summarised in Sked A *Britain's Decline, Problems and Perspectives* Oxford 1987 pp 28–35; tax burden cit in FRUS 1952–54 Vol VI p 1005; cf Cairncross *Years of Recovery* cit pp 231–3
32. Burnham op cit p 175; Worswick GDN and Ady PH (eds) *The British Economy in the Nineteen-Fifties* Oxford 1962 Ch 1
33. Rioux op cit p 134

34. Minutes, Conference of Information Officers, Paris, 28 Aug 1950, in NA RG 286, OSR Information Divn, Office of Director, General Subject Files 1949–50, *Information Officers* sub-file
35. As n 14
36. FRUS 1951 Vol IV p 350; Carew op cit p 215
37. Hogan op cit p 410
38. Carew loc cit; Kuisel op cit p 243
39. Carew op cit pp 215–16
40. These paragraphs are based on Lynch F *The Impact of Rearmament on French Reconstruction* European University Institute Florence 1986 (cits at pp 6,39)
41. FRUS 1951 Vol IV pp 395–7; on de Gaulle, Crozier B *De Gaulle The Statesman* 1973 pp 434–40
42. Rioux op cit p 188
43. Nicholls A The Other Germany–the 'Neo-Liberals'. In Bullen RJ et al (eds) *Ideas into Politics: Aspects of European History 1800–1950*
44. Bark DL and Gress DR *A History of West Germany* Vol 1 Oxford 1989 p 262
45. Erhard L *Prosperity through Competition* 1958 p 38
46. Bark and Gress op cit p 263
47. Ibid p 268; cf Carlin op cit pp 60–1
48. Carew op cit p 218
49. Hardach G The Marshall Plan in Germany, 1948–52. In *Journal of European Economic History* Winter 1987 pp 447–48
50. Ibid pp 465, 471–72, 477
51. Ibid pp 455, 458, 483–4; Abelshauser W The Role of the ERP in German Recovery and Growth unpublished ms pp 16–18
52. Hardach op cit pp 483–5; Abelshauser The Role of the ERP in German Recovery and Growth cit pp 32–3
53. Hardach op cit p 468; cf Abelshauser The Role of the ERP in German Recovery and Growth pp 28–33
54. Ibid pp 480,470
55. Ibid p 475
56. Ibid p 485; Abelshauser The Role of the ERP in German Recovery and Growth cit p 37
57. Berghahn V *The Americanisation* op cit
58. Carew op cit p 218
59. Ibid p 219
60. Berghahn *The Americanisation of West German Industry* cit pp 155–81 (*Wall Street Journal* cit p 175)
61. Bark and Gress op cit p 257
62. These pages are based on Sorensen op cit Ch 8; cf Hans Christian Johansen *The Danish Economy in the Twentieth Century* 1987 pp 104–9
63. *New York Times* 3 June 1949
64. Ellwood Il Piano Marshall e il processo di moderniszazione in Italia. In Aga-Rossi E (ed) *Il Piano Marshall e l'Europa* Rome 1983 pp 153–5
65. Translated text of Costa speech, Rome, 8 Nov 1951 in NA RG 469, Mission to Italy, Office of Director, Subject Files (Central Files) 1948–1957 *Productivity Drive* sub-file
66. Carew op cit p 211

67. Ginsborg P op cit Ch 4; cf. Zamagni *Dalla periferia al centro* op cit pp 418–20; for the dramatic experience of a region like Emilia Romagna in these years, Ellwood Il Piano Marshall in Emilia Romagna. In D'Attorre PP (ed) *La ricostruzione in Emilia Romagna* Parma 1985
68. Ginsborg P op cit pp 118–20, 186–8
69. D'Attorre PP Il piano Marshall: politica, economia, relazioni internazionali nella ricostruzione italiana. In *L'Italia e la politica di potenza in Europa – 1945–50* Milan 1988 pp 520–35
70. USIS-FOA *Cooperazione economica Italia – Stati Uniti 1944–54* nd pp 18–19
71. D'Attorre *Il piano Marshall* cit pp 525–45
72. Jones H op cit p 234
73. McNeill WH *Greece: American Aid in Action 1947–1956* NY 1957 p 48
74. Ibid pp 63–4; Jones H op cit Ch 13 n 20
75. McNeill *The Metamorphosis of Greece since World War II* Oxford 1978 pp 91–3
76. Candilis WO *The Economy of Greece 1944–66. Efforts for Stability and Development* NY 1968 Ch 5 (cit at p 65)
77. McNeill *The Metamorphosis* cit pp 94–5
78. Ibid pp 95–6
79. Ibid pp 97–8
80. Kondonassis AJ et al Political Instability and Economic Development: An Economic History Case Study of Greece, 1948–66. In *Journal of European Economic History* Fall 1983 pp 354–55, 359
81. Vergopoulos K L'hégémonie américaine après la seconde guerre mondiale et la formation de la bourgeoisie périphérique en Grèce. In *Les Temps modernes* mars 1979; Kondonassis op cit pp 361–2; cf Lianos TP Political Stability and Economic Development. The Case of Greece, 1948–66. In *Journal of European Economic History* Winter 1986 pp 617–19

CHAPTER ELEVEN

Hoping for Prosperity 1953–54

THE FUTURE EMERGES: 1953

The recovery from the war was generally thought to be complete by 1953. Many other reasons point to 1953 as a milestone year in the postwar era. Its key events included:

- The arrival in January of Eisenhower in the White House and Dulles in the State Department.
- The death of Stalin in March.
- The first popular uprising in a Soviet bloc country, East Berlin, in June.
- The end of De Gasperi's political career after the failure of an electoral reform manoeuvre in the June general election in Italy.
- A permanent ceasefire in the Korean War in July, followed by the establishment of a dividing line (still existing) between North and South Korea.
- The nomination of Nikita Krushchev as First Secretary of the Soviet Communist Party.
- The first US–Spanish accord, in September, for the construction of military bases and the granting of military aid to Franco. This agreement signalled the beginning of Spain's re-entry into the international system.
- The substantial victory of the CDU in the German elections of November.

Now the worst is over

Beyond all these auspicious events, the signs of a new upward lift in everyday life, beyond stability and hope to a different kind of progress, were to be seen on all sides. The contours of a postwar baby boom became clear, and commentators everywhere, noting that it was 'far greater than the normal postwar rise from postponed marriages and return of husbands', took it to be a great affirmation of faith in the future, especially as it was shared between Europe and America.

The figures for births per thousand people in the leading countries were:

	1937	1949
Austria	12.8	16.3
Belgium	15.4	17.2
France	15.0	20.9
Ireland	19.2	21.5
Netherlands	19.8	23.7
Norway	15.0	19.5
UK	15.3	17.0
United States	17.1	24.0

'One of the great and ignored facts about France is that the French are having babies again', Theodore White announced in his survey of 1953. The birth rate was now 20 per cent higher than before the war, giving the country first place in the European league. Following de Gaulle's appeal in March 1945 for 'douze millions de beaux bébés', the welfare state was subsidising babies once again, but as elsewhere, 'the individual determination of French couples to refresh the nation' was probably just as important in White's view.[1]

A panoramic survey of Western Europe offered by a special correspondent of the *Economist* in November well illustrates the sense of change. The writer talked of 'the remarkable, and now complete, recovery of Western Europe from Hitler's war', and believed that 'a minor social revolution' had happened, bringing everywhere a 'fundamentally new attitude to social problems'. He continued: 'large and in some cases major, redistributions of income and wealth have been carried out as part of a conscious policy. Expanded systems of social security have been introduced. And there is pretty general agreement everywhere on the need to keep unemployment as low as possible.'

The division of Europe and the consequent defence burden had been hard to bear, the 'idealistic conceptions' going beyond sovereignty in search of unity had languished. But the 'much greater degree of mutual understanding and broad agreement' evident was surely a major advance. As for the contest with the Soviets, the recovery in the West constituted an achievement which 'more than match[ed] anything on the other side of the iron curtain'.[2] Yet there was no hint of why, in spite of everything now known about Stalinist Communism and all the efforts to counter it, not least by America, Communist parties in France and Italy were holding on to or increasing their vote. Everyone was satisfied that the worst was over, but the sense of well-being was fragile, the fear of atomic war at times overpowering. And the first notions of the price to be paid for all the innovations were also filtering through.

Italy for instance was a country whose progress was remarked on by every visitor. Seen from within the benefits were not so clear-cut. In 1953 one of Italy's best-known popular writers of the time, Guido Piovene, was commissioned by the state radio network, RAI, to draw up a comprehensive 'inventory' of postwar Italy, travelling to every corner and offering his experiences and impressions on weekly pro- grammes. The journey took Piovene three years and in book form his *Viaggio in Italia* became a classic work of reportage, the equivalent of Priestley's *English Journey* of the mid-1930's. The exploration began in the north-eastern region of the Veneto, the author's birthplace.

The area was clearly in the process of dividing between the traditional countryside of archaic beauty and extreme rural backward- ness, and those places where an awkward modernity was imposing itself. In Cortina the ski resort was deciding to restrict the height of proposed 'skyscrapers'; in the foothills of the Alps to the south the majority of the population were peasants living with half an acre and a byre. Venice was becoming an industrial port. While in its byways and islands subsistence living on fishing carried on listlessly in the time-honoured ways, to the south the planned industrial settlement of Marghera already employed 25,000. The majority of them, however, voted Communist.

Piovene appreciated the new economic impulses on display but commented critically:

> The countryside is being spoiled by ugly new buildings and ways of doing things, the country villas decay and industry fails to flourish. Rather than a real change one sees before one's eyes an ancient way of life disappear into itself. The frame of the picture remains traditional, old habits and sentiments linger, but are deeply felt no longer by the people who share them. One frequently feels in Italy now a drastic break between all the historical traditions, the deep background of everyone, and life today, which as a result feels empty.[3]

In the French countryside too a revolution was taking place; French agriculture was taking its first hesitant steps on the road to a new way of life. 'The last thing one might have expected in 1950 was the modernisation of agriculture in Aquitaine', an eyewitness recalled. Life there had changed very little over the years, and postwar attempts at land reform had been ignored. 'Although not a great deal was produced, the markets were so short of everything that good prices were earned.' But by 1953 the rush for tractors was on, financed from the gains of the years when food was so scarce: 'It was a considerable investment, and this made the farmer keep proper accounts, which he had never done before. This in turn made him realize the need for increasing his output by using his tractor for spreading fertilizer and sowing some of the new wheats which were appearing.' Introduced under the Marshall Plan, American hybrid grains with higher yields and uniform growth for easier reaping were challenging the old ways. By 1955 half of the growers in the Aquitaine were planting them.[4]

Yet 1953 was the year when the small-town shopkeeper Pierre Poujade launched his movement of 'little men' against the Fourth Republic. In a broad wave of unrest which linked farmers, shopkeepers and large parts of the public sector, the political parasitism and unaccountability of the Fourth Republic – incarnated in its tax regime – was the specific object of attack. Underneath, much of the movement's dynamic came from its attack on modernity, and its defence of the ancient feeling of French fraternity rooted in 'small towns, gentle change and the beauty of the French countryside'.[5]

In England Theodore White continued his grand European tour of 1953 looking for the effects of six years of Labour Party socialism. He was struck by how much it had achieved and how much of it was taken for granted by Churchill's government. He travelled to Doncaster to interview the local director of labour relations for the Coal Board, Joe Curry a former miner. The American reporter wished to study at first-hand the results of the years when, after decades of scorn and threats to their livelihood, miners had become the object of patriotic appeals – 'for Dunkirk, for the Middle East, for Italy, for the Invasion of France, for the Dollar Drive' – and had seen the mines nationalised as the reward for their efforts:

> I look around me here in Doncaster [continued Joe Curry]. It's not so long since I saw people ill-nourished, ill-clad, their homes sparsely furnished. Now you see them well-dressed, well-fed. You go into their homes and they have decorations, pianos, carpets, radios, some of them are getting TV sets. It's all changed.

Nationalisation on the other hand appeared to be just a 'soulless machine', threatening to produce bureaucracy and alienation. Absenteeism was already becoming a problem.[6]

In general White found the West European peoples he visited in 1953 irritable and restive, powerless in the face of the now-institutionalised East–West confrontation, and unhappy to be the ward of one of the two strange descendent civilisations which now faced each other so dangerously. Not even the 'half-reality' of European unity nor the renaissance of Germany could comfort the peoples involved, since these were both developments born of American aid and prompting. And they left uncertain what Europeans and Germans had really learned for themselves from their own recent history. To the unequivocal 'No' given to Russia, an 'equally steadfast "Yes"' offered to America was conspicuously missing, argued White. The problem was not the Left opposition: 'As if by instinct, without deep thought, Europe has rejected in every state in the West the gospel of communism without finding any other gospel to match it in vitality.'[7]

Faith in the future as faith in production

Would productivity be that gospel? André Siegfried, for many years the best-known French commentator on the international scene, was doubtful. The scale of mass production and consumption, the organisation and standardisation of men, machines and markets on view in America was unthinkable in the 'established and rigid European system', he asserted. Addressing the readers of *Foreign Affairs* in mid-1952, Siegfried highlighted all the contrasts which put Western Euope at a disadvantage compared to the United States:

> It can be said truthfully that in Europe technical progress does not necessssarily 'pay'. There are too many people and too few raw materials; the social system is too complicated. After two wars, the second of which came when we had not even recovered from the first, the Old World certainly does not give the impression of moving forward on a rising tide.

It was to overcome this sort of scepticism, and the realities which produced it, that the European Productivity Agency was born, as a branch of the OEEC, in May 1953. Half funded by the United States, its job was to continue the great crusade for ever more productive efficiency, and ensure long-term support for the defence drive at all levels of economic activity. The Anglo-American Productivity Council was immediately taken over by the EPA, just as its chief publicist, the economist Graham Hutton, published his panegyric to productivity, entitled *We Too Can Prosper*. It proclaimed more efficient output to be: 'the brightest hope for every man, woman and child that the standard of living can be maintained and improved. Its importance and the universal concern in its achievement therefore cannot be exaggerated.'[8]

THE UNITED NATIONS ANALYSIS OF POSTWAR RECOVERY

Promises and performance in economic policy

The eventful year 1953 also saw the publication by the sceptics of the UN Economic Commission on Europe of their first comprehensive survey of the continent's progress since the end of the war. Their introduction confirmed that the years since 1945 had seen continuous expansion, 'in accordance with wartime pledges for high and stable employment'. But it was now clear, said the UN economists, that the efforts of the political generation which had assumed the responsibility of those pledges 'contributed less to the expansion in these years than was sometimes believed.' They continued: 'In retrospect, this pro-longed boom is seen to have been carried on waves of successive external stimuli which enabled the expansion to continue each time it was threatened, either from the side of supply or from that of demand.'

On the supply side the Commission listed the UNRRA programme and the first US loans, then the Marshall Plan, immediately followed by the Mutual Security drive. On the demand side the survey included the devaluations of September 1949, the 'violent outburst of speculative demand' which accompanied the Korean crisis, and finally the national rearmament efforts. The general economic turbulence following all this, particularly on the inflation and payments fronts, appeared likely to bring the boom to a halt, 'in sharp contrast to the . . . resolve of OEEC countries [in the 'European Manifesto' mentioned above] to secure an increase in production of 25 per cent in five years.'[9]

The UN experts noted that, as intended, most governments had succeeded in increasing exports while holding back imports, their promises on liberalisation and integration notwithstanding. They had increased investment and had generally restricted the share of consumption, in spite of their commitments to welfare. Adding in such factors as the loss of prewar investment income from overseas, a significant general deterioration in the terms of trade and population increases, the result was that national income per head had improved much more slowly than the physical expansion of output would imply: 'In particular, it was much more difficult to regain prewar levels of consumption in food and housing than to increase the consumption of manufactured products.'[10]

Everywhere the share of resources absorbed by governments increased over the prewar era, with the exceptions of Germany and Italy where totalitarian regimes had ruled pre–1939. And the causes were always the same: increased spending on defence and social security. The UK and France reached their prewar levels of defence spending by 1951, while countries such as Greece, but also Belgium, the Netherlands and Denmark, were dedicating far larger shares of their national incomes to this sector than they had done before the war.[11] Social security spending rose to an average of 9.3 per cent of GNP through the 1950s, with the trend accelerating in the wake of increased prosperity: 'the absolute growth of the national product formed the basis for the *relative* growth of the welfare state', says the director of the first large-scale comparative research report on the subject.[12]

The UN report described how investment as a proportion of national output was higher almost everywhere than in the prewar years. In Britain only was there a partial shortfall, due to the impossibility of reaching the very high level of housebuilding characteristic of the immediate prewar years. Otherwise the amount of capital dedicated to productive output had gone up at the same rate as elsewhere. Generally this result was an outcome of deliberate political choice and new varieties of macroeconomic management, particularly in north-western Europe. But expanded forms of government intervention in the economies of Scandinavia, Denmark, Holland and Britain had not succeeded in combining monetary stability with full employment, and the result was inflation.

> In the other western European countries, the picture – very broadly speaking – was either one of full employment accompanied by violent price inflation, as in France and Finland, or one of monetary stability together with unemployment, as in Belgium, Italy and western Germany. Switzerland alone managed to combine a virtually stable price level with sustained full employment, helped in part by variations in the number of foreign workers admitted to the Swiss labour market.

Meanwhile the problems of Southern Europe – including Greece and Turkey – remained essentially unaltered. Long-term development still stood as the principal challenge, more specifically the modernisation of agriculture and the start of industrialisation. Only Yugoslavia showed significant signs of progress in this sense in 1953: after the break with the Soviet Union in 1949, the country had begun to accept credits from the United States, some West European countries and the International Bank. The original Soviet-style five-year plan had not been abandoned but had been modified to concentrate on investment projects which could be completed quickly. 'Undoubtedly', said the Geneva experts, 'industrialisation is proceeding at a faster rate than in the other southern European countries and is in less danger of suffering from periodic relapses.' But in general a new dualism seemed to be emerging between Northern and Southern Europe which the impulses to integration were quite insufficient to halt.[13]

The verdict from Geneva

So the UN observers were by no means uncritical of the achievements of reconstruction, and there is no sense whatever in their assessment that a historically new era of prosperity and abundance was opening. They noted the perverse workings of the contrast between cheap money (interest rates often as low as 2.5 per cent), and high taxes. They deplored the lack of incomes policy and the random nature of investment policy, which combined general stimulation with a mass of usually inefficient controls introduced to overcome passing shortages of raw materials, labour or foreign exchange. When inflation threatened there would immediately be cuts in public spending, but these would often hit investment where it was most needed, including building and 'some of the socially most desirable investments, such as houses, hospitals and schools.' The consequences were most evident in Britain, but were visible throughout Western Europe:

> In the face of these limitations, . . . Governments constantly compromised with the major aims of their policy. Their efforts were diverted into coping with the day-to-day problems of foreign exchange reserves and inflation. They had to maintain the emergency controls introduced during the war: not in order to bring about changes in the structure of their economies and in the efficiency of industry, but to interfere, from the long-term point of view unnecessarily, with the freedom of consumers and producers. This compulsion to petty and unsystematic interferences was an important factor in the gradual loss of popularity of the first postwar Governments.[14]

But the greatest uncertainties were still to be found in Europe's economic relationships with the rest of the world. As a result of the war and its aftermath, the international economy had gone through 'radical structural changes'. The result was to make the vision of global free trade not easier but harder to realise, with Europe's place in it even more difficult to discern.

The almost total cessation of trade with Eastern Europe, the deterioration of the relationship between the prices of exports and the cost of imports, above all the loss of invisible income, had all brought far greater difficulties to the reconstruction plans than could possibly have been foreseen at the end of the war. In the UN estimate the terms of trade by 1953 were 25 per cent worse than in 1938, requiring an increase in export volume of 44 per cent over 1938 to compensate. As for the drop in invisible earnings: 'the (external) income of 1950–51 was equivalent to only 9 per cent of the 1938 volume of exports, compared with 32 per cent before the war. This may be taken as an approximate measure of western Europe's loss from the effects of the war on external capital.'[15]

These were the problems which had fed inflation, the payments worries and the still unbridgeable dollar gap. Only by increasing exports 80 per cent in volume over 1938 could Western European countries aspire to pay for the import volume of that year, let alone hope to increase living standards.[16] By 1951 the increase was only 40 per cent, and most of that had gone to the 'affiliated' (mostly ex-imperial) areas. The increase to the dollar area was impressive at 65 per cent, but considering the pressures of necessity and the attention given to the problem, the result was a disappointing one.[17]

It was of course this reality which gave such prominence to the role of US supplies, US aid, and US trade and payments policies. By 1952 Europe's annual dollar receipts from all sources had dropped by over \$1 billion compared with the pre-Korean era, and in general terms, said the UN analysts, all the aid furnished since the war seemed to have done 'little more over the whole period than alleviate [the structural] difficulties without providing a basic cure'.[18] Moreover, a new factor was now appearing which made prospects look even more dubious: the emergence of Japan in a dollar-hungry condition very similar to that of Western Europe: 'So far . . . European countries have been spared the necessity for reconciling themselves to the inevitable consequences of Japan's recovery only because it, too, has been receiving dollars in extraordinary forms which can scarcely continue indefinitely.' The UN economists took it for granted that the United States would start cutting back its dollar support to Japan and Europe as soon as the military build-up was complete, and warned their readers that Europe could only look the dollar area in the face in terms of export capability and reserves if a total readjustment of the order of \$4 billion was achieved. That was the magnitude of the increase in exports to the United States, Canada and Latin America which had to be brought about if Europe seriously wished to participate in a new, liberal system of trade and payments, with full currency convertibility as its supreme goal.[19]

THE CONTINUING ROLE OF US AID

In 1953 there seemed very little prospect that such a turnround could take place. Like Japan, Europe continued to receive dollar aid 'in extraordinary forms' for many years after Korea. This was partly because the arms race ensured that the military build-up would never be considered complete, partly because in some countries the political and economic divisions which had set off the original ERP still persisted.

The *Economist* calculated that aid to western Europe in 1953 was in reality worth no less than $6 billion. The figure was made up of $1.4 billion of explicit 'defence support and economic aid', $1.5 billion of 'offshore procurement' – contracts for military supplies – $500 million of troop expenditure and general expenses for NATO (such as air-bases), and three billion dollars' worth of military hardware donated to national armed services.[20]

France was the nation most dependent on continued US support. Economically, it was considered the 'black spot' of the entire West European picture by Robert Marjolin of OEEC. Long-standing rigidities in the structure of occupations – the numbers dedicated to peasant agriculture and old-fashioned trade and artisan activities – had by now revealed their capacity to put spokes in the wheels of the technocrats' planning and modernisation effort. Although on the increase, agricultural production lagged far behind the requisites of the planners. Mechanisation remained too low and credit scarce; yields were still only half those of her neighbours and France was a net importer of food.

The targets planned by the Monnet Commissions and their Marshall Plan supporters for most of the basic industries had almost been met (oil refining and cement were the successes). But these achievements were clearly not enough to ensure political stability, let alone satisfy expectations. The 'wage-earning class [was] by common agreement held outside effective political power' (as the Geneva observers put it), while wide-spread tax evasion and the use of farm subsidies as political favours tended to unsettle the ways and means of *la France profonde*. Poujadism was one of the symptoms of this sense of exasperation.[21]

Although levelling off – at a point 43 per cent above the 1949 figure – inflation remained by far the greatest issue troubling those interviewed by opinion polls, 'a preoccupation', says Rioux, 'which must be interpreted as a sign of rising popular expectations, one which completely overshadowed the questions of world peace, the European Defence Community, or Algeria.'[22] But the anxieties were real enough since the persistent budget and trade deficits aggravated the oscillations between inflation and deflation, and increased dependence on American support. Dollar aid ran at a level of $690 million in the year ending June 1953, and was expected to *double* in the following year. By then the United States would, among other items, be paying for two-thirds of the cost of the war in Indo-China.

West Germany, by way of contrast, was expected to receive no more than $13 million dollars in the first half of 1954.[23]

Italian dependence was not so obvious as France's, at least in dollar terms, and it was set to decline from half to less than a third of the French share in 1953–54. But as in France most of the money went on the 'defense support program', particularly on raw materials for arms production. Again the proceeds were recycled by way of a counterpart fund, which continued to be devoted to industrial and agricultural modernisation using devices like the Cassa per il Mezzogiorno (which flourished until 1984).[24]

All the tools of American power and influence were mobilised for the June elections of 1953, their deployment being handled by a new ambassador of unusual anti-Communist fervour even for those times: Clare Booth Luce, the controversial senator and wife of *Time–Life* proprietor Henry Luce. Yet not even her dedication, or the millions once again channelled to favourable elements, or an electoral law manipulation on the Greek and French models, could produce the right result. The Communist vote increased to ten million. The ambassador knew the reasons for this were partly destitution and unemployment, and wondered openly what effect the billions of dollars poured into Italy since the war had really obtained. The proceedings of parliament's extraordinary inquiry into national poverty and misery, set up in 1953, revealed in graphic detail the depths of poverty endured by a quarter of Italian families. This was a reality which provided solid leverage as well as potential votes for the Italian Communist Party's claims and denunciations. But Mrs Luce was tired of the government's endless pleas for more aid. She demanded that the Left be tackled frontally, with force.[25]

By mid-1954 the US Congress had decided that purely economic aid to Europe would be terminated within two years, and the total for 1954–55 – $3.4 billion – was almost entirely military in nature. But when looking for more working capital for the ECSC in the spring of 1954, Monnet had again turned to Washington. He was promised $100 million as a loan, a cautious commitment recognising his organisation's achievements after two years as still dominated by intention rather than by realisation. (The general pattern of the coal and steel trade remained 'overwhelmingly traditional', according to the *Economist*.)[26]

Very many observers assumed that whenever the United States went into its next significant recession, Western European countries, and Britain in particular, would be just as disturbed as they had all been in 1948–49. So when a different trend of expansion began to assert itself in the course of 1954 it was unexpected, and not seen as such by any of the experts watching so closely over the west European scene.

1954 – A NEW KIND OF BOOM

The British awakening

All the authorities had preached caution when 1953 came to an end. The *Economist* was pleased to note in October that unemployment in Britain was down to 1.4 per cent and that the increase in consumption was up to 5 per cent annually, even 21.5 per cent in household goods. But their warning against optimism could hardly have been sterner: '. . . let nobody suppose that the rate of improvement in the standard of living that (the figures) indicate is a rate that can continue for long.'[27] One of the inventors of contemporary macroeconomics, Colin Clark, was reported as predicting a major recession in the United States, with effects in Europe too strong to be arrested 'by any measures that one can put within the bounds of political probability'.

The OEEC's report on 1953 considered inflation to have been brought under control on the whole, but at the price of a widespread stagnation in output. Underneath a superficial improvement, the structural problem of the dollar gap persisted, whose only solution was 'increasing and modernising industrial capacity'.[28] From their observatory in Geneva the UN experts also welcomed the relaxation in strains on the payments front and the reduced controls on markets. But they discerned 'no return of the climate of confident expansion which had characterised the years up to 1950', and worried that 'a substantial decline in private investment demand' was taking place, 'in spite of the generally acknowledged need for a further extension and renewal of the capital base of European industry'.[29]

The change which came over Western Europe's prospects and confidence during the course of 1954 can easily be gauged by tracing the evolution of the *Economist*'s attitude in that year. In January a survey of 1953 was unable to decide whether the world had 'struck a happy equilibrium between inflation and deflation' or was facing instead 'the twilight of the boom'. It was the year when Germany and Japan 'proved themselves fully re-established in world markets', threatening British exports in particular, and when raw materials prices steadied back to their pre-Korean average: 'economic conditions as a whole looked altogether too normal to last'. In March the magazine complained of Britain's slow expansion in industrial output, which at 2–2.5 per cent per annum (against West Germany's 5 per cent) produced only £250 million of usable new wealth. Even when it was discovered that GDP had risen £500 million and GNP (i.e. including foreign earnings), $800 million in 1953 – making it the most prosperous year ever – there was said to be 'disturbingly little of lasting value' to show for it. All the increase had gone in consumption, defence, housing, the nationalised industries, leaving the reserves no stronger and investment flat.[30]

May brought more news of record output, but the commentators of the *Economist* focused on productivity: it was reported to have gone up 14 per cent in the previous five years. However, in the same years it had grown 20 per cent in Sweden, 27 per cent in France and the Netherlands, 60 per cent in Italy, 100 per cent in Germany: 'there is no getting away from the significance of these figures', they warned. With the spring and early summer came the end – finally – of food rationing in Britain, as well as of restrictions on hire purchase. The pound surged to new heights but the *Economist* talked austerely of 'another step back from the siege economy to more normal conditions', and demanded the removal of the travel allowance.[31]

Only with the end of the summer did a different spirit become visible in the weekly journal's pronouncements. Instead of all the usual symptoms of autumn crisis, the indicators clearly stated that only 1 per cent remained without work, wages were rising at an annual rate of 5 per cent or more, personal spending at a rate of 2.5–3 per cent. In the short run, in other words, 'the British economy has never had it so good'.[32]

Soon it was possible to rejoice that Europe and Britain had weathered America's 1953–54 recession with hardly any ill effects: output was expanding at 6 per cent per annum and productivity appeared to be increasing as fast as production. A representative of the Board of Trade declared: 'This government's theory of expansion implies steadily increasing earnings, incomes and – dare I say it – dividends.'[33] But the great milestone in the British recognition process came with R.A. Butler's speech as Chancellor to the Conservative Party conference in October. It was on this occasion that a famous pledge was made: 'I see no reason why, in the next quarter of a century, if we run our policy properly and soundly, we should not double our standard of living in this country'. It was a call, enthused the *Economist*, 'for a return to the theory and practice of capitalism', an invitation to imitate the United States, where the progressive effects of their vast increases in wealth could be seen in the wholesale 'levelling-up' of the living standards of the poor, offering among all its other benefits a comprehensive response to Leftism in all its forms.[34]

Looking back on the year in its annual survey the magazine admitted it had never believed possible an increase in British output at the rate of 6 per cent per annum, and was happy to offer congratulations all round for the 'remarkably satisfactory showing in exports'. The fruits of the newly created wealth had largely gone, of course, on a 'splurge on consumer durables', of which the supreme example was the motor car. Furniture, television and radio and other items of 'domestic equipment' came next in the order of preferences, buoyed by hire purchase. A particularly striking and unexpected change had taken place in the labour market. In contrast with a predicted 'natural increase' of 55,000, mostly men, the workforce had expanded by 175–200,000, of which 120,000 were women entering or re-entering the working population.[35]

The boom in Europe

When the OEEC and the ECE produced their year-end surveys of the West European situation at the beginning of 1955 they were hardly less surprised. Over the whole of Western Europe (including Scandinavia) the rise in output was on average 8 per cent, according to the ECE. The chemical industries had reached 15 per cent, but by far the most conspicuous increase was in motor vehicles: 20 per cent. For the majority of countries export volumes had risen between 10 and 25 per cent, with intra-European trade once again out-performing the increase to the rest of the world. A similar upswing had taken place in 1951, noted the UN economists, but the great and positive contrast of 1954 was the general picture of monetary stability which had emerged, together with the virtual elimination of unemployment everywhere (except Italy). The shocks produced by the Korean War had finally been absorbed, and the new upswing contained another 'remarkable' feature: a 'rapid expansion in the markets for durable consumer goods, largely of new types'.[36]

The OEEC's sixth report, published in March 1955, was entitled *From Recovery towards Economic Strength*. The introduction explained:

> The task which Western Europe now faces is to build a better economy than that existing before the war. For Member countries have completed – indeed exceeded – the economic recovery which, when the Marshall Plan

began, was no more than a hope and, according to the first report of the OEEC (1948), a doubtful hope at that. Their recent achievements have paved the way for further progress.

The OEEC admitted that its members were not likely to fulfil the target of the European Manifesto, and that while they had improved consumption by 12 per cent over the prewar level, America's increase had been 45 per cent. Military dollars continued to compensate for inadequate exports to the US, whose level had in fact declined. But the organisation was proud to point out that 80 per cent of trade between its members had been liberalised (if agriculture and invisibles were excluded), and that productivity had increased between 15 and 20 per cent compared with the immediate prewar phase. Yet not enough had been done in this direction, which should now, asserted the OEEC, be 'one of the central and most constant preoccupations of governments': 'In the 1930s the great common problem was unemployment, and in the postwar years it was reconstruction; today, however, the problem of raising productivity has pre-eminence.' Only by recognising this priority could Western Europe turn into reality the two great watchwords for the future: '*expansion* and *liberalisation*'.[37]

When the OEEC came to write its seventh report, at the beginning of 1956, it confirmed that 'a new phase of postwar economic development' was under way, with total output 'on a sharply rising trend' for the third consecutive year. But by far the most portentous novelty in the report's text was the use of new words to describe and characterise the processes unfolding. Alongside 'upsurge', 'expansion', 'development' and 'prosperity', there appeared for the first time the phrase 'economic growth'.[38]

In the remainder of the decade, as the consumer durable-led 'miracles' surged forth in Western Europe, it was this word 'growth' which came to sum up the newness of the era and to dominate the objectives of economic policy, if not of all policy, for governing classes throughout the West. Not by chance had the word first been used in this manner in the United States, in the Marshall Plan era. In 1960 the OEEC was refounded, with the United States and Canada now entering as full members, to become the OECD, the Organisation for Economic Cooperation and Development. Article 1 of its founding convention states the agency's purpose as 'to achieve the highest sustainable economic growth and employment and a rising standard of living in Member countries, while maintaining financial stability, and thus to contribute to the development of the world economy.'[39] Ten years earlier almost all these objectives would have been familiar to European statesmen and their advisers. But the arrival of the concept of economic growth, at the maximum rate possible, as a supreme goal of policy, brought a new and significant evolution in the idea of progress itself to advanced industrial societies.

NOTES

1. Birthrate figures in United Nations *Demographic Yearbook 1952* cit and discussed in Brinton C *The Temper of Western Europe* Cambridge Mass. 1953 pp 116–17; White op cit p 97. On French pro-natal policy Shennan op cit Ch 9
2. The *Economist* 14 Nov 1953
3. Piovene G *Viaggio in Italia* Milan 1957 pp 11–41 (cit at pp 39–40)
4. Cit in Dupeux G *French Society 1789–1970* 1976 pp 244–5
5. Vinen R Pierre Poujade and Margaret Thatcher. In *History Today* Aug 1991; cf Rioux op cit pp 219–21
6. White op cit pp 212–3, 232–13 (cit at p 232)
7. Ibid Ch 1 (cit at p 17)
8. Siegfried A Can Europe Use American Methods? In *Foreign Affairs* July 1952 (cit at p 663); Hutton G *We Too Can Prosper* 1953 pp 150–1 (cit at p 5). Siegfried was opposed by Hutton's equivalent in France, Jean Fourastie, author of *La Civilisation de 1960* (1947), *La Productivité* (1947), *Grand espoir du siècle* (1949 and 1958), *Machinisme et bienêtre* (1951 and 1962). 'On the threshold of the 1950s,' says Rioux, 'no one better than he expressed the ideology of progress and modernity, or wrote the history of a future which was to be that of comfort and work'; op cit Ch 16 n 1
9. *UN Economic Survey* 1953 cit pp 51–2 (cit at p 51)
10. Ibid pp 55–6
11. Ibid p 55, 57, 60
12. Flora P (ed) *Growth to Limits. The West European Welfare State Since World War II* Vol 1 Berlin/NY 1986 pp xxii–v (cit at p xxii). Tables summarizing trends in defence and social security spending are presented in an Appendix below.
13. *UN Economic Survey* 1953 cit pp 60, 66EP
14. Ibid pp 66–8 (cit at p 67)
15. Ibid pp 10–12
16. Ibid p 13
17. Ibid p 100
18. Ibid p 127, 81; a paradox of the entire postwar situation regarding Europe's dollar earnings was the great difficulty of exporting to the United States due to the wide range of tariff and non-tariff barriers which persisted, protecting various US industries and interests. This rarely explored subject is discussed briefly in ibid pp 106–08
19. Ibid pp 131–3
20. *Economist* 10 Oct 1953
21. *UN Economic Survey* 1953 cit pp 78–81

22. Rioux op cit pp 197, 218–21
23. *Economist* 17 Oct 1953, 21 Nov 1953
24. Ibid 9 Jan 1954
25. Ginsborg op cit pp 142–5; Zamagni *Dalla periferia al centro* op cit pp 406–7; Mrs Luce's activities are documented officially in FRUS 1952–54 Vol VI W Europe and Canada Pt 2; discussion in Ellwood, Italy, Europe and the Cold War. Paper presented at the conference 'The Politics of Power' Reading Oct 1990
26. *Economist* 1 May 1954, 14 Aug 1954
27. Ibid 10 Oct 1953
28. Ibid 28 Nov 1953; Fifth Report of the OEEC Paris Feb 1954
29. UN Economic Commission for Europe *Economic Survey of Europe in 1953* Geneva 1954 Ch 1
30. *Economist* 2 Jan, 27 March, 3 April 1954
31. Ibid 8 May, 17 July 1954
32. Ibid 7 Aug, 14 Aug 1954
33. Ibid 21 Aug, 2 Oct 1954
·34. Ibid 16 Oct 1954; (but in the same number the journal also reported strikes in the docks, the buses, the newpapers, and the ship repairers, calling it 'the most disturbing week of strike action since the war')
35. Ibid 1 Jan 1955
36. UN Economic Commission for Europe *Economic Survey of Europe in 1954* Geneva 1955 Ch 1
37. Sixth Report of the OEEC Paris March 1955 pp 15, 24, 27, 175
38. Seventh Report of the OEEC Paris March 1956 pp 13–16, 19–20
39. Arndt op cit Ch 4; cit from Convention of the OECD 14 Dec 1960 Art 1

CHAPTER TWELVE
Expecting Growth 1955–61

REALISATIONS

With the success of the West European economies in the 1950s came the canonisation of the growth idea and its propagation as a full-scale model of society. When the expansion gathered speed it was seen to depend on intra-European exports as much as any other factor. As a consequence the impulses to integration regained confidence and momentum. The processes which led to the Treaty of Rome and the founding of the European Economic Community in March 1957 sprang then not so much from supranational idealism or visionary American- ism as from the imperatives of expansion in the growth era. Article 2 of the Rome Treaty, defining the purpose of the EEC, states:

> It shall be the aim of the Community, by establishing a Common Market and progressively approximating the economic policies of Member States, to promote throughout the Community a harmonious development of economic activities, a continuous and balanced expansion, an accelerated raising of the standard of living and closer relations betwen its Member States.

Just how far the development of the growth vision progressed in a very few years is well illustrated by a series of prestigious lectures put on by the outgoing OEEC in January 1961 in Madrid. Spain had become a full member of the organisation in 1959 as part of a milestone accord, also involving the IMF, which was aimed at launching a new investment and internationalisation process in what was a near- bankrupt and still largely autarkic country.[1] Emphasising the change from OEEC to OECD in Europe's 'spectacular postwar recovery and further remarkable progress', the Secretary-General, Kristensen, explained in technical terms the new prerequisites of progress. Each nation was expected to take advantage of the 'smooth functioning of the world economy' now guaranteed by agencies such as his own, to bring about radical changes in its policies, attitudes and structures. 'The general philosophy', the Secretary-General summed up, 'is economic growth.'

Succeeding high-ranking members of West Europe's new establishment explained to the distinguished Spanish audience the lessons of the preceding years and what this 'general philosophy' should be understood to mean. Monnet's successor as Commissaire General du Plan, Pierre Massé, emphasised the quantity, quality and direction of investment. With rising productivity as a common method and measure, a coherent strategy of growth could be evolved if 'target planning' at the national level was combined with careful technical programming in each firm. Yet Monsieur Massé hinted that there were in reality no fixed recipes:

> It is . . . a remarkable fact that from 1950 to 1959 national product per head of the working population in France, Italy and Germany increased by roughly similar proportions (44, 45 and 52 per cent), despite the application of fundamentally different methods, whereas in the United States and the United Kingdom the corresponding figures for the period were under 20 per cent.

As a former head of the French social security system, M Massé explained another discovery of the era of high living standards:

> . . . above all, greater welfare has to be financed. In fact, the European social security systems came into being because industrial growth justified the claims of the trade unions, and enabled the new schemes to be financed on the basis of employers' and workers' contributions.

So no welfare state without growth. But the other half of this story was by now beyond doubt. As the Marshall Planners had long predicted: 'up-to-date solutions for a country's social problems may help to maintain economic equilibrium'.

The most significant intervention in Madrid was that of Dr Emminger, a Director of the Federal Republic's Central Bank, on 'Economic Growth Without Inflation'. Nations everywhere, said Dr Emminger, had *'become aware of the problem of growth'*. In his victorious presidential campaign of 1960, John F. Kennedy had declared that a 3.5 per cent rise in GNP per annum was not good enough: 5 per cent should be the target. The British were talking of 3–4 per cent as a commitment to be recognised on a par with that to full employment; in France the planners were constantly under pressure for more expansion. But at the same time, all now realised that along with growth came the risk of creeping inflation and instability. Now among all the remedies for inflation said to exist only one was certain to work: not deflation, nor Keynesian demand management, but higher productivity: 'the more productivity can be increased the less danger there will be of high demand putting an excessive strain on the economy'. What stood at the roots of higher productivity? Changes in the '*attitude of management and labour to wages and prices*', meaning refusal to employ monopoly power to demand higher wages or prices, redistribution of profits through 'fair taxation', openness to 'vigorous and dynamic free competition'.[2]

As a model society the United States was never mentioned in Madrid. But the Americans could be satisfied: their lessons had been learned most faithfully by West Europe's new leaders, their victory seemed complete. In 1961 the book that was to be the bible of the growth philosophy had just appeared: *The Stages of Economic Growth*, a historical view of growth as the culmination of a long development process by an already distinguished MIT economist W.W. Rostow. Subtitled 'A Non-Communist Manifesto', it sought to offer a liberal alternative to the determinism of the classical Marxist analysis, and at the same time a practical programme to apply to all the rest of the world which desired what the West possessed. The five stages of growth delineated by Rostow passed from traditional society, through the beginnings of industrialisation to 'take-off' and maturity, before culminating in 'the age of high mass consumption'.

In this supreme phase all consumption, as well as production, took place on a mass scale. Urbanisation accompanied the triumph of the white-collar classes and 'society ceased to accept the further extension of modern technology as an overriding objective'. Instead,

> Western societies have chosen to allocate increased resources to social welfare and security. The emergence of the welfare state is one manifesta-tion of a society's moving beyond technical maturity; but it is also at this stage that resources tend increasingly to be directed to the production of consumers' durables and to the diffusion of services on a mass basis, if consumers' sovereignty reigns. The sewing-machine, the bicycle, and then the various electric-powered household gadgets were gradually diffused.

But one innovation above all supplied the mainspring of the new way of life: 'Historically . . . the decisive element has been the cheap mass automobile with its quite revolutionary effects – social as well as economic – on the life and expectations of society.'

America had invented the age of mass consumption with Fordism, had embraced it as a way of life in the 1920s and pressed it to its 'logical conclusion' in the postwar decade. Now it was the turn of

Western Europe and Japan to fully enter this phase, 'accounting for a momentum in their economies quite unexpected in the immediate postwar years'.[3]

By 1978 Rostow had developed this view and with the help of fellow economists had further elaborated his historical perspective. The postwar success had come, he agreed, because 'the major nations did all the things they should have done between the wars; and, in considerable part, this was because the lessons of the earlier period were well learned'. So the increased determination of governments to manage their national economies had worked, even if with differing methods and rates of success. But the crucial point in Rostow's analysis was that Western Europe in the 1950s had invented nothing which had not been seen already in the high points of America's twentieth-century development. The technical mechanism at work was explained as follows by E.F. Denison (quoted approvingly by Rostow):

> What distinguishes postwar Europe is that increases in output in the fast-growing countries have systematically been particularly marked in those products that Europe produced only on a small scale and at high cost *compared to the United States* in the early 1950s, and for which techniques for lowering costs with an increase in the scale of production already existed in the United States and did not need to be developed gradually and expensively as markets expanded.

Thanks to American experience Europeans enjoyed a short-cut to affluence:

> As incomes rose in Europe, demand for and production of these income-elastic products rose sharply and their unit costs were reduced by applying American techniques that could not have been adopted until per capita incomes were sufficient to provide a market. . . .
>
>   Automobiles and consumer durables provide classic and obvious examples of the process but it was quite pervasive and, I believe, applied to a great range of detailed products.[4]

After the revolution of rising expectations

In reality debate continues among economists to this day on the relative contribution of all the major technical elements to the boom. But it was the spirit at the heart of the extraordinary expansion of the 1950s which was unprecedented, according to the 1967 account by the economic historian Michael Postan: 'What was really remarkable . . . was that economic growth was so powerfully propelled by public sentiments and policies. . . . In all European countries economic growth became a universal creed and a common expectation to which governments were expected to conform.'

225

Full employment had developed 'into a policy and economic philosophy much wider in its implications . . . all classes of society gradually came to expect continued – indeed perpetual – rises in the material standards of life'. Politicians and economists nurtured this optimism: 'their policies and plans came to be geared to certain irreducible *minima* of growth . . . in this way fast growth, rather than just growth, became the principle of state policy'.[5]

Writing in the 1970s on the French case, Jean-Paul Rioux confirms Postan's judgement. Beyond the specific economic factors, whose exact weight remains impossible to measure,

> . . . growth occurred because it was actively sought after, because behaviour had changed, because knowledge had increased: thus the French were prepared to accept growth even before they could actually promote it. A new-found confidence in the future, a taste for education, possibly a less deferential attitude to the status quo, were all changes as important as the rate of capital formation or the intensity of competition.

'In the final analysis then', concludes Rioux, 'an explanation of the economic leads us back to the domains of the social and the mental.'[6] And in none of these domains was any influence so powerful or all-pervasive in these years as that of the United States.

AMERICANISATION AND THE POLITICS OF GROWTH

The force of the American example

'The urge to follow the American way of life is strong in a number of countries', the head of one of the biggest US advertising agencies told the *New York Times* after a tour of Western Europe in spring 1955. American-style retailing, with its self-service groceries, chain stores and 'installment selling' (hire-purchase), was expanding to deal with the new purchasing power of all those now entering the middle class, 'realizing [their] desire for a better life after so many years of a hardship economy'.

Michael Postan eloquently explains the processes at work:

> Transatlantic inspiration to European policies of growth . . . came not only from what the USA gave or preached but also from what the USA was. . . . Both openly and discreetly the wish to catch up with the USA became the ambition of governments and the public. . . . American affluence and American levels of consumption – motor cars, domestic gadgets, and all – were held up as rewards to come. In short, America's very presence

provided an impulse to European growth and a measure of its achievements.[7]

After scaling down its economic significance, protagonists and experts still agree on the political and psychological impact of American influence, whose most expressive form, at the time and historically, was the Marshall Plan. 'You Too Can Be Like Us': that was the original message of the Marshall Plan, and it was the task of the extraordinary propaganda effort accompanying it to bring that promise home to Europeans everywhere. As Administrator Hoffman wrote in his memoirs: 'They learned that this is the land of full shelves and bulging shops, made possible by high productivity and good wages, and that its prosperity may be emulated elsewhere by those who will work towards it.'[8]

'Prosperity Makes You Free' proclaimed the slogans on the Marshall Plan Freedom Trains as they brought aid and comfort in the dark days of the late 1940s. 'We Too Can Prosper' cried the Anglo-American Productivity Council in 1953. If European governments hoped for prosperity, the Americans expected growth. American power was turned into American influence by their comprehensive and systematic insistence on the individual, subjective dimensions of the recovery–modernisation process. A British Ministry of Labour analysis of the reports sent in by the industrial teams on their return from the United States noted how the 'psychological factor' always commanded the attention of the visiting workers and managers: 'Almost without exception the reports dwell on what is variously called "the American Way of Life", the "will to work", the "stimulating environment", the American "attitude of mind", the "climate of opinion" and the "energising and effective atmosphere".'[9]

And by pointing the most credible, alluring way forward from recovery to modernisation in a hundred different ways – personalities, products, magazines, advertising, films, television, fashions, 'lifestyles' – this kind of influence was turned into 'Americanisation'.

The changes in market relationships involved in the Americanised 'era of high mass consumption' touched every social class and brought new groups forward to enjoy its benefits: most of the working class, women, youth. American myth and American model merged in the Hollywood cinema, never more powerful in Europe than in the years 1945–54. While productivity stood as the key to the supply side, a force like Hollywood's worked on the demand side of the economic and social transformation, speeding and channelling the changes in mentality and behaviour. Thus if the inspirational message of Marshall

Plan documentaries was in reality an invitation to follow the American example all the way, the feature films on the same programmes helped show how, and where the road might lead.[10]

A new political culture

Politics began to adapt as progress was redefined in economic, consumerist, terms and the very bases of legitimacy shifted. This process still awaits its historians and so can only be suggested in these pages. At first sight, for instance, the West German electorate would seem to have experienced the change earlier than the others. In the 1953 elections 'Adenaeur virtually ran on an American ticket', the American Ambassador told his colleagues shortly afterwards:

> He campaigned with the aid of a moving picture of his trip to the US, which presented him as being intimately identified with America. His explanation is that it was good politics because the Germans are thoroughly convinced that their future lies with the US, and this tended to show that he could deal effectively with the Americans and had succeeded in raising Germany to the level of an equal.[11]

If that 'American invention' Erhard is to be believed, the growth idiom was the keynote of the CDU campaign. As early as April 1953 he had told a technical fair in Hanover that the aim should be to 'go beyond the people's basic needs and their day-to-day demands'. Accordingly: 'We must see to it that in German households, and particularly in working-class households, durable goods, such as refrigerators, washing machines, vacuum cleaners amongst others, will be used.' For Erhard, his party's victory confirmed the rightness of this vision, fruit of the 'social harmony' which came from 'that trinity, which for every modern market economist must be the ideal picture': 'Rising production and productivity accompanied by rising nominal wages, and the increase in prosperity, thanks to stable or lower prices, [bringing] all-round benefits.'

Over the subsequent years, say today's German historians, the Federal Republic's economic success and its 'belief in unlimited economic growth' were fundamental forces in shaping that artificial nation's sense of identity, realities 'that muted nationalism and any strong initiatives to overcome the division of Germany.'[12]

The British general election of 1955 was the first in which the presence of television was felt, with the BBC and the new commercial network having doubled the audience in less than five years to ten million viewers. The government's campaign was opened by an expansionary budget and an 'Economic Survey' for the year which transposed the American message in language doubtless appropriate to British conditions at the time: 'Productivity should benefit . . . from the added incentive to effort which the prospect of rising consumption affords . . . general confidence in the possibilities of expansion will do much to ensure that expansion is in fact achieved'.[13]

But the 1959 election under Harold Macmillan's premiership was carried on in quite different tones. 'Compared with prewar, most people are a good deal better off', agreed the leader of the opposition, Gaitskell. The consequences were worrying for a Labour politician: 'There are signs of the breaking up of traditional political loyalties.' Specifically, wrote British commentators, 'polarisation between worker and management was dissolving into the subtler hierarchies of a world based upon "status symbols", as measured by consumer goods – badges of the new affluence'. Labour accused the Tories of substituting these symbols for issues, of selling Macmillan like a detergent, and of introducing 'the worst sort of Americanisation'.

But in reality both the major parties were busy submerging the important choices in a generalised consensus on the mixed economy, the welfare state and the supremacy of growth. As the political historians Bogdanor and Skidelsky point out:

> Economic growth was essential to the consensus. It enabled the Conservatives to offer for the first time a viable alternative to Socialism with their idea of a property-owning democracy. No one need be defeated in the class war because no war was being fought. Capitalism could provide affluence for the working class while at the same time preserving the gains of the well-to-do.

As for the Labour opposition, growth held out a vision of: 'victory to the working class in the class struggle without the necessity of having to do battle with capitalism. Redistribution could be financed from the proceeds of growth without hurting the better-off'. But if growth was now the supreme political objective, it was the Tories who were thought best able to supply it. 'You've never had it so good', was a slogan Macmillan had launched in 1957, and his decisive victory two years later ensured its attachment to a memorable slice of British postwar life.[14]

As early as 1949 Monnet had disarmed his critics in the French parliament with 'a new economic analysis', writes Richard Kuisel:

> 'We are in a world undergoing a total transformation', he had told them; 'You can no longer think of the future in the context of the past. We Europeans are still haunted by past notions of security and stability. Today the principal idea is that of expansion. That is what is happening in the United States. They are always ready to evolve and search out progress.'

So the Frenchman should take on 'the psychology of an American . . . the disposition to change constantly'.[15]

Monnet's Second Plan was launched in 1954, seeking to use coordinated productivity increases to build a modern economy 'capable of responding to the challenge of free trade and able to offer the consumer a wide choice'. In France, too, cars led the way to the growth revolution: they more than doubled in number between 1951 and 1958. In late 1955 the first major productivity bargain was negotiated in French industry, at the Renault plant. It brought guaranteed future wage increases and fringe benefits in exchange for 'a measure of labour peace and acceptance by the unions that the pursuit of efficiency was in the interests of both sides'.[16]

The pact was one of the most visible fruits of the non-inflationary expansion at last established. In Rioux's account:

> Economic growth was rising by 5 per cent a year, national income had grown by 25 per cent between 1952 and 1955; trade was expanding, notably in the most dynamic sectors, and in 1955, for the first time since the war, the commercial balance was positive. And higher demand in turn stimulated production; increased currency earnings eased the budgetary imbalance, reducing the humiliation of the search for foreign loans and advances . . . the steady diffusion of growth's economic and social benefits fostered a climate of peace and optimism.

By this time the centrist politicians who wrangled incessantly for control of the Fourth Republic had also learned 'that for the bulk of the population sharing the fruits of expansion and economic modernisation, with better standards of living, improved amenities, and more social services, counted for more than questions over the Atlantic Alliance, Europe, Germany, and colonial wars'.[17] Although these questions dominated formal politics and elections as the Fourth Republic staggered towards its collapse in 1958, beneath the surface a fundamental historical shift in values had occurred. Economic considerations had replaced politics, the 'mission civilisatrice', the nation's cultural aura, gold and savings, in France's evaluation of her own power. Modernization understood in the terms of growth gained priority, writes Robert Frank: 'presented either as an absolute precondition of the power of France or as an end in itself, a replacement ideal'.[18]

In a country like Italy, where Catholic influence was so strong, adapting the culture of solidarity and austerity to the new opportunities seemed at first sight deeply problematic. The Christian Democrats appeared to walk into the era of the 'economic miracle' looking backwards. The party secretary (and former economics professor), Amintore Fanfani, struggled hard to reconcile the traditional priorities with the new spirit of expansion as he addressed his party's congress in late 1956:

Politically we work to carry out the second industrial revolution, the personal, solidaristic and hence Christian revolution, even as we favour technical progress. That progress which multiplies goods and reduces human effort will lessen the hardness of the struggle for existence, lessen burdens in the economic sector, lessen the weight and number of temptations wherever misery prevails. That progress will bring a greater abundance of goods, an easier escape from hard times for individuals, for groups, for peoples.

In reality, most of the Democrazia Cristiana was looking forward to the prospect of modernisation on the American pattern without reserve, writes Paul Ginsborg. At the same congress a possible means to this end was adopted, an economic framework plan of the French type which promised to bring full employment, eliminate the North–South gap and balance the foreign payments accounts. How? By 5 per cent growth a year and a series of institutional and structural innovations.

But this most ambitious Italian planning effort of the postwar period was never realised. It was neither liberal nor protectionist, and so had little appeal for the industrialists. At the same time it cut across the Christian Democrats' own methods for organising patronage in the public sector, institutionalised in a new Ministry of Public Intervention.[19] The language of growth politics in fact never took hold in Italy. There was little or no connection between the declared policies of office-holders, their actual behaviour and the performance of the real economy. And voters were not encouraged to expect any, least of all in terms of numerical pledges on growth, employment, inflation, etc.

Yet the outcome of Italy's 'miracle' (thus called because it was so unexpected) has led some historians to include Italy as among the most Americanised of all the Western European countries in these years. Its need for a strong development model became more deeply felt as expectations rose and the technological possibilities of fulfilling them were made more readily available. Urbanisation (seven to eight million people moved to the cities in the 1950s), the expansion of welfare, the development projects and the DC system for spreading its influence by distributing public money, all pushed consumption upwards. Wages grew less than productivity, but still consumption increased on an average of 5–6 per cent per year. It was high social mobility which made the American model seem so appropriate and attractive, says Vera Zamagni, providing 'a common pattern which succeeded in homogenising the Italians and at the same time preserved their localistic traditions'.[20]

In no country was the impact of the motor car revolution more

231

tremendous, led by a company, FIAT, which had been a privileged beneficiary of ERP aid and made no secret of its admiration for American methods of production, distribution and selling. Yet the car which put the Italians on wheels, the FIAT 600 of 1955, was a small utility model, in no way resembling the Detroit product. As the great source of models and methods in the new Europe, America's propositions were always adopted in this stage as far as they were useful and no further.

THE OUTCOME OF EUROPEAN RECONSTRUCTION

The old world remade the American way?

In April 1955 President Eisenhower announced that the original Marshall Plan nations would receive no new financial aid in the US government's budget for 1956. Only Spain and Yugoslavia would get new money to add to the existing US commitment, as would West Berlin, 'that outpost of freedom'. When 1956 came, the permanent US forces in Europe were spending about one billion dollars in military hardware, goods and services, as the main pillar of the NATO front line, or, as Theodore White put it, 'the flesh of America's pledge that Europe's destiny is ours'.

> One hundred thousand of the finest men in America's army are strung out between the Rhine and the Thuringian ridges, on the alert day and night. They sleep with combat packs beside them, helmets by their pillows, rifles and ammunition stacked in company quarters, their tanks, guns, trucks, ammunition carriers, ready to roll on an hour's notice.[21]

In the meantime they could wonder at the changes visible all around them in those territories where they had last fought, amidst ruins and desperation, only a few years before. They were changes which American observers now claimed to be the successful outcome of all the dollars and all the economic aid – $25 billion's worth, said the *New York Times* – poured into Western Europe since the end of the war. An American correspondent in Geneva judged that 'The booming state of the Western European economy offers the best possible evidence that, on the whole, the massive American-aid programs of the immediate post-war years accomplished what they were supposed to do.'[22]

Although leaders and laggers in the growth race were already emerging across Western Europe, everyone could see the benefits of rising output and wages. In Sweden, Switzerland and Britain, said the same observer, 'the belief is very strong that the day of the car-owning wage earner is dawning'. This happy result was ascribed to the victory of the productivity message, which now began appearing everywhere, in newspaper debates, the annual reports of companies, the judgements of bankers, the exhortations of politicians.

It was less frequently found on the lips of trade unionists. They demanded, first of all, a fuller share of each country's growing national product for their members. Their power derived from what the *Economist* called 'the frantic demand for labour', which had gripped Britain in 1955, as it gripped all the West European countries except Italy. Immigration now began to fill the gaps, with 50,000 Italian workers admitted to West Germany in 1956 and the first significant entry of Commonwealth immigrants into the British workforce. The inadequate supply of skilled labour however emerged as a serious bottleneck, especially in Germany, where ten vacancies were reported for each motor mechanic. On the over-crowded Clyde delivery dates for new merchant ships slipped from three to five years.[23]

Inflation emerged definitively as the great price to pay for all this. Phrases such as 'over-heating' and 'over-full employment' began their contemporary careers; they were tackled with the old weapon of deflation dressed up in new form, the 'credit squeeze'. Interest rates rose significantly and a variety of controls on credit and wage trends were tried in the various countries. Everywhere, said the Chairman of a British bank in his New Year 1956 message to shareholders, 'the problem remains how to persuade the man in the street to consume a little less than he is producing for the time being'. Deploring the practice of collective bargaining to drive up wages as opposed to individual effort, a fellow Chairman pointed to the American example:

> . . . if the people of the United States of America were prepared to accept today the standard of living they had twenty-five years ago, they would need to work only one day a week under current industrial conditions.
> As it is they prefer to take full advantage of every labour-saving device, work hard while on the job and so have all the advantages that they now enjoy.[24]

As it was the Americans were happy to see the style and some of the substance of their way of life being adopted so enthusiastically throughout Western Europe. They assumed that everyone by now had learned their lessons on the 'cunning inter-relationship between technology, the market and the forces of communication', as a British social historian characterised it.[25]

In the summer of 1955 Reuters news agency reported the results of a world-wide survey of its correspondents who had been asked the simple question, 'Is all the free world being Americanized?' There were responses from Tokyo and Melbourne, from Canada and Brazil, as well as from the Middle East and Europe.[26]

A new process of change and development had undoubtedly arrived with the spread of American power, said the Reuters correspondents. But the transition was varied and its effects not always the ones to be predicted. In Iran – the 'desert' which Roosevelt had once dreamed of transforming – 'Americanisation' had already reached the point where Moslem leaders were mobilising to put a stop to it. Hollywood was a particularly disturbing presence in such a setting, as it was in a country like Spain, where American films were thought however to be a positive influence, breaking down that country's isolation and encouraging the emergence of a new middle class. Greece was described as resisting the adoption of American clothes, food, mass communication styles and mass production methods, although 'teenagers' were known to be much more receptive to them than older generations. Still, the great effort to bring the Greek road system, industry and farming into the twentieth century was continuing and the national department of foreign commerce was being run directly by an American, in the employ of the Greek government.[27]

But it was in the major countries of Europe that the greatest American impact was in evidence, according to the Reuters survey. In each of them, different emphases and preferences could be seen, but the underlying patterns were clear: American methods and customs were being adopted, even 'without acknowledgment to the source. They become part of life in a natural way, especially where the younger people are concerned.' Everyone mentioned popcorn, Coca Cola, blue jeans and hamburgers. The new socialising effects of Hollywood and jazz and transatlantic dance music were commented on widely, (still to come was rock'n'roll, which began to arrive in Europe in 1956 with the film *Rock Around the Clock*). But more long-lasting would be the changes to factories and farms, to advertising and shops and restaurants.

In the face of all these challenges the British were responding with a determination 'to stay more doggedly British than ever'. But they were bound to succumb: 'They stubbornly resist central heating, but it is making inroads. And women of all classes are demanding kitchens planned on American lines. Frozen food is becoming more popular and self-service shops are coming into vogue.' Working-class teenagers in particular liked the new leisure products, comic strips, advertising and commercial television, all of them infused with American styles.

Industry was adopting personnel relations and public relations. Still, Britain was the country with the strongest low-intensity anti-Americanism, and there was much deploring among 'thoughtful people' of the 'candy-floss' standards said to be taking hold.[28]

In France only a few of the American influences were thought likely to be long-lasting. Again young people were likely to be the chief beneficiaries, since they were the ones most enthusiastic about jukeboxes, snack-bars and 'le be-bob', and the sense of personal liberation that went with them. Meanwhile, the 'little shop around the corner' stayed at the centre of distribution because of the lack of refrigerators. On the output front the 'principle of the small independent proprietor remains the basis of most industry and agriculture in spite of all campaigns for more mass production'.[29]

In Naples twenty years of mingling with American servicemen had brought a new sense of 'hurry and urgency' to that sleepy old city, according to the Reuters man on the spot. In general, however, US influence in Italy touched only the big cities and the few big factories. Teenagers could be seen in centres such as Florence, Genoa and Rome wearing blue jeans and sports shirts, while their mothers were lured by the advertisements for 'American-style kitchen furniture' and washing machines. But in the villages, 'especially those in poverty-stricken southern Italy', the inhabitants knew there was such a place as the United States 'only because an uncle emigrated there thirty years ago'.[30]

While comments such as these showed the limits of the survey's 'snapshot' character, its judgement that West Germany was the most Americanised nation of all has become generally accepted over the years.[31] Ludwig Erhard now appeared as the champion of the free enterprise way, and German trade unions, with their emphasis on economic gains rather than political power, appeared closer to the American equivalent than those in neighbouring countries. Architects followed transatlantic building methods, advertising was 'high-powered', and 'the prominent place given to American authors in the playbills of German theatres show that the country is willing to accept American ideas'. There was still a long way to go: 'a working man with his own car is almost unknown. Television is still in its infancy. The equality of women exists only on paper.'

Less than a year later, the image of 'young women running around in slacks', would be taken by a *New York Times* correspondent in Bonn as yet another symbol of the widening Americanisation of Germany. The process was now well-recognised in Europe, simply taking different forms in the various local contexts. A quiz show in Italy had become a national event, watched *en masse* on outdoor television screens. The 'fast-food' invasion was clearly not a passing fad: in a country like Belgium it was seen to alter rhythms and create new industries. Only in Denmark, where the state owned the great breweries, were barriers erected against it. While few of the new arrivals were strictly original inventions, 'the garb in which they spread fastest is likely to be American', judged Michael Hoffman. An obvious example was the transformation of the Frankfurt sausage into the hot dog. As Hoffman concluded: 'The least one can report is that a permanent-looking layer of American customs has spread itself across the old Continent in the last ten years, to the consternation of the élite, the delight of the masses and the solid satisfaction of the vendors.'[32]

Varieties of modernisation

In historical terms Americanisation appears as a particularly distinctive form of modernisation, superimposed with great political, economic and cultural force, but more or less randomly, on each European country's own variant. The Marshall Plan and the productivity drive together represented only elements in this process, exceptional and temporary interventions when the United States attempted deliberately to remake the old world in the image of the new.

For the most part West European societies were free to resist the projection of American power in all its forms, to take what they wanted from the American model and to cultivate their own versions of neo-capitalism. Entirely free they were not: the imperatives of the Cold War and generalised anti-Communism provided dominant themes in European politics all the way through the 1950s and caused continuous tension between the defence and welfare priorities in national budgets. It was the reality of expansion of course, which supplied the means to make these tensions politically manageable, thereby fostering the spread of the growth consensus.

Every nation arrived at its own synthesis of production and consumption, of collective and individual spending, of traditional ways and new practices directed to growth. Whatever the impulses to functional integration and homogenised consumption patterns, national identities were jealously defended and the nation-state itself emerged stronger, not weaker, from the processes of recovery and modernisation.

An explanation for this result was offered in 1964 by Simon Kuznets, another of the American economists who led the great effort to theorise the postwar experience of expansion so as to make it reproducible elsewhere. Kuznets talked of an 'intensification of nationalism', most obviously visible where the aspiration to growth was setting off development processes in non-industrial cultures, but apparent also in the newly affluent societies. Only the nation was possessed of a consensus strong enough to withstand the disruptiveness of contemporary economic change, suggested Kuznets: 'Modern economic growth is revolutionary in the rapidity of its structural shifts, the changes in relative position among various groups in society; and the modern nation-state is the mechanism usually employed to channel and contain such a revolution.'[33]

In 1968 the banker Eric Roll noted the paradox of the Bretton Woods and UN commitments to full employment, highlighting how 'the full employment objective of national policy had ... basically more affinity with commercial and financial measures based on national autonomy than with those designed to circumscribe the freedom of national action and to restore a large measure of free international trade'.[34]

More recently Alan Milward has argued that the priorities of welfare, of defence, of strategic industrial intervention, of agricultural protectionism (which burgeoned as soon as US economic aid stopped), of growth itself, led to a vast expansion in the power of the national state in the postwar era. Understanding this, the statesmen most outwardly committed to organised interdependence – Spaak, De Gasperi, Adenauer, Schuman, Monnet himself – saw European integration as a means to promote national security above all, and to 'control and distribute the gains and losses which might arise' as new industrial sectors came forward and others fell behind following the processes described previously by Denison. The various forms of weak Keynesianism which emerged to reconcile the key priorities were all applied in strictly national frameworks, Milward asserts, and GNP comparisons became the test of their success.[35]

No one could doubt that the EEC Europe of 1957 was a very different place compared with the 1948 scene of bilateral trade deals, blocked bank accounts, barter transactions and controls. However, seen from the national perspective, the American idea of full-scale economic integration seemed almost totally out of place: 'As soon as that example was brought to the level of practical policy-formulation for a future Europe ... the irreducible complexity of history and national interest made it seem utterly remote and implausible.'[36] It is no exaggeration to say that the single-market Europe which the Americans wished to see created by 1952 would only appear, in weak and distorted form, in the course of 1992.

Winners and losers

Every European society and social group constructed its own filtering mechanisms for taking what it wanted from the American model and rejecting the rest. Even in industrial culture there was resistance. A 1959 study on the German case reported that 'a synthesis between traditional forms of behaviour and imports only occurred where they clearly overlapped . . . only those innovations were taken over which did not conflict with indigenous values'. But judging their performance in the long term, argues Berghahn, the filtering mechanisms can be seen to have worked differently according to which groups and branches were in the ascendancy at any given time, and which generation was running them.[37]

The scarcity mentality – Malthusianism, as it was called in Continental Europe – persisted in a thousand different forms, proving extraordinarily impervious to the new economics. British trade unions, French farmers and industrialists, Italian artisans and retailers all persisted in a restricted view of the possibilities of employment and income which no amount of exhortation, social security or affluence could shift. One reason was that the benefits of affluence were far from evenly distributed, in time, by geographical area, or by social group. The old, the homeless, the chronically poor, the small farmers, those working in outdated industries or living on the periphery of Europe all failed to participate in the new kind of abundance. An Italian survey of 1957 revealed that:

> 1 per cent of the workers owned a washing machine and 38 per cent stated that they would like one but did not think that they would ever have one. As for refrigerators, the proportions are . . . 2 per cent (who own one) and 41 per cent (who would like one but did not think they would ever have one). For automobiles the figures are 1 per cent and 66 per cent.[38]

Looking at per capita income in France in 1955–56 and taking the average to be a hundred, the denizens of the region round Paris had the highest figure – 167. In Corsica, the poorest region, the figure was forty-five. The average citizen of Milan enjoyed four times the income of the average inhabitant of Calabria. It was no surprise then that France and Italy witnessed internal migrations of historical significance in the 1950s. Each year 140,000 people abandoned farming in France; in Italy the overall movement each year was no less than 1.5 million. 'Inequality remained, in fact it was the motive power of the whole system', argues a French historian; 'The secret of neo-capitalistic growth was to get inequality accepted in the hope and promise of a better future.'[39]

The moderate Left pleaded for a new egalitarianism; the radical Left (and Right) appealed to the excluded with a vague anti-consumerism and a strident anti-Americanism. But if anti-Americanism flourished in these years it was due mostly to the work of the intellectuals. The more radical on the Left rejected neo-imperialism and the imperatives of the Cold War (while enjoying a private relationship with American culture which excluded nothing); conservatives found a new outlet for their traditional anti-industrialism and refusal of mass society. Others simply resented the situation of being the targets of so much power projection, particularly the force applied to them to choose sides in the East–West confrontation.

In a country like France, where it was most diffuse, anti-American-ism represented an active, comprehensive rejection of the myths and symbols of America as well as the American model of society: street battles and a furious political confrontation had broken out when Coca Cola arrived in 1949, and there were struggles too over the Hollywood 'invasion' (as there were in many European countries).[40]

Yet such emotions were in many ways just the outward sign of the problems encountered by intellectuals and the Left in general in redefining their role as guardians of national identity in the new era of limited sovereignty and high mass consumption. Individual figures in the political centre managed the transition without great difficulty. Voices like those of Raymond Aron in France, Anthony Crosland in England, the editors of *Der Monat* in West Germany represented a new intellectual synthesis of reformism and Americanism, and it was to such 'opinion-makers' that the American effort of persuasion directed its attention when direct mass propaganda was abandoned and the culture of 'Atlanticism' took its place.[41] In 1949 Crosland had satirised the 'countless ECA officials, businessmen and visiting trade unionists [who] preach the doctrine of mass production for mass markets and a rising standard of life – essentially, in American eyes, a capitalist ideology'. Yet his 1956 book entitled *The Future of Socialism*, one of the most ambitious efforts of the non-communist Left anywhere to rejig its purposes in the age of affluence, has been characterised as, among other things, the 'quintessential expression of Marshall Plan values as applied to British social democracy'.[42]

In far-off 1941 Keynes had lectured the Treasury: 'The chief thing that matters is that Ministers should not suppose that the chief thing that matters is to avoid the mistakes made last time.'[43] Doubtless with this lesson in mind, the new and not-so-new ruling groups in Europe came to apply an extraordinary range of correctives to the societies whose wreckage they inherited. But the radiant expectations of war-time seemed very far away by the mid-1950s and their outcome quite different from what had been predicted.

François Bédarida, a French historian, has chosen a scene from John Osborne's famous play of 1956, *Look Back in Anger*, to capture the English version of the new sense of ambiguity. Alison, the wife of the violently anti-social hero, says to her father, a retired colonel: 'You're hurt because everything's changed. Jimmy's hurt because everything's the same. And neither of you can face it.' The transition from reconstruction to modernisation left the West Germans 'oscillating between cosmic fear and satisfaction with their prosperity', wrote the Italian critic Cesare Cases in 1956.[44] It was a condition which, in their own way, as peoples and individuals, all but the 'under-privileged' in Western Europe would eventually come to know.

NOTES

1. Preston P Spain. In Graham A and Seldon A (eds) *Government and economies in the postwar world. Economic policies and comparative performance, 1945–85* 1990 pp 130–5
2. OEEC/EPA *Series of Lectures on Economic Growth* University of Madrid Jan–Feb 1961 Paris 1961 (emphases in original)
3. Rostow WW *The Stages of Economic Growth* cit pp 10–11 and Ch 6 (cit at p 11)
4. Rostow WW *The World Economy, History and Prospect* 1978 pp 261–3, 270 (cit, from Denison EF *Why Growth Rates Differ* Washington DC 1967, at p 261; Denison's emphasis)
5. Economic debate on origins of boom summed up in Maier The two postwar eras cit pp 174–5; cf Milward op cit pp 477–8, 490–1; Postan op cit p 25
6. Rioux op cit p 335; Zamagni also insists on non-economic variables as the key factors in Italy's transformation: peace, 'the presence of the Americans', the Christian Democrats' 'popular inspiration . . . capability of mediation . . . pragmatic approach'. In The Italian 'Economic Miracle' op cit
7. *New York Times* 8 May 1955; Postan op cit p 49
8. Hoffman PG *Peace Can Be Won* NY 1951 p 53
9. Cit in Carew op cit pp 143–4
10. 'Hollywood in Europe 1945–54', a conference at the European University Institute Florence March 1989
11. FRUS 1952–4 Vol VI p 672
12. Erhard op cit pp 57, 51; Schröder op cit p 303
13. Bailey H Britain's Political Pendulum. In *The Reporter* 16 June 1955; Economic Survey cit in *Economist* 2 April 1955

14. Butler D *The British General Election of 1955* 1956; Bogdanor V and Skidelsky R *The Age of Affluence 1951–1964* 1970 pp 10–11
15. Kuisel op cit p 244
16. Rioux op cit pp 318, 327; Carew op cit p 216
17. Rioux op cit pp 240–41, 243
18. Frank op cit pp 263–4
19. Ginsborg op cit pp 205–6, 222–3, (cit at p 205 n 21)
20. Gundle S L'americanizzazione del quotidiano. Televisione e consumismo nell'Italia degli anni Cinquanta. In *Quaderni storici* n 62 1986; Zamagni The Italian 'Economic Miracle' op cit
21. Eisenhower announcement reported in *New York Times* 21 April 1955; figure of $1bn cit in ibid 23 Jan 1956; an effective summary of the aid story since the war is in ibid 4 May 1956
22. White op cit p 7; *New York Times* 23 Jan 1956
23. *Economist* Jan–Feb 1956
24. Reports of Chairman of Williams Deakins Bank and of Chairman of Martin's Bank published in *Economist* 21 Jan 1956
25. Marwick A op cit p 115
26. *New York Times* 21 Aug 1955
27. Ibid; case of American director of Greek foreign trade cit in ibid 23 Oct 1955
28. The most famous commentary – though with little explicit reference to the American model – was in Richard Hoggart's *The Uses of Literacy* 1957; cf Marwick op cit Chs 7–8. Marwick has always doubted the existence of any specific reality of 'Americanisation' in the general process of change; cf Marwick Society and Culture: Britain 1951. In *History Today* April 199
29. Cf Body-Gendrot S Une vie privée des français sur le modèle américan. In Ariès P and Duby G (eds) *Histoire de la vie privée V. De La première guerre mondiale à nos jours.* Paris 1987
30. Cf D'Attorre PP Sogno americano e mito sovietico nel-l'Italia contemporanea. In D'Attorre PP ed *Nemici per la pelle* Milan 1991
31. Cf Willett R *The Americanisation of Germany, 1945–1949* 1989
32. *New York Times* 24 June 1956
33. Kuznets S *Postwar Economic Growth* Cambridge, Mass 1964 p 28
34. Roll op cit pp 92–3
35. Milward 'Nations and Integration in Postwar Europe', talks at the Johns Hopkins University, School of Advanced International Studies, Bologna Center, 25 April 1988, 15 May 1989; cf Milward Exporting a Mistake. In *Times Literary Supplement* 26 Jan 1990, and *The Reconstruction of Western Europe* cit p 498
36. Milward *The Reconstruction of Western Europe* cit p 499
37. Berghahn *The Americanisation of West German Industry* cit pp 252–4; cf Zamagni The Italian 'Economic Miracle' op cit for the Italian experience
38. Pizzorno A The Individualistic Mobilisation of Europe. In *Daedalus* Winter 1964 pp 208–9
39. Ibid p 219; Bedarida F *A Social History of England, 1851-1975* 1979 p 254; cf Galbraith JK *The Affluent Society* 1958 Ch 7
40. On intellectual anti-Americanism, Brinton op cit pp 105–8; Kuisel R

Le Coca-Cola et la France. In *L'Histoire* n 94 1986; papers in the conference 'Hollywood in Europe' cit; the British case is the only one to have been studied extensively: Swann P *The Hollywood Feature Film in Postwar Britain* 1987

41. The monthly review *Encounter*, founded in 1953 (expired 1990) was the meeting point for many of these currents of opinion. Its older and newer generations, and their American peers, are gathered together in a special number of the American journal *Daedalus*: A New Europe Winter 1964. Cf Crosland A *The Future of Socialism* 1956; Maier The Two Postwar Eras cit pp 178–9; on anti-Americanism, papers from the symposium 'Anti-Americanism in Europe', European University Institute Florence April 1984

42. Carew op cit pp 131, 245

43. Cit in Cairncross *The Price of War* op cit p 17

44. Bedarida op cit p 170; Cases C Alcuni vicende e problemi della cultura nella Repubblica democratica tedesca. In Cases *Saggi e note di letteratura tedesca* Turin 1963 (cit at p 135)

Tables

Table 1 Expenditures as percentage of GDP

	Total public expenditure				Defence				Social services			
	1938	*1949*	*1954*	*1960*	*1938*	*1949*	*1954*	*1960*	*1938*	*1949*	*1954*	*1960*
Denmark	17.0	20.9	22.4	23.6	0.9	1.8	3.4	2.6	9.4	9.9	11.1	13.6
France	22.2	26.2	28.1	24.4	9.0	5.7	9.1	6.8	5.1	8.2	8.2	8.9
Germany	29.9+	28.7*	30.0	27.6	7.4+	4.8	3.7	3.6	10.1+	14.3	14.6	12.8
Italy	24.7	22.0	18.9	19.8	8.0	3.4	3.2	2.9	3.3	5.2	5.5	5.9
Holland	17.6	26.6	27.7	21.3	2.7	4.4	7.5	4.3	4.4	4.7	6.3	8.7
Britain	28.6	35.1*	33.8	37.1	8.5	6.5	9.6	6.3	10.8	16.2	14.8	15.3
Belgium	23.4	n.a.	19.2−	20.5	2.5	n.a.	4.5−	3.1	4.2	n.a.	5.2−	6.2

Note + = 1935; * 1950; − = 1953

'Social services' include social insurance and assistance, other social transfers, health, housing, education and science.

Source Peter Flora, *State, Economy and Society in Western Europe 1815–1975. A Data Handbook* The Macmillan Press Ltd, London, 1983 Vol I, Ch. 8

Table 2   Highest year for defence expenditure 1949–60

Country	Year	Percentage of GDP
Denmark	1954	3.4
France	1953	10.1
Germany	1951	6.6
Italy	1951	4.0
Holland	1954	7.5
Britain	1952	10.5
Belgium	1953	4.5

Source As above

Table 3   Private cars in use in major West European countries

	France	Britain	Germany	Italy
1946	1,550	1,770	n.a.	150
1949	1,520	2,131	352	267
1951	1,600	2,380	682	425
1952	1,800	2,508	900	510
1953	2.020	2,762	1,126	613
1954	2,677	3,100	1,393	744
1955	3,016	3,526	1,663	879
1956	3,477	3,888	2.030	1,051
1957	3,972	4,187	2,436	1,237

Note Numbers in thousands
Source Rostow WW *The Stages of Economic Growth* 2nd edn (Cambridge 1971) Appendix A

Table 4   Indices of industrial production in Western Europe 1948–51

	1948	*1949*	*1950*	*1951*
Austria	85	114	134	148
Belgium	122	122	124	143
Denmark	135	143	159	160
France	111	122	123	138
West Germany	50	72	91	106
Greece	76	90	114	130
Italy	99	109	125	143
Holland	114	127	140	147
UK	120	129	140	145

Note 1938 = 100
Source Wexler p 94

Table 5   Average annual rate of growth of output 1913–59

	1913–50	*1950–59*
Austria	n.a.	5.8
Belgium	1.0 (0.7)	2.9 (2.3)
Denmark	2.1 (1.1)	3.3 (2.6)
France	0.7 (0.7)	4.6 (3.5)
West Germany	1.2 (0.4	7.8 (6.5)
Greece	n.a.	5.9
Italy	1.3 (0.6)	5.8 (5.3)
Holland	2.1 (0.7)	4.7 (3.6)
UK	1.7 (1.3)	2.7 (2.2)

Note Percentages in brackets: per capita
Source Van Der Wee p 50

Table 6   Volume indices of GNP at market prices

	1938	*1947*	*1948*	*1949*	*1950*	*1951*	*1952*	*1953*	*1954*	*1955*
Denmark	72	81	85	87	95	94	95	100	103	102
France	76°	79°	75°	85	92	95	97	100	105	113
Germany	80°	46°	54°	63	75	88	93	100	108	120
Italy	80°	72	74	79	84	91	93	100	105	112
Holland	69°	71°	79	85	88	89	92	100	105	112
Britain	83°	85	87	90	94	97	96	100	105	108
Belgium	74°	80°	85	87	91	95	97	100	103	108

Note 1953 = 100
   °   = OEEC estimate.
Source OEEC *Statistics of National Product and Expenditure No 2* (Paris 1957) p 19

Bibliography

(Place of publication London except where indicated otherwise)

BOOKS

Acheson D *Present at the Creation. My Years in the State Department* NY 1969

Addison P *Now the War is Over* 1987

Adenauer K *Memoirs 1945–53* 1966

Aga-Ross E (ed) *Il Piano Marshall e l'Europa* Rome 1983

Arndt H W *The Rise and Fall of Economic Growth* Melbourne 1978

Bark DL and Gress DR *A History of West Germany* Vol 1 Oxford 1989

Becker J and Knipping F (eds) *Power in Europe? Great Britain, France, Italy and Germany in a Postwar World, 1945–1950* Berlin/New York 1986

Bedarida F *A Social History of England, 1851–1975* 1979

Berghahn VR *The Americanisation of West German Industry 1945–1973* Leamington Spa 1986

Berghahn VR *Modern Germany. Society, Economy and Politics in the Twentieth Century* Cambridge 1987

Bogdanor V and Skidelsky R *The Age of Affluence 1951–1964* 1970

Bottiglieri B *La politica economica dell'Italia centrista (1948–1958)* Milan 1984

Brinton C *The Temper of Western Europe* Cambridge, Mass 1953

Bullen RJ et al (eds) *Ideas into Politics. Aspects of European History 1880–1950* 1984

Bullock A *Ernest Bevin. Foreign Secretary 1945–1951* Oxford 1985
Burnham P *The Political Economy of Postwar Reconstruction* 1990
Butler D *The British General Election of 1955* 1956
Cairncross A *Years of Recovery. British Economic Policy 1945–51* 1985
Cairncross A *The Price of War. British Policy on German Reparations 1941–1949* Oxford 1986
Calleo DP and Rowland BM *America and the World Political Economy* Bloomington 1973
Calvocoressi P *The British Experience 1945–75* Harmondsworth 1979
Candilis WO *The Economy of Greece 1944–66. Efforts for Stability and Development* NY 1968
Carew A *Labour Under the Marshall Plan* Manchester 1987
Carr EH *Conditions of Peace* 1942
Carr EH *Nationalism and After* 1945
Cerquetti E *Le forze armate italiane dal 1945 al 1975* Milan 1975
Cook D *Charles de Gaulle. A Biography* 1984
Council of Foreign Relations *The Problem of Lend-Lease: Its Nature, Implications and Settlement* NY April 1944
Crosland A *The Future of Socialism* 1956
Crozier B *De Gaulle The Statesman* 1973
DAFR – see *Documents on American Foreign Relations*
de Gaulle General *War memoirs. Salvation 1944–1946* 1960
D'Attorre PP (ed) *La ricostruzione in Emilia Romagna* Parma 1985
DIA – see *Documents on International Affairs*
Di Nolfo E (ed) *Vaticano e Stati Uniti 1939–52. Dalle carte di Myron C.Taylor* Milan 1978
Divine RA *Second Chance. The Triumph of Internationalism in America During World War II* New York 1967
Djilas M *Conversations with Stalin* 1963
Djilas M *Wartime* NY 1976
Documents on American Foreign Relations World Peace Foundation Boston (yearly)
Documents on International Affairs 1947–1948 Royal Institute of International Affairs 1952
Donovan RJ *The Second Victory. The Marshall Plan and the Postwar Revival of Europe* NY 1987
Dupeux G *French Society 1789–1970* 1976
Eatwell R *The 1945–1951 Labour Governments* 1979
Ellwood DW *Italy 1943–1945* Leicester 1985
Ellwood DW(ed) *The Marshall Plan Forty Years After: Lessons for the International System Today* Bologna 1989
Erhard L *Prosperity through Competition* 1958

European Recovery and American Aid A Report by the President's Committee on Foreign Aid Washington DC Nov 1947

Flora P (ed) *Growth to Limits. The West European Welfare State Since World War II* vol 1 Berlin/NY 1986

Foreign Relations of the United States The Conferences at Malta and Yalta. 1945 Washington DC 1955

Id 1946 vol V Washington DC 1969

Id 1947 vol III Washington DC 1972

Id 1951 vol IV Washington DC 1985

Id 1952–54 vol VI Parts 1 and 2 Washington DC 1986

Freeland RM *The Truman Doctrine and the Origins of McCarthyism* NY 1972

FRUS – see *Foreign Relations of the United States*

Gaddis JL *The United States and the Origins of the Cold War 1941–1947* NY 1972

Ginsborg P *A History of Contemporary Italy. Society and Politics 1943–1988* 1990

Griffiths RT *Economic Reconstruction Policy in the Netherlands and Its International Consequences, May 1945–March 1951* European University Institute Working Paper n 76 Florence 1984

Grosser A *The Colossus Again. Western Germany from Defeat to Rearmament* NY 1955

Harper JL *America and the Reconstruction of Italy 1943–1948* Cambridge 1986

Hoffman PG *Peace Can Be Won* NY 1951

Hogan MJ *The Marshall Plan: America, Britain, and the reconstruction of Western Europe, 1947–52* Cambridge 1987

Holt RT and van de Velde RW *Strategic Psychological Operations and American Foreign Policy* Chicago 1960

Hutton G *We Too Can Prosper* 1953

Iatrides JO *Revolt in Athens. The Greek Communist 'Second Round', 1944–45* Princeton 1972

Jansen M and De Vree JK *The Ordeal of European Integration, 1945–1985* Bilthoven 1985

Jones H *'A New Kind of War'. America's Global Strategy and the Truman Doctrine in Greece* NY 1989

Kaplan JJ and Schleiminger G *The European Payments Union. Financial Diplomacy in the 1950s* Oxford 1989

Kendall W *The Labour Movement in Europe* 1975

Keynes JM *The Economic Consequences of the Peace* 1919

Kindleberger CP *Marshall Plan Days* Boston 1987

Kolko G *The Politics of War. The World and United States Foreign Policy 1943–1945* NY 1968

Kolko J and G *The Limits of Power. The World and United States Foreign Policy, 1945–1954* NY 1972

Kuisel R *Capitalism and the State in Modern France* Cambridge 1981

Kuznets S *Postwar Economic Growth* Cambridge, Mass 1964

Lieberman S *The Growth of European Mixed Economies 1945–1970* Cambridge, Mass 1977

Lipgens W *A History of European Integration* vol 1 1945–1947 Oxford 1982

Lippmann W *The Method of Freedom* NY 1934

Lippmann W *The Cold War* NY 1947;

Lynch F *The Impact of Rearmament on French Reconstruction* European University Institute Florence 1986

Macmillan H *The Blast of War* 1967

McNeill WH *The Greek Dilemma* 1947

McNeill WH *Greece: American Aid in Action 1947–1956* NY 1957

McNeill WH *The Metamorphosis of Greece since World War* Oxford 1978

Mallalieu WC *British Reconstruction and American Foreign Policy* NY 1956

Marjolin R *Europe in Search of its Identity* NY Council on Foreign Relations 1980

Marwick A *British Society since 1945* Harmondsworth 1982

Matloff M (ed) *American Military History* Office of the Chief of Military History Washington DC 1969

Mayne R *Postwar. The Dawn of Today's Europe* 1983

Middlemas K *Politics in Industrial Society. The experience of the British system since 1911* 1980

Miller JE *The United States and Italy, 1940–1950* Chapel Hill 1986

Milward A *The Reconstruction of Western Europe 1945–51* 1984

Ministry of Foreign Affairs *Road to Recovery The Marshall Plan Its Importance for the Netherlands and European Co-operation* The Hague 1954

Monnet *Memoirs* NY 1978

Montgomery JD *Forced to be Free: the Artificial Revolution in Germany and Japan* Chicago 1957

Mortimer E *Roosevelt's Children. Tomorrow's World Leaders and Their World* 1987

Ninkovich FA *Germany and the United States. The Transformation of the German Question Since 1945* NY 1988

OEEC/EPA *Series of Lectures on Economic Growth* University of Madrid Jan-Feb 1961 Paris 1961

Pelling H *Britain and Marshall Plan* 1988

Penrose EF *Economic Planning for the Peace* Princeton 1953

Piovene G *Viaggio in Italia* Milan 1957

Postan MM *An Economic History of Western Europe 1945-1964* 1967

Power in Europe – see Becker J and Knipping F

Prefaces to Peace. A Symposium NY 1943

Price HB *The Marshall Plan and its Meaning* Ithaca 1955

The Public Papers and Addresses of Franklin D. Roosevelt. 1940 Volume NY 1941

Rearden SL *History of the Office of the Secretary of Defense. Vol.1. The Formative Years 1947–1950* Historical Office, Office of the Secretary of Defense, Washington DC 1984

Reitzel W *The Mediterranean: Its Role in America's Foreign Policy* NY 1948

Rioux JP *The Fourth Republic, 1944–1958* Cambridge 1987

Robertson AJ *The Bleak Midwinter 1947* Manchester 1986

Roll Sir E *The World After Keynes. An Examination of the Economic Order* 1968

Rostow WW *The Stages of Economic Growth, a Non-Communist Manifesto* Cambridge 1960

Rostow WW *The World Economy, History and Prospect* 1978

Rostow WW *The Division of Europe after World War II* Aldershot 1982

Salvati MA *Stato e industria nella ricostruzione* Milan 1982

Shennan A *Rethinking France: Plans for Renewal 1940–1946* Oxford 1989

Sherry MJ *Preparing for the Next War. American Plans for Postwar Defense 1941–45* New Haven 1977

Sked A *Britain's Decline, Problems and Perspectives* Oxford 1987

Sked A and Cook C *Post-War Britain. A Political History* Harmondsworth 1979

Smith HK *The State of Europe* NY 1949

Smith ML and Stirk PMR (eds) *Making the New Europe. European Unity and the Second World War* 1990

Sorensen V *Social Democratic Government in Denmark Under the Marshall Plan, 1947–1950* PhD thesis European University Institute 1987

Speir H *From the Ashes of Disgrace. A Journal from Germany 1945–1955* Amherst 1981

Spriano P *The European Communists and Stalin* 1985

Survey – see :

Survey of International Affairs 1939–1946 *The Realignment of Europe* ed Arnold Toynbee and Veronica M Toynbee 1955

Survey of International Affairs, 1949–50 1953

Tomasevich J *The Chetniks, War and Revolution in Yugoslavia 1941–1945* Stanford 1975

Turner ID (ed) *Reconstruction in Post-war Germany. British Occupation Policy and the Western Zones. 1945–1955* Oxford 1989

Tusa A and J *The Berlin Blockade* 1988

UN Economic Commission for Europe *Economic Survey of Europe in 1948* Geneva 1949

Id *Economic Survey of Europe in 1949* Geneva 1950

Id *Economic Survey of Europe in 1953* Geneva 1954

Id *Economic Survey of Europe in 1954* Geneva 1955

United Nations Dept of Economic Affairs *Economic Survey of Europe Since The War* Geneva 1953

The United States in World Affairs 1945–1947 Council on Foreign Relations NY 1947

Urwin DW *Western Europe since 1945* 3rd edn 1981

Urwin DW *The Community of Europe: A History of European integration since 1945* 1991

USIS-FOA *Cooperazione economica Italia – Stati Uniti 1944–54* nd

USWA – see *The United States in World Affairs*

Van Der Wee H *Prosperity and Upheaval. The World Economy 1945-1980* Harmondsworth 1987

Ward B *The West at Bay* NY 1948

Welles S *The Time for Decision* NY 1944

Wexler I *The Marshall Plan Revisited. The European Recovery Program in Economic Perspective* Westport 1983

When Hostilities Cease. Papers on Relief and Reconstruction Prepared for the Fabian Society 1943

White TH *Fire in the Ashes. Europe in Mid-Century* NY 1953

Wilson TA *The Marshall Plan* Foreign Policy Association NY 1977

Woodward Sir L *British Foreign Policy in the Second World War* 1962

Worswick GDN and Ady PH (eds) *The British Economy in the Nineteen-Fifties* Oxford 1962

Young JW *France, the Cold War and the Western Alliance, 1944–49* Leicester 1990

Zamagni V *Dalla periferia al centro. La seconda rinascita economica dell'Italia 1861–1981* Bologna 1990

ARTICLES

Abelshauser W West German Economic Recovery, 1945–1951: A Reassessment. In *Three Banks Review* Sept. 1982

Abelshauser W *The Role of the ERP in German Recovery and Growth: A Macroeconomic Perspective.* Unpublished ms

Abelshauser W American Aid and West German Economic Recovery: A Macroeconomic Perspective. In Maier CS and Bischof G (eds) *The Marshall Plan in Germany: West German Development within the Framework of the European Recovery Program* Leamington Spa 1991

Adamthwaite A Overstretched and overstrung: Eden, the Foreign Office and the making of policy. In *International Affairs* Spring 1988

Agosti A Il partito comunista italiano e la svolta del 1947. In *Studi storici* n 1 1990

Anstey C Foreign Office Publicity, American Aid and European Unity. Mobilising Public Opinion, 1947–1949. In *Power in Europe* qv

Baldwin HW The Recruitment and Training of the New Armed Forces. In Kerwin JG (ed) *Civil–Military Relationships in American Life* Chicago 1948

Berghahn VR Ideas into Politics: The Case of Ludwig Erhard. In Bullen et al qv

Blom JCH and ten Have W Making the New Netherlands: Ideas about renewal in Dutch politics and society during the Second World War. In Smith ML and Stirk P qv

Boyle PG Britain, America and the Transition from Economic to Military Assistance, 1948–51. In *Journal of Contemporary History* July 1987

'A British Official' (sic) Liberated Europe: The Economic Inexorables. In *Foreign Affairs* July 1945

Bullen R An Idea Enters Diplomacy: the Schuman Plan, May 1950. In Bullen et al qv

Carlin W Economic Reconstruction in Western Germany, 1945–55: The Displacement of 'Vegetative Control'. In Turner ID qv

Cases C Alcuni vicende e problemi della cultura nella Repubblica democratica tedesca. In Cases *Saggi e note di letteratura tedesca* Turin 1963

Cleveland H Van Buren Reflections on the Marshall Plan: Then and Now. In Ellwood *The Marshall Plan Forty Years After* qv

Crofts SW The Attlee Government's Economic Information Propaganda. *Journal of Contemporary History* vol 21 1986

D'Attorre PP Il piano Marshall: politica, economia, relazioni internazionali nella ricostruzione italiana. In *L'Italia e la politica di potenza in Europa – 1945–50* Milan 1988

De Cecco M Economic Policy in the Reconstruction Period, 1945–51. In Woolf SJ (ed) *The Rebirth of Italy 1943–50* 1972

Delmas J Reflections on the Notion of Military Power through the French Example (1945–1948). In *Power in Europe* qv

Düwell K Germany 1945–1950 Problems of the 'Economic Miracle'. In *History Today* Sept 1983

Ellwood DW Classe operaia e occupazione alleata in Piemonte, 1945–46. In *Rivista di storia contemporanea* n 3 1974

Ellwood DW Allied Occupation Policy in Italy 1943–46 PhD thesis Reading University 1977

Ellwood DW From 'Re-Education' to the Selling of the Marshall Plan in Italy. In Pronay N and Spring DW (eds) *The Political Re-Education of Germany and her Allies after World War II* 1985

Emerson B 'Belgian Political Parties and European Integration 1940–1944'. Paper presented at the conference, 'European Unity in Context' Hull 1988

Emerson B 'Paul-Henri Spaak and European Integration'. Paper presented at the conference, 'European Unity in Context' Hull 1989

Fish Armstrong H Europe Revisited. In *Foreign Affairs* July 1947

Foa V La ricostruzione capitalistica nel Secondo dopoguerra. In *Rivista di Storia Contemporanea* n 4 1973

Frank R The French Dilemma: Modernization with Dependence or Independence and Decline. In *Power in Europe* qv

Gardner RN Sterling–Dollar Diplomacy in Current Perspective. In Louis WR and Bull H (eds) *The 'Special Relationship'. Anglo-American Relations Since 1945* Oxford 1986

Gordon L in Ellwood *The Marshall Plan Forty Years After* qv

Gundle S L'americanizzazione del quotidiano. Televisione e consumismo nell'Italia degli anni Cinquanta. In *Quaderni storici* n 62 1986

Hardach G The Marshall Plan in Germany, 1948–52. In *Journal of European Economic History* Winter 1987

Henau BP Shaping a new Belgium: the CEPAG – the Belgian Commission for the Study of Postwar Problems (1941–1944). In Smith and Stirk qv

Hürten H Farewell to the Power State? The Perception of the Political Environment and the Idea of the State in Public Opinion in the Western Occupation Zones of Germany between 1946 and 1948. In *Power in Europe* qv

Ilari V Le forze armate italiane dal Trattato di Pace al Patto Atlantico. In *Strategia globale* n 3 1985

Jervis R The Impact of the Korean War on the Cold War. In *Journal of Conflict Resolution* Dec 1980

Kennan G The Marshall Plan and the Future of Europe. In *Transatlantic Perspectives* Winter 1988

Kondonassis AJ et al Political Instability and Economic Development: an Economic History Case Study of Greece, 1948–66. In *Journal of European Economic History* Fall 1983

Kuisel R Le Coca-Cola et la France. In *L'Histoire* n 94 1986

Leffler MP The American Conception of National Security and the Beginnings of the Cold War, 1945–48. In *American Historical Review* April 1984

Loth W German Conceptions of Europe during the Escalation of the East-West Conflict, 1945–1949. In *Power in Europe* qv

Lundestad G Empire by Invitation? The United States and Western Europe, 1945–1952. In *Journal of Peace Research* n 3 1986

Maier CS The Politics of Productivity: Foundations of American International Economic Policy after World War II. In Katzenstein PJ (ed) *Between Power and Plenty. Foreign Economic Policies of Advanced Industrial States* Madison, Wisconsin 1978

Maier CS The Two Postwar Eras and the Conditions for Stability in Twentieth-Century Western Europe. In *American Historical Review* April 1981

Maier CS Why Was the Marshall Plan Successful? In *Transatlantic Perspectives* Winter 1988

Marwick A Society and Culture: Britain 1951. In *History Today* April 1991

Messerschmidt M et al West Germany's Strategic Position and her Role in Defence Policy as Seen by the German Military, 1945–1949. In *Power in Europe* qv

Miller JE Taking Off the Gloves: The United States and the Italian Elections of 1948. In *Diplomatic History* Winter 1983

Nachmani A Civil War and Foreign Intervention in Greece 1946–49. In *Journal of Contemporary History* Oct 1990

'Origins of the Postwar Crisis', London Oct 1967. In *Journal of Contemporary History* April 1968

Overesch M Senior West German Politicians and their Perception of the German Situation in Europe 1945–1949. In *Power in Europe* qv

Papers on The Socialist Party, Economic Problems of Liberated Belgium and Financial Reconstruction of Belgium. In *Belgium in Transition* vol 247 of the Annals of the American Academy of Political and Social Science Sept 1946

Pizzorno A The Individualistic Mobilisation of Europe. In *Daedalus* Winter 1964 pp 208–9

Potter CJ Europe's Coal Problem. In *European Recovery* Proceedings of the Academy of Political Science Columbia University NY Jan 1946

Preston P Spain. In Graham A and Seldon A (eds) *Government and Economies in the Postwar World. Economic Policies and Comparative Performance, 1945–85* 1990

Lord Roberthall International Economic Cooperation after 1945. In *History Today* Sept 1983

Schöder HJ The Economic Reconstruction of West Germany in the Context of International Relations 1945–1949. In *Power in Europe* qv

Siegfried A Can Europe Use American Methods? In *Foreign Affairs* July 1952

Smith H K An American Looks At Europe. In *International Affairs* Oct 1950

Van der Bruggen C Belgium: A Survey of Recent Events. In *International Affairs* July 1950

Varsori A De Gasperi, Nenni, Sforza and their Role in Post-War Italian Foreign Policy. In *Power in Europe* qv

Vergopoulos K L'hégémonie américaine après la seconde guerre mondiale et la formation de la bourgeoisie périphérique en Grèce. In *Les Temps Modernes* mars 1979

Vigezzi B Italy: the End of a 'Great Power' and the Birth of a 'Democratic Power'. In *Power in Europe* qv

Vinen R Pierre Poujade and Margaret Thatcher. In *History Today* Aug 1991

'War Damage in Western Europe'. In *The World Today* April 1946

Warner G Belgium, France and Italy 1944–1950. *History Today* Sept 1983

Warner G Britain and Europe in 1948: the View from the Cabinet. In *Power in Europe* qv

Warner G The Division of Germany 1946–1948. In *International Affairs* Jan 1975

Warner G The Labour Governments and the unity of Western Europe. In Ovendale R (ed) *The Foreign Policy of the British Labour Governments, 1945–1951* Leicester 1984

Warner G The United States and the rearmament of Germany, 1950–54. In *International Affairs* Spring 1985

Warner G The Belgian Crisis of November, 1944: A Case Study in the Politics of Liberation (unpublished paper)

Watt DC American Aid to Britain and the Problem of Socialism,

1945–51. In Watt (ed) *Personalities and Policies. Studies in the Formation of British Foreign Policy in the Twentieth Century* 1965

Watt DC British Military Perceptions of the Soviet Union as a Strategic Threat, 1945–1950. In *Power in Europe* qv

Zamagni V Betting on the Future. The Reconstruction of Italian Industry, 1946–1952. In *Power in Europe* qv

Zamagni V The Italian 'Economic Miracle' Revisited: New Markets and American Technology. In E Di Nolfo (ed) *Power in Europe? II* Berlin 1992

Guide to Further Reading*

Four volumes are now available in English dealing comprehensively and impressively with the major countries of Western Europe since the war. All include substantial sections on the reconstruction period. They are: JP Rioux's brilliant study of the French experience, *The Fourth Republic 1944–1958*; Paul Ginsborg's outstanding book *A History of Contemporary Italy. Society and Politics 1943–1988*, deeply influenced by the strong and mature left wing culture of that country; the volumes by the Americans Bark and Gress dedicated to West Germany, *A History of West Germany*, the first of which, covering the years 1945–63, provides a balanced and accessible study of the period; and Kenneth O Morgan's widely praised treatment of Britain *The People's Peace. British History 1945–1989* (1990) which builds on the most comprehensive quantity of sources and published studies available in any of the countries.

As long as the years 1945–1955 continue to be the object of intense research effort, collections of conference papers will always be important keys to further study. The 'Perceptions of Power in Western Europe' series started in Sèvres in 1982, went on to Augsburg in 1984 then to Florence in 1987. The proceedings of the 1984 event, *Power in Europe? Great Britain, France, Italy and Germany in a Postwar World, 1945–50*, (Becker and Knipping), and the Florence conference *Power in Europe? II* (Di Nolfo) are prime indicators of the current debate on reconstruction. The series of conferences at Hull on 'European Unity in Context' has produced so far *Making the New Europe*, (Smith and Stirk) and *Shaping Postwar Europe* (Stirk and Willis). The conference of

---

* Texts already cited are not supplied with date and place of publication. In other instances place of publication is London, unless otherwise indicated.

Luxemburg 1987 is recorded in Clesse and Epps *Present at the Creation: the Fortieth Anniversary of the Marshall Plan* (NY 1990), a good introduction to the Marshall Plan in the light of subsequent developments which should be compared with *The Marshall Plan. A Retrospective* (Maier and Hoffmann), the product of a Harvard anniversary symposium of 1982. The research results of the conferences held regularly at the European University Institute, Florence, are available in that institution's *Working Papers* and *Colloqium Papers* series. To these should be added, of course, the output of scholarly journals, in particular *Diplomatic History, International Affairs*, the *Journal of European Economic History*, the *Journal of Contemporary History* and the *European History Quarterly*.

In terms of conventional subject areas the story of European integration and of the Cold War continues to dominate the production of those who concentrate their attention on the postwar years. While the first of these areas may now be approached by DW Urwin's companion volume in this series, *The Community of Europe. A History of European Integration since 1945*, the Cold War is the province of American historians above all, particularly John Lewis Gaddis, Lawrence Kaplan, Lloyd C Gardner and Thomas G Paterson. In general the transatlantic relationship has always concerned American scholars more than European ones, except in the British case where the work of a great number of scholars, but particularly Geoffrey Warner, John Young, Andrew Hurrell and Anne Deighton, provides a reading from the perspective of British preoccupations. Meanwhile the major volumes on relations between the United States and Italy, and the United States and Greece have all been supplied by American scholars, J Harper and JE Miller in the first case, H Jones and J Iatrides in the second. The outstanding new study of the Marshall Plan, *The Marshall Plan. America, Britain and the Reconstruction of Europe, 1947–1952*, by Michael J Hogan, is again a product of American scholarship. While American policies and their impact in Germany have been approached from many different angles (occupation policies, the Berlin blockade, the role of Clay, the workings of the Marshall Plan, 'Americanisation'), the first serious study of United States – French relations appeared as this text was completed: IM Wall *The United States and the Making of Postwar France 1945–1954* (Cambridge 1991).

As indicated in the introductory pages, major influences on reconstruction studies have been provided by the work of the American Charles Maier and the British economic historian Alan Milward. The range of Maier's interests is indicated by the title of the volume now including all his major articles in this area: *In Search of Stability:*

Explorations in historical political economy (Cambridge 1987). Maier's comparisons of the two postwar eras and his synthesis of political and economic logic in the concept of the 'politics of productivity' have been particularly fruitful. Milward has suggested that in 1947 European powers were strong enough politically and economically to follow an independent course from that laid down by the Americans. While the economic evidence for this hypothesis is debatable, the political and social facts point in almost all cases in quite the opposite direction. The most accessible expression of his viewpoint is in Was the Marshall Plan Necessary? a review essay centring on the Hogan book, in *Diplomatic History* (Spring 1989). The importance of Milward's major volume on reconstruction is that it was the first to analyse the confrontation between the various national reconstruction plans – which, as he makes clear, all depended *a priori* on American help – and the propositions the Americans actually put forward in the ERP. In their original form the American designs took none of the European schemes into account in any way.

A glance at studies on reconstruction in single countries provides interesting contrasts. The German experience continues to be intensively researched by economic historians such as W Abelshauser, C Bucheim, K Borchardt and L Niethammer. In Italy economic history is dominated by the work of Vera Zamagni (now brought together impressively in *Dalla periferia al centro. La seconda rinascita economica dell'Italia*) with useful contributions from B Bottiglieri, M Salvati and PP D'Attorre. In France the work offered by François Bloch-Lainé and Jean Bouvier in *La France restaurée 1944–1954 . . . Dialogue sur les choix d'une modernisation* (Paris 1986), and by Henri Rousso (ed) in *De Monnet à Massé: enjeux politiques et objectifs économiques dans le cadre des quatre premiers Plans (1946–1965)* provides detailed access to recent debates on the postwar economic choices (as does the excellent bibliography furnished by Rioux). Except in Britain, where the work of the new Institute of Contemporary British History offers stimulating reflections on political affairs (especially by way of its journal *Contemporary Record)*, in most of the major countries economic history appears to have made significantly greater contributions to recent progress than its political counterpart. The most significant recent volumes of comparative economic history, the Flemish scholar Van der Wee's *Prosperity and Upheaval. The World Economy 1945–1980* and *Government and economies in the postwar world* (Graham and Seldon) both offer suggestive new readings of the basic story: Van der Wee with such chapters as 'Economic Growth as the Mainspring of Government Policy' and 'The Imperative of Demand', and Graham and Seldon with their contributions on 'Economic Policies and Traditions' and 'The Meaning of Hard Work'. Thus economic history is finding a way forward from its uncritical dependence on macroeconomic numbers whose relationship with live experience, whether social, political or even economic, seems so often tenuous, especially in years of general upheaval such as those under study in this volume.

Documentary sources

Documents on Germany, 1944–1985 Washington DC Dept of State 1985

ECA *Report of the ECA – Commerce Mission to Investigate the Possibilities of Increasing Western Europe's Dollar Earnings* Washington DC 1949

ECA *A Report on Recovery Progress and United States Aid* Washington DC 1949

Documents on British Foreign Policy (yearly)

IMF *Bretton Woods at Forty 1944–84* Washington DC 1984

OEEC *Interim Report on the European Recovery Program* 3 vols Paris 1948

The State Department Policy Planning Staff Papers, 1947–1949 NY 1986

UN Department of Economic Affairs *The European Coal Problem* NY 1952

UN Department of Economic Affairs *The Quest for Freer Trade* NY 1955

UN Department of Economic Affairs *Recent Changes in Production* NY 1952

UN Economic Commission for Europe *Growth and Stagnation in the European Economy* Geneva 1954

UN Economic Commission for Europe *Postwar Shortages of Food and Coal* Geneva 1948

Some significant articles

Abelshauser W The First Post-Liberal Nation. Stages in the Development of Modern Corporatism in Germany. In *European History Quarterly* n 3 1984

Anstey C The projection of British socialism. Foreign Office publicity and American opinion 1945–50. In *Journal of Contmporary History* 1984

Carden RW Before Bizonia: Britain's Economic Dilemma in Germany, 1945–46. In *Journal of Contemporary History* July 1979

Deighton A The 'frozen front': the Labour government; the division of Germany and the origins of the Cold War. In *International Affairs* Summer 1987

Folly MH Breaking the Vicious Circle. Britain, the US and the Genesis of the North Atlantic Treaty. In *Diplomatic History* Winter 1988

Gaddis JL The emerging post-revisionist synthesis on the origins of the Cold War. In *Diplomatic History* Fall 1983

Gardner LC Lost Empires. In *Diplomatic History* Winter 1989

Homan PT Economics in the War Period. In *American Economic Review* Dec 1946

Kalecki M Political Aspects of Full Employment (1943). In id *The Last Phase in the Transformation of Capitalism*. NY 1972

Leffler M The United States and the Strategic Dimensions of the Marshall Plan. In *Diplomatic History* Summer 1988

Matthews RCO Why has Britain had full employment since the war? In *Economic Journal* Sept 1968

May ER The American Commitment to Germany. In *Diplomatic History* Fall 1989

Mueller-Armack A The principles of the social market economy. In *The German Economic Review* n 2 1965

Newton CCS The Sterling Crisis of 1947 and the British Response to the Marshall Plan. In *Economic History Review* Vol 32 1984

Pharo H Bridgebuilding and reconstruction; Norway faces the Marshall Plan. In *Scandinavian Journal of History* 1, 2 1976

Reynolds D Origins of the Cold War: the European Dimension. In *Historical Journal* June 1985

Reynolds D Rethinking Anglo-American Relations. In *International Affairs* Winter 1988–89

Rostow WW The Past Quarter Century as Economic History and the Tasks of International Organization. In *Journal of Economic History* March 1970

Smith TE From Disarmament to Rearmament: the United States and the Revision of the Italian Peace Treaty of 1947. In *Diplomatic History* Summer 1989

Williams JH Europe after 1952: the Long-Term Recovery Problem. In *Foreign Affairs* April 1949

William JH Marshall Plan Halfway. In ibid April 195

William JH The End of the Marshall Plan. In ibid July 1952

Books for further reading

Alexander GM *The Prelude to the Truman Doctrine. British Policy in Greece, 1944–1947* Oxford 1982

Andreas-Freidrich R *Battleground Berlin. Diaries 1945–1948* NY 1990

Arkes H *Bureaucracy, the Marshall Plan and the National Interest* Princeton 1972

Aron R and Lerner D *France Defeats EDC* 1957

Backer JH *Priming the German Economy; American Occupational Policies, 1945–48* Durham NC 1971

Balogh T *The Dollar Crisis* Oxford 1949

Balogh T, Burchardt FA, Kalecki M *The Economics of Full Employment* Oxford 1946

Barnet RJ *Allies. America, Europe, Japan Since the War* 1984

Bernstein BJ (ed) *Politics and Policies of the Truman Administration* NY 1974

Beveridge WH *Full Employment in a Free Society: 'Misery generates hate'* 1945

Bourneuf A *Norway: The Planned Revival* Cambridge, Mass 1958

Brown WA jr *The United States and the Restoration of World Trade* Washington DC 1950

Clarke Sir R *Anglo-American Economic Collaboration in War and Peace 1942 – 1949* Oxford 1982

Cook D *Forging the Alliance. NATO 1945 to 1950* 1989

Crowther G *The Economic Reconstruction of Europe* Claremont NH 1948

Deighton A *The Impossible Peace: Britain, the German Problem and the Origins of the Cold War* Oxford 1990

Diebold W jr *The End of the ITO* Princeton 1952

Diebold W jr *The Schuman Plan* NY 1959

Dobson AP *The Politics of the Anglo-American Economic Special Relationship 1940–1987* Brighton 1988

Dow JCR *The Management of the British Economy 1945–60* Cambridge 1964

Edmonds R *Setting the Mould: the US and Britain 1945–1950* Oxford 1986

Eisenstadt SN and Ahimeir O *The Welfare State and its Aftermath* 1985

Ellis HS *The Economics of Freedom. The Progress and Future of Aid to Europe* NY 1950

Farquharson JE *The Western Allies and the Politics of Food: Agrarian Management in Postwar Germany* Leamington Spa 1985

Flora PJ and Heidenheimer AJ *The Development of Welfare States in Europe and America* New Brunswick, NJ 1981

Foot R *The Wrong War. American Policy and the Dimensions of the Korean Conflict 1950–53* Ithaca 1985

Footitt H and Simmonds J *France 1943–1945* Leicester 1988

Fursdon E *The European Defence Community: a history* 1980

Gaddis JL *The Long Peace. Inquiries into the History of the Cold War* NY 1987

Galantière L (ed) *America and the Mind of Europe* 1951

Geiger T, Van Buren Cleveland H *Making Western Europe Defensible* Washington DC 1951

Gimbel J *The Origins of the Marshall Plan* Stanford 1976

Grosser A *The Western Alliance: European–American Relations since 1945* 1980

Hansen AA *America's Role in the World Economy* NY 1945

Harris SE (ed) *Postwar Economic Problems* NY 1943

Harris SE *The European Recovery Program* Cambridge Mass 1948

Harrod RF *Are These Hardships Necessary?* 1947

Hawtrey RG *The Balance of Payments and the Standard of Living* 1950

Heale MJ *Anti-Communism: Combatting the Enemy Within 1930–1970* Baltimore 1990

Hieronymi O *Economic Discrimination against the US in Western Europe 1945–58* Geneva 1973

Ireland TP *Creating the Entangling Alliance: The Origins of the North Atlantic Treaty Organisation* Westport 1981

Kaplan LS *NATO and the US: the Enduring Alliance* Boston 1988

Keezer DM *Making Capitalism Work; a Program for Preserving Freedom and Stabilising Prosperity* NY 1950

Kidron M *Western Capitalism since the War* 1968

Kindleberger CP *Europe's Postwar Growth: the Role of Labour Supply* Cambridge, Mass 1967

Kofas JV *Intervention and Underdevelopment: Greece during the Cold War* University Park 1989

Lacey MJ (ed) *The Truman Presidency* Cambridge 1989

Lacouture J *De Gaulle* 1990

Lewchuk W *American Technology and the British Vehicle Industry* Cambridge 1987

Lindbeck A *Swedish Economic Policy* 1975

Maddison A *Economic Growth in the West* 1964

Marjolin R *Europe and the United States in the World Economy* Durham NC 1953

Marjolin R *Architect of European Unity. Memoirs 1911–1986* 1989

May ER *'Lessons' of the Past. The Use and Misuse of History in American Foreign Policy* Oxford 1973

Milward AS *War, Economy and Society 1939–45* 1977

Northrop FSC *European Union and United States Foreign Policy* NY 1954

OECD *From Marshall Plan to Global Interdependence. New Challenges for the Industrialized Nations* Paris 1978 (proceedings of official conference on thirtieth anniversary of the Marshall Plan, grouping many important protagonists)

Pollard RA *Economic Security and the Origins of the Cold War* NY 1988

Range W *FDR's World Order* Athens Ga. 1959

Robertson AJ *The Bleak Midwinter – 1947* Manchester 1987

Rosenstein Rodan PR *Problems of the Industrialisation of Eastern and South Eastern Europe* Washington DC 1943

Roubatis YP *Tangled Webs: the United States in Greece, 1947–1967* NY 1987

Sassoon D *The Strategy of the Italian Communist Party* 1981

Sassoon D *Contemporary Italy. Politics, Economy and Society since 1945* 1986

Schwarz TA *America's Germany: John J. McCloy and the Federal Republic of Germany* Cambridge, Mass 1991

Shonfield A *Modern Capitalism: The Changing Balance of Public and Private Power* Oxford 1965

Stavrakis PJ *Moscow and Greek Communism 1944–1949* Ithaca 1989

Stein G *The World the Dollar Built* 1952

Sternberg F *The Coming Crisis* 1947

Stuart DT and Tau WT *The Limits of Alliance: NATO Out of Area Problems since 1949* Baltimore 1987

Tomlinson J *Employment Policy: the Crucial Years 1939–55* Oxford 1987

Urban JB *Moscow and the Italian Communist Party* Ithaca 1986

Van Buren Cleveland H *The Atlantic Idea and its European Rivals* NY 1966

van der Beugel EH *From Marshall Aid to Atlantic Partnership* Amsterdam 1966

van Dormael A *Bretton Woods: Birth of a Monetary System* 1978

Whelan R *Drawing the Line: The Korean War 1950–53* 1990

Whitfield JW *The Culture of the Cold War* Baltimore 1991

Willis RF *France, Germany and the New Europe 1945–1967* Stanford 1976

Wilson T *Modern Capitalism and Economic Progress* NY 1950

Young JW *Britain, France and the unity of Europe, 1945–1951* Leicester 1984

Index